TRUMPED
AN ALTERNATIVE MUSICAL

This edition first published in 2020 by Blue Lens
Blue Lens is an imprint of Blue Lens Films Limited

Blue Lens Films Limited, 71-75 Shelton Street,
Covent Garden, London, WC2H 9JQ, United Kingdom

ISBN 978 1 913408 26 8
1 3 5 9 10 8 6 4 2

Printer and binder may vary between territories of
production and sale

LICENSE INFORMATION

Subject to the terms and conditions set out in this book, the purchase* of this book entitles you to be granted a one-time non-transferable performance license for the material with the following conditions:

VERSION	TRUMPED: An Alternative Musical, Extract (Up to fifteen scenes)
LICENSE TYPE	Educational Two Performance *See terms for eligibility criteria*
LICENSE AREA	Australia, Canada, European Economic Area, New Zealand, South Africa, United Kingdom, United States
NUMBER OF PERFORMANCES	Maximum of two performances
MAXIMUM AUDIENCE	Not to exceed 300 in aggregate
TICKET PRICE RESTRICTIONS	Not to exceed USD 10.00 (or foreign equivalent) per ticket, or USD 2,400 (or foreign equivalent) in aggregate.

*Only the first purchaser of this book is entitled to be granted a performance license. Used or resold copies do not entitle you to a performance license.

To register for your license, please complete the online for at analternativemusical.com/performancelicenses.

TERMS OF LICENSE

1) Subject to these terms, the first purchaser of this book ("the licensee") (defined as the individual/ organization to first purchase this copy from a recognized registered book retailer), is entitled to be granted by Toupee or Not Toupee Limited (a UK based company managing the rights to TRUMPED: An Alternative Musical on behalf of the rights holders), a one-time non-transferable performance or use license for the material contained within this book.

2) No performance license will be granted for purchasers of used or resold copies of this book.

3) No performance or performance-related work may begin until a performance license has been granted to the licensee.

4) The granting of a performance license is subject to the successful registration of the licensee and their purchase of this book. Satisfactory proof of first purchase is required before a license is granted.

5) Licensees can register their book purchase at analternativemusical.com/performancelicenses.

6) The license must register before January 1, 2022. No license will be granted for registrations after this date. All licenses (except educational use) will be valid for a period of twelve months. Any and all performance-related work and performances must take place within this period. Educational use licenses will be valid for a period of three months. Any use, performance-related work or performances undertaken outside of this period will be deemed unlicensed use.

7) Licenses will be granted subject to the terms and with the conditions as set out within this book. License terms or conditions will not be varied under any circumstance.

8) Only one license will be granted per book and each licensee is limited to a maximum of five licenses.

9) Educational licenses are available only to registered non-profit educational organizations within the license area.

10) Non-profit licenses are available only to registered non-profit organizations within the license area.

11) Amateur licensees are available only to amateur performance groups within the license area and with annual revenues not exceeding USD 25,000 (or foreign equivalent) in the previous financial year.

12) Licenses are valid only within the license area, defined as: The United States, United Kingdom, European Economic Area, Canada, Australia, New Zealand, and South Africa.
13) Once a purchase is registered, a license cannot be canceled for any reason.
14) Once a license is granted, the licensee is required to enter the license number on each page of this book in the designated area, after which, copies of the material may be made in order to distribute for performance or education use as the license allows. No copying is permitted without a license number being entered on each page. Licensees are required to control and note the number of copies of the material being made. All copies must be returned to the licensee and destroyed at the end of the material's licensed use.
15) Once licensed, subject to the conditions of that license and these terms, the licensee is permitted to produce the material contained within this book for public performance. This does not apply to educational use licenses which grant the license to use the material in a purely educational environment with performances permitted to non-paying audiences not exceeding 30 persons.
16) Licensees must produce the material in full with no edits of any kind (substitutions, additions or subtractions) permitted. In the circumstance of extract licenses, the licensee is permitted to choose up to fifteen scenes to produced. These scenes must be produced in full with no edits of any kind (substitutions, additions or subtractions) permitted.
17) Performances must take place at a premises which is owned and/or controlled by the licensee. No performances may take place as part of a festival in any territory or within 50 miles of a city where a current arts festival is taking place during that festival.
18) No additional rights, including, but not limited to, artwork, likeness, trademarks (registered or otherwise), or any other intellectual property is included as part of any license. No license is granted for any music, tune, incidental music, or any other material which may, in some circumstances, be held by third party rights holders.
19) Licensees are required to observe all relevant local, state, and national laws, and any relevant union agreement. Under no circumstances will the retailer, distributor, publisher, Toupee or Not Toupee Limited, the

rights holders, or any other third party be liable to the licensee or any person, group, or organization associated with the licensee, for any loss or liability which the licensee experiences or which is incurred as a result of a license being granted.

20) In no circumstance will the livability of the retailer, distributor, publisher, Toupee or Not Toupee Limited, the rights holders, or any other third party be liable to the licensee or any person, group, or organization associated with the licensee, exceed the United States list price of this book at the time of purchase.

21) For performances taking place in the United Kingdom or the European Economic Area, the licensee may be required to pay VAT in addition to the purchase of this book. No performance license will be granted until this is paid.

22) The licensee and any person, group, or organization associated with the licensee, must not bring the the retailer, distributor, publisher, Toupee or Not Toupee Limited, the rights holders, or any other third party into disrepute. This includes, but is not limited to, by sharing hateful messages and/or content, and using the licensed material in any way except that explicitly permitted in their license. Should Toupee or Not Toupee Limited decide that the licensee or any person, group, or organization associated with the licensee has breached this term, the license granted will be revoked without compensation to the licensee.

23) The licensee must ensure that they do not associate themselves or lead any person to believe they are associated with the retailer, distributor, publisher, Toupee or Not Toupee Limited, the rights holders, or any other third party.

24) Should the purchaser of this book be ineligible for a license, no refund of this book will be given. Should the licensee breach any term or condition of the license, the license granted will be revoked without compensation to the licensee.

INTRODUCTION

Written in four acts presented across two parts, TRUMPED:
An Alternative Musical is a satirical stage play that
parodies the 2016 Presidential Election campaign of Donald
Trump and his subsequent time in office as the 45th
President of the United States.

Opening on the final day of the July 2016 Republican
National Convention in Cleveland, Ohio, Act I tells the
story behind the Trump campaign's journey from the outsider
of the Republican field to the unexpected winner of the
Electoral College with a questionable victory.

Covering the Russia meeting at Trump Tower, all three
election debates against the Democratic opponent, Hillary
Clinton, and the attempts of the Russian President,
Vladimir Putin, to ensure a win for the Trump campaign in
the state of Wisconsin, Act I concludes at the end of
November 8, election day, as the final results come in.

With the election over and Donald Trump set to become the
4th President, Act II opens the day following the election
as both the world and the current President, Barack Obama,
are all still in shock at the previous day's result.

Concluding toward the end of Trump's first year in office,
Act II covers his and his Vice President, Mike Pence's
inaugurations, a visit to the White House by his German
counterpart, Angela Merkel, and the apparent early collapse
of the Trump regime brought about through the actions of
Robert Mueller, the tweets of Donald Trump Junior, and the
gullibility of Eric Trump, forcing the family to make a
quick escape and leave another to fall in their place as
Part One comes to a close.

Picking up some weeks after the conclusion of Part One, Act
III opens as the President is presumed missing by his
closet supporters, and Vladimir Putin is becoming tiresome
of ruling from the front lines.

With the job of bringing Trump back to the United States
tasked to him, Fox News anchor, Sean Hannity, soon sets off
to South America to discover that his journey home is to

(CONTINUED)

CONTINUED:

be hindered by the measures he supported.

Coming to a close as the 2018 Midterm elections approach,
Act III follows the President as, despite his America-first
attitude, he attempts to forge new international ties with
world leaders and royalty alike, while domestically, his
party works to secure a new seat on the Supreme Court.

Act IV opens with an opportunity to discover how Trump's
predecessor is coping with his post-presidential life and
his thoughts on the upcoming Midterm elections. Leaving
island life behind, the action then returns to Trump as he
discovers that under his leadership, the Republican Party
is set for a historic loss.

Following the Midterms being brought to you live from
Florida and Texas, Act IV goes on to tell the story of a
government shutdown and fine dining Trump-style as the
Democrats begin searching for their 2020 nominee.

Coming to a close in late 2019, this final act builds up to
an interpretation of events as they should have been, with
the President finally being held to account.

CAST OF CHARACTERS

All characters are listed in order of appearance.

HILLARY CLINTON, Presidential Candidate/ Former Sec. State
DONALD TRUMP, Presidential Candidate/ 45th President
MICHAEL COHEN, Lawyer to Donald Trump
KELLYANNE CONWAY, Campaign Manager to Donald Trump
STEPHEN MILLER, Advisor to Donald Trump
NYT JOURNALIST, Journalist from the New York Times
THE NARRATOR, Narrator of TRUMPED: An Alternative Musical
DONALD TRUMP JR, Son to Donald Trump
IVANKA TRUMP, Daughter to Donald Trump
ERIC TRUMP, Son to Donald Trump/ Eric
LAWYER, Lawyer to the Narrator
MIKE PENCE, Running Mate to Donald Trump/ Vice-President
JARED KUSHNER, Son-in-Law and Advisor to Donald Trump
VLADIMIR PUTIN, President of Russia/ American Supreme Ruler
DELIVERY DRIVER, Takeout Delivery Driver
CHRIS CHRISTIE, Governor of New Jersey
DMITRY SUREFIRE, Agent of the Kremlin
PETROV SUREFIRE, Agent of the Kremlin
RUDY GIULIANI, Former NYC Mayor/ Lawyer to Donald Trump
LESTER HOLT, NBC News Anchor/ First Debate Moderator
CLINTON AIDE, Aide to Hillary Clinton
TIM KAINE, Running Mate to Hillary Clinton
MIDWESTERN VOTER, Voter from the Midwest
BILL CLINTON, 42nd President/ Husband to Hillary Clinton
ANDERSON COOPER, CNN News Anchor/ Second Debate Moderator
MARTHA RADDATZ, ABC News Anchor/ Second Debate Moderator
BARACK OBAMA, 44th President
MICHELLE OBAMA, First Lady
BERNIE SANDERS, Senator from Vermont/ Democratic Candidate
JOHN OLIVER, TV Host/ Comedian
MIKE HUCKABEE, Former Governor of Arkansas
SARAH PALIN, Former Governor of Alaska
CHRISTOPHER WALLACE, Fox Anchor/ Third Debate Moderator
RECORDED MESSAGE, Trump Grill Phone Message
ELECTION OFFICIAL, Election Official
STEVE DOOCY, Fox & Friends Host
AINSLEY EARHARDT, Fox & Friends Host
BRIAN KILMEADE, Fox & Friends Host
WISCONSIN VOTER, Voter from Wisconsin
SEAN HANNITY, Fox News Anchor

(CONTINUED)

CONTINUED:

PRESS #1, CNN Journalist
PRESS #2, New York Times Journalist
PRESS #3, Washington Post Journalist
PRESS #4, NBC Journalist
PRESS #5, Fox News Journalist
PRESS #6, MSNBC Journalist
SEAN SPICER, White House Press Secretary
ANGELA MERKEL, Chancellor of Germany
PAUL RYAN, Speaker of the House
PRODUCTION ASSISTANT, Assistant to Anderson Cooper
DAY CARE ASSISTANT, White House Day Care Assistant
ANTHONY SCARAMUCCI, Director of Communications
SARAH HUCKABEE SANDERS, White House Press Secretary
DELIVERY MAN #1, White House Delivery Worker
DELIVERY MAN #2, White House Delivery Worker
FBI AGENT #1, Agent for the FBI
FBI AGENT #2, Agent for the FBI
ROBERT MUELLER, Former FBI Director/ Special Counsel
CHECK-IN AGENT, Airport Check-In Agent
FOX NEWS PRODUCER, Producer for Fox & Friends
JUSTICE KENNEDY, Supreme Court Justice
EMMANUEL MACRON, President of France
JUSTIN TRUDEAU, Prime Minister of Canada
PRINCE PHILIP, Husband to The Queen
PRINCE CHARLES, Son to The Queen
THE QUEEN, The Queen of the United Kingdom
GUARD, Buckingham Place Guard
JUDGE, Member of the Judiciary
BARTENDER, Bartender in DC
BRETT KAVANAUGH, Supreme Court Justice Nominee
JOHN CORNYN, Senator from Texas
TED CRUZ, Senator from Texas
JEFF FLAKE, Senator from Arizona
LINDSEY GRAHAM, Senator from South Carolina
CHUCK GRASSLEY, Senator from Iowa
ORRIN HATCH, Senator from Utah
DIANNE FEINSTEIN, Senator from California
WAITER, Tahiti Restaurant Waiter
MITCH MCCONNELL, Senate Majority Leader from Kentucky
NANCY PELOSI, Speaker of the House
CHUCK SCHUMER, Senate Minority Leader from New York
LOCAL, Texas Local

(CONTINUED)

CONTINUED:

STORE OWNER, Texas Store Owner
BETO O'ROURKE, Democratic Senate and Presidential Candidate
MARCO RUBIO, Senator from Florida
MOTHER, Texas Mother
JIM ACOSTA, CNN White House Correspondent
INTERN, White House Intern
ELIZABETH WARREN, Senator from Massachusetts/ 49th VP
JOE BIDEN, Former Vice President/ 46th President
GENERIC WHITE MAN, Democratic Presidential Candidate
GEORGE CONWAY, Husband to Kellyanne Conway
RACHEL MADDOW, MSNBC News Anchor/ Dem. Debate Moderator
CHUCK TODD, MSNBC News Anchor/ Dem. Debate Moderator
KAMALA HARRIS, Senator from California/ Dem. Candidate
PETE BUTTIGIEG, Mayor of South Bend/ Dem. Candidate
MARIANNE WILLIAMSON, Dem. Candidate
ADAM SCHIFF, House Intelligence Committee Chair
DEVIN NUNES, Congressman from California/ Farmer
ERIC SWALWELL, Congressman from California
JIM JORDAN, Congressman from Ohio
MATT GAETZ, Congressman from Florida
SMALL BOY, Donald Trump Fan
CASHIER, Store Cashier

PRODUCTION NOTES

At all performances, the production crew should ensure that a message is played to audiences in order to inform them that while based upon and satirizing true events, TRUMPED: An Alternative Musical, Part One and Two, should not be considered a true or accurate record or representation of those events, nor should it be considered to portray the individuals satirized within accurately.

At all performances, a seat should be resaved at the end of the row within the audience for the character of Hillary Clinton to make her entrance from in Act I, Scene 7. This seat should be within the front orchestra section and be viewable, as far as reasonably possible, by all sections of the auditorium.

To cover the high number of characters within TRUMPED: An Alternative Musical, the majority of company members should perform multiple roles. This excludes the company member who is playing the role of the Narrator.

Where the script refers to the Ensemble, this should be taken to mean all company members, who are available at the time of that scene (i.e., not performing a different role within the scene or undertaking a wardrobe change), except for where specific exemptions are noted within the script.

The note that follows the introduction of the ensemble provides additional information on the role which the ensemble is performing in that scene (e.g., "ENSEMBLE (as PRESS").

In some instances, specific characters will be included as part of the ensemble (e.g., "Press #1").

At no point should company members performing the role of the Narrator or Donald Trump be included within the ensemble.

Performances of TRUMPED: An Alternative Musical should not require additional ensemble members outside of principal company members and understudies.

(CONTINUED)

CONTINUED:

The role of the Narrator is nonspecific for casting purposes, and freedom should be offered to this company member to perform their own style of narration (within the direction of the written material and director).

With the majority of characters in TRUMPED: An Alternative Musical based upon real people and to be performed as impersonations and parodies, company members should be given the freedom (within the direction of the written material and director) to perform the impersonation as they feel most appropriate. This may include the changing of minor words, the mispronunciation of words and phrases, or varying the pace of delivery.

"Cardboard Melania" should be achieved through the creation of a life-size cardboard cutout of Melania Trump being attached to an RC vehicle, which is controlled from offstage.

Dialogue   Indicates that dialogue should be
                  mispronounced.

Dialogue   Indicates that dialogue should be
                  emphasized.

/DIALOGUE/   Indicates that dialogue should be sung.

PART ONE

ACT I : "THE CAMPAIGN"

ACT I, PRE-SHOW | PRE-SHOW

> On an otherwise empty and dark
> stage, a dimly lit flagpole
> stands front stage right with a
> United States flag moving gently
> in a wind that comes from
> somewhere offstage.
>
> With the audience seated, the
> lights in the auditorium go down
> to leave the flag as the only
> thing in the room that's lit.

                    CLINTON (PRE-RECORDED)
Well, hello there, everyone. I'm Hillary Rodham Clinton,
and I'm here to thank you for coming to watch this here
performance of 'Trumped: An Alternative Musical' today, or
as I sometimes call it, fifty shades of orange.

Incidentally, did you happen to know that I've been to see
shows like this one many times myself before? Going to the
theater is a thing that people do, and I'm a people. I'm
Hillary Rodham Clinton, and I'm relatable. You could even
say that I'm Hillary Relatable Clinton.

So before we begin the performance, I would just like to
give you a quick reminder that all forms of electronic
devices and phones should be switched off now for the
duration of the performance. Did you know that I still use
a Blackberry personally? It does everything I need it too.
My calls, my messages and, of course, all of my em --
electronic letters.

I know what you're saying, "typical Hillary, spoiling all
the fun for us," but I say if for everyone's benefit, just
like when I warned you all about Bernie Sanders.
                         (MORE)

                                              (CONTINUED)

                                    CLINTON (PRE-RECORDED) (CONT'D)

Those texts and those calls can wait until after the show
for you, and as for your emails, well, they can wait even
longer. We don't need to worry about the emails. We never
need to worry about the emails.

Thank you for your co-operation and enjoy the show.

ACT I, SCENE ONE | THE REPUBLICAN NATIONAL CONVENTION

                                    In a CONFERENCE HALL in Ohio,
                                    the flag remains the only thing
                                    lit as we begin to hear the
                                    voices of a conversation from
                                    backstage.

                                    TRUMP (OFF)

Do you promise me, lawyer man, that if I sign this document
here, nobody will ever find out?

                                    COHEN (OFF)

Of course, Mister Trump. It's a non-disclosure agreement.
It's an effective way of keeping things, and people, that
should be kept quiet, quiet, if you know what I mean, boss?

                                    TRUMP (OFF)

And all I have to do is sign my name here?

                                    COHEN (OFF)

Almost, boss. You sign your name on the line, but you also
need to sort out the money to pay them off too.

                                    TRUMP (OFF)

And how much is this one?

                                    COHEN (OFF)

One hundred and thirty thousand dollars.

                                    TRUMP (OFF)

Can you sort out the money? I will pay you back one day in
the future, probably.

                                    COHEN (OFF)

Are you sure, sir?

                                        (CONTINUED)

                         TRUMP (OFF)
Of course, I am sure, Michael Cohen. You can trust me. I am
the most trustworthy person that you know.

                         COHEN (OFF)
Well okay, if you're certain. But what about the signature
though, boss?

                         TRUMP (OFF)
That will have to wait. I have to go on stage to talk to a
bunch of losers right now.

                         COHEN (OFF)
But it only takes a second to sign.

                         TRUMP (OFF)
I have to find the correct spelling before I can sign it.

                         COHEN (OFF)
Okay, boss. But don't forget to sign it, the entire
agreement would be worthless if you do. You don't know how
it might come back on you.

                         TRUMP (OFF)
Do not worry yourself, I would never be that stupid.

                         COHEN (OFF)
I believe you, boss. Well, I'd love to stay and watch your
big speech, but Sean Hannity wanted to see me about
something. Good luck.

                              Silence falls before the United
                              States National Anthem begins to
                              play, and a podium appears next
                              to the flag.

                              A moment later, TRUMP enters and
                              stands behind the podium as the
                              music stops.

                         TRUMP
Privet, mo kollegi-Amerikantsy --

                                                      (CONTINUED)

> KELLYANNE CONWAY runs on stage
> in a panic and whispers in his
> ear.

                    TRUMP
Thank you for letting me know that, Kellyanne Conway.

> CONWAY exits.

                    TRUMP
Friends, delegates, and fellow Americans, except for those
who look foreign even though they are not, by the way, I am
the most American person you have ever met. Trust me, okay
folks.

Anyway, I, Donald J. Trump, do hereby right now accept
humblebee... no, Huckabee... no, humbly accept, because I
am a very humble man, your nomination for the Presidency of
the United States...

> He trails off into a silent mime
> as lights find CONWAY and
> STEPHEN MILLER watching from
> across the stage.

                    MILLER
Such elegance in all of his words.

                    CONWAY
Isn't there?

                    MILLER
And he's finally speaking in English too.

                    TRUMP
I loves these uniqueded swates of awericma!

                    MILLER
Well, almost.

                    CONWAY
He was reluctant for a while, but I just told him that
English is alternative Russian, and he went with it.

                                              (CONTINUED)

                              Unnoticed, an NYT JOURNALIST
                              enters and begins taking notes
                              behind them.

                    MILLER
How is that going? Teaching him Russian, I mean.

                    CONWAY
It's going really well. He says that Russian is his new
language of love.

                    MILLER
Let me tell you what I think for a moment. I think it's
quite annoying. We should have just colluded with a country
that speaks English.

                    CONWAY
Because none of those countries like us.

                    MILLER
                  (nodding)
Fair point. How is the collusion going?

                    CONWAY
It's going okay. The Russians can give us some real help.
We haven't told Mike about everything that's going on yet,
though.

                    MILLER
What haven't you told him?

                    CONWAY
We thought it would be best not to tell him everything
about all the help Russia is giving Mister Trump.

                    MILLER
Why not?

                    CONWAY
Well, Mike is just a little old-fashioned...

                              MILLER looks at her perplexed.

                                                    (CONTINUED)

CONTINUED:

                         CONWAY
We don't know if he actually approves of treason.

                                        MILLER glances back at her as
                                        the NYT JOURNALIST sneezes,
                                        prompting them both to look.

                         CONWAY
Who are you?

                         NYT JOURNALIST
Oh... I'm just --

                         MILLER
Let me speak for a moment. I know who you are. I've seen
you before. You work for the New York Times.

                         CONWAY
The New York Times? You're a journalist? But we don't like
journalists do we, Stephen?

                         MILLER
How much of our conversation did you just overhear?

                         CONWAY
Did you overhear the bit when I said that the Trump
campaign is actively colluding with the Russian Government
in order to fix the election?
                         (beat)
Because you shouldn't know about that.

                                        A pause, and then a flash of a
                                        camera as the NYT JOURNALIST
                                        takes a photo of them.

                                        CONWAY and MILLER step closer.

                         NYT JOURNALIST
Please, have mercy on me. Just let me go. I've got two
children.

                                        Another step closer.

                                                        (CONTINUED)

MILLER
We're Republicans. We don't care about the children.

As they take another step
closer, at the front of the
stage, TRUMP begins to hug the
flagpole.

NYT JOURNALIST
(noticing TRUMP)
What is he doing?

CONWAY and MILLER look at TRUMP.

MILLER
Oh my Comrade Putin...

CONWAY
He's hugging the flag again.
(to NYT JOURNALIST)
You wait here for us. We'll deal with you in a moment.

As CONWAY and MILLER move to
push TRUMP and the flag
offstage, the NYT JOURNALIST
takes another photo then makes a
run for it.

ACT I, SCENE TWO | THE JOURNEY TO NEW YORK

Aboard HAIR FORCE ONE in the
main cabin of TRUMP's private
jet where he paces up and down
while CONWAY, ERIC TRUMP, IVANKA
TRUMP, DONALD TRUMP JUNIOR,
JARED KUSHNER, and MIKE PENCE,
sit watching him.

NARRATOR
(entering)
And so it is to be that on July eighteen, two thousand and
sixteen, Donald Trump becomes the Republican --

(CONTINUED)

                              TRUMP
It's Donald J. Trump. Not Donald Trump. The J is important.
It stands for Jenius.

                             NARRATOR
And so it is to be that on July eighteen, two thousand and
sixteen, Donald...

                              TRUMP
J...

                             NARRATOR
Trump becomes the Republican candidate for the Presidency
of the United States of America. A historic moment, for it
marks the first time a person orange in color has received
such a nomination, a feat that could only have come about
with the help of Russia --

                    A LAWYER enters and coughs.

                             NARRATOR
Allegedly.

                    The LAWYER nods then exits.

                             NARRATOR
But the election is still many months away, and there's
still much for old Donald to do, for still he is yet to
battle, debate and argue with both Hillary Clinton and with
all of you.

So with his spray tan at the ready and his chief of staff
his former caddy, there's a campaign ahead, and in
preparation, both Steve Bannon and Chris Christie have been
fed.

It's time to hit the trail, all expecting them to fail. But
first, we journey to New York, for more than just so Mister
Trump can eat his K-F-C with a fork.

                    The NARRATOR exits.

                                                     (CONTINUED)

CONTINUED:

                    TRUMP
I think I have managed to get away with it. With Russia's
help, I am now the presidential candidate of the Russian
National Convention --

                    CONWAY
No! Mister Trump, sir. It's the Republican National
Convention.

                    TRUMP
Republican? But they were the people I once called the
dumbest bunch of voters in the country.

                    CONWAY
Yes, that's them, sir. But it won't matter, they're all too
dumb to remember that you said it.

                    TRUMP
I am confused. What is the Russian National Convention,
Kellyanne Conway?

                    CONWAY
That doesn't exist, sir.

                    TRUMP
Oh, does it not? Never mind then. Mike Pence, where are
you, Mike Pence?

                    PENCE
I'm right here, sir.

                    TRUMP
Okay, join me, Mike Pence.

             PENCE joins him pacing.

                    PENCE
Mister Trump, why exactly are we doing this, sir?

                    TRUMP
We are doing this, Mike Pence, because this is what people
call walking and talking, and as we know, both bits, both
the walking and also the talking too, is what my favorite
president is famous for doing.

                                              (CONTINUED)

                              PENCE
And who is your favorite president, Mister Trump?

                              TRUMP
My favorite president, Mike Pence, is President Mister
Martin Sheen, Mike Pence. I can relate to him. Much like
me, he did not win the Emmy that he deserved, but also, the
thing that we have most in common is that no matter how
realistic it might look if I win, people will never believe
I am a real president.

                         Beat.

                              PENCE
You were truly robbed of that Emmy, sir.

                              TRUMP
Thank you, Mike Pence. I like you, Mike Pence.

Clearly, you have a lot of intelligent in you, and it is
such intelligence insight like that which is why I chose
for you to have the honor of being my walking mate.

                              PENCE
Your walking mate, sir?

                              TRUMP
Yes, Mike Pence. My walking mate. A walking mate is just
like a running mate, only it requires less exercise.

                              PENCE
Well, thank you, sir. It really is an honor to be chosen by
you.

                              TRUMP
You may sit now, Mike Pence.

                         PENCE sits.

                              JUNIOR
Hey dad, me and...

                              ERIC
Eric...

                                                      (CONTINUED)

CONTINUED:

                              JUNIOR
We're both wondering, why are we going back to New York?
Don't we need to be hitting the campaign trail straight
away?

                              TRUMP
We are going back to New York, Donald Trump Junior, because
we need to get our campaign team together and work out a
strategy.

I never actually thought I was going to win the nomination,
not even I thought the Republican party would be this
stupid, and so I never planned a campaign.

I do know that I need you and Eric Trump to be there with
me, though.

                              ERIC
Hey, it's not Eric. It's Eric.

                              JUNIOR
Thanks, dad. It's nice to know that you really value us.

                              TRUMP
Oh, it is not that, Donald Trump Junior. It is that you are
both stupid enough to do all of the really illegal things
for me.

                              ERIC
I'm stupid.

                              TRUMP
We were going to say in Ohio and meet at the end of the
convention, but Chris Christie wanted to be there too, and
as we all know, he is illegal in forty-six states.

                              ERIC
My name is Edward.

                              CONWAY
Mister Trump, if I may make a suggestion? Perhaps you
should spend this journey coming up with some policy ideas?

                                                    (CONTINUED)

                          TRUMP
That is a very great idea, Kellyanne Conway. But I have a
better one.

                          CONWAY
What is your idea, sir?

                          TRUMP
I am going to spend this journey, this one that we are all
on now, coming up with some policy ideas.

                          IVANKA
Daddy.

                          TRUMP
Yes, darling?

                          IVANKA
I think that you should work on a policy that helps out
women who struggle.

                          CONWAY
Melania suggested that, but Donald said he doesn't want a
divorce. Where is Melania anyway?

                          TRUMP
She said she had a doctor's appointment.
                    (to IVANKA)
I like your idea, babycakes. Stand up and come to me so
that daddy can kiss you.

                              IVANKA stands and approaches
                              until the NARRATOR runs on and
                              gets in the way to end up being
                              kissed on the cheek by TRUMP.

                              There's a pause before the
                              NARRATOR wipes their face.

                          NARRATOR
This is supposed to be a family show. We're not going
there.
                    (beat)
                         (MORE)

                                              (CONTINUED)

CONTINUED:

                    NARRATOR (CONT'D)
But Ivanka has a point, because like it or not, and Donald
certainly doesn't, women are entitled to vote --

                    JUNIOR
I don't think it's a good idea either, and neither does
Eric, do you, buddy?

                    ERIC
What's a woman?

                    NARRATOR
And as such, they do need policies to appeal to the group
that few of them know. Unfortunately for the campaign,
Donald Trump is not a man who knows what appeals to women.

                    TRUMP
How does this sound, Ivanka Trump darling? Each and every
woman in America will be given, for free, a calendar where
me, Steve Bannon, and Mike Pence all dress up and pose as
firemen.

                    IVANKA
No.

                    CONWAY
Definitely not.

                    TRUMP
What would be wrong with it? It would be so great. Just so
great.

                    CONWAY
Two things. The first being Steve, and the second being
Bannon.

                    NARRATOR
And so with his first idea out, Trump begins to think,
until eventually inside his head, a light begins to blink.

                    TRUMP
I have got it. A genius idea. I am telling you all, this is
a genius idea. I am going to invent a new sort of pant that
will be made, and this is the really genius part, just for
women.

                                          (CONTINUED)

                              CONWAY
Sir?

                              TRUMP
Also, and this is the bit that will really blow all of your
minds so hold on to your toupees and your g-strings --

                              ERIC
But I don't own a guitar.

                              TRUMP
These pants will be called three quarters in length pants,
and they will, you would never have been able to guess
this, be three quarters the length of men's pants.

                              CONWAY
Mister Trump, sir?

                              TRUMP
Not now, Kellyanne Conway... These pants are going to also
cost, this is genius, three quarters the price of men's
pants.

There, your minds are all so blown, just so blown. I have
just solved the issue of women earning less. All women will
now be able to buy cheaper and shorter pants, because as we
all know, women all earn less and are shorter, except for
those who are not, but they are just losers.

Also, these new pants will all be beige and two sizes too
small.

                         A pause.

                              JUNIOR
                       (breaking the silence)
Well, I for one think that you've got a really good idea,
dad. I can't wait to see them come off.

                              TRUMP
Spoken just like your father, Donald Trump Junior.

                                                     (CONTINUED)

                    JUNIOR
I think we could have them produced in foreign sweatshops
too. I know Ivanka has some. Not only would it save money,
but we'd be contributing to foreign aid.

                    TRUMP
I like your thinking there. What do you think, Jared
Kushner?

          KUSHNER remains silent.

                    IVANKA
Jared?

          Again, he's silent.

                    TRUMP
That guy is always quiet. That is why I like him. A guy who
is quiet cannot leak.
                (beat)
Anyway, I am certain all women will have to thank me for
this invention. If they do not, then they are just mean and
sexist.

                    ERIC
I met a woman once. She came close to me and my Eric grew.
She's Missus Eric now.

                    IVANKA
Your Eric?

                    ERIC
My Eric, that's right. I have an Eric, so does dad, and
Junior too.

                    IVANKA
What do I have then?

                    ERIC
Oh, you? You have a Missus Eric.

                    IVANKA
Missus Eric? Are you talking about your wife?

                                        (CONTINUED)

CONTINUED:

                              ERIC
That's right, Missus Eric. Have you met her? She's just
like me except she has man boobs like dad.

                              Beat.

                            NARRATOR
While there is one idea down, there is still many more to
come, and nothing is off the table, from the bad.

                             TRUMP
How about we deport anyone who speaks more than one
language for showing disrespect to the American language...
English.

                            NARRATOR
To the very bad.

                             TRUMP
Or how about we force every newborn child to be called
Donald Trump in my honor?

                            NARRATOR
To how did this guy actually get the nomination?

                         VLADIMIR PUTIN crosses the back
                         of the stage unnoticed.

                             TRUMP
We should create an American monarchy.

                            NARRATOR
Ideas were shared and thrown around until the journey to
New York has in full been flown, Eric excluded, of course,
for he needed a prop to be entertained, a hat that allowed
him to pretend to fly the plane.

                         JUNIOR places a pilot's hat onto
                         ERIC.

                             ERIC
Welcome aboard this Eric Airlines flight E-R-I-C to
Ericville. I am your pilot, Eric.
                            (MORE)

                                              (CONTINUED)

CONTINUED:

                          ERIC (CONT'D)
                    (beat)
This is so cool!

ACT I, SCENE THREE | CONWAY & CHRISTIE

                          TRUMP'S OFFICE in Trump Tower
                          where a desk sits waiting and
                          nearby, tall curtains hang.

                    NARRATOR
And so before long, we arrive in New York, landing on the
tarmac runway four at LaGuardia airport. And as we arrive,
the cars are waiting to take the family to Midtown for
meetings of much anticipating. For on the corner of Fifth
and Fifty-Sixth stands tall the fifty-eight stories of
Trump --

                          TRUMP enters while eating from a
                          box of chicken.

                    TRUMP
No. It is actually sixty-eight stories.

                    NARRATOR
It's fifty-eight. You just miss ten out when numbering them
to make it sound taller... It's almost as if you're trying
to compensate for something.

                          Beat, and then TRUMP offers the
                          box.

                    TRUMP
Would you like some chicken?

                          The NARRATOR takes a piece and
                          eyes it suspiciously.

                    NARRATOR
Has Eric touched it?

                    TRUMP
Who is Eric?

                                               (CONTINUED)

CONTINUED:

                              TRUMP goes to sit at his desk.

                         NARRATOR
And so stands on the corner of Fifth and Fifty-Sixth stands
Trump Tower, all fifty-eight --

                         TRUMP
Sixty-eight --

                         NARRATOR
Stories high, where on one of the top floors, is taking
place a meeting of great importance that shall not be told
by I.

                              The NARRATOR exits as CONWAY
                              enters.

                         CONWAY
Mister Trump, sir.

                         TRUMP
Hello, Kellyanne Conway.

                         CONWAY
Mister Trump, I've been thinking --

                         TRUMP
No! Do not think, Kellyanne Conway. I did not make you my
campaign manager so that you could think. I made you my
campaign manager so that I could spread the illegal things
I am doing across more than one person in case Paul
Manafort ever flips. If you wanted to think, you should
have joined the campaign of Crooked Hillary Clinton.

                         CONWAY
Crooked Hillary, sir?

                         TRUMP
Yes, Crooked Hillary Clinton. I am going to call her that
from now on. I think that it is a good name for her because
she is both crooked, but she is also Hillary Clinton. It is
lucky she is called Hillary Clinton, otherwise it would not
work.

                                                  (CONTINUED)

PERFORMANCE LICENSE EDITION   LICENSE # _ _ _ _ _ _ _ _

                              CONWAY
It's --

                              TRUMP
It is. It is so great that I am actually going to go and
tweet about it right now.

                    TRUMP stands.

                              CONWAY
Mister Trump, where are you going?

                              TRUMP
My golden tweeting room, Kellyanne Conway.

                              CONWAY
Your golden tweeting room?

                              TRUMP
Let us just say that I am going to create a Republican
health care bill.

                              CONWAY
                         (nodding)
Oh, I understand.

                         TRUMP exits as CONWAY turns her
                         attention to the curtains.

                              CONWAY
                         (to herself)
What are these here for? This is an internal wall, there's
no window behind here.

                         Pulling them back, she reveals a
                         giant 6ft portrait on TRUMP and
                         attached to it, a label.

                              CONWAY
                         (reading the label)
"To Donald J. Trump. Thank you for all you do for the Trump
Foundation. From Donald J. Trump."

                                              (CONTINUED)

CONTINUED:

                              CONWAY closes the curtains as
                              TRUMP returns.

                         TRUMP
So, where were we?

                         CONWAY
Mister Trump, as I was just saying --

                              A knock on the door interrupts.

                         TRUMP
Not now, Kellyanne Conway.
                    (shouting)
Enter.

                              A DELIVERY DRIVER enters
                              carrying food.

                         DELIVERY DRIVER
Your burger, Mister Trump.

                         TRUMP
Thank you.

                              The DELIVERY DRIVER exits.

                         CONWAY
Mister Trump, if you don't mind me asking, why are you
eating chicken if you've ordered a burger?

                         TRUMP
The chicken is a starter, I have time for one before Chris
Christie arrives. Also, I get the burger for free because I
let the local restaurant use Eric Trump as a stand-in for a
clown at a birthday party.

                              The DELIVERY DRIVER returns.

                         DELIVERY DRIVER
I'm sorry, Mister Trump. I forgot about your drink. It was
diet cola, wasn't it?

                                             (CONTINUED)

PERFORMANCE LICENSE EDITION   LICENSE # _ _ _ _ _ _ _

                         TRUMP
Yes. Two of them.

                         DELIVERY DRIVER
I'll go get them.

                         They exit again.

                         CONWAY
Just two? Are you cutting down?

                         The DELIVERY DRIVER returns,
                         this time carrying two large
                         barrels with "Diet Cola" written
                         on them.

                         DELIVERY DRIVER
Here you go, sir.

                         TRUMP
Thank you, delivery driver person.

                         The DELIVERY DRIVER exits.

                         TRUMP
Oh no. They did not give me a straw.

                         CHRIS CHRISTIE enters carrying a
                         deckchair.

                         CHRISTIE
Hey everyone.

                         TRUMP
Chris Christie, you just walked through a closed door.

                         CHRISTIE
Oh, did I? Jeez, I'm sorry, Mister Trump. That is new for
me. I usually manage okay with the doors, it's the bridges
that trouble me. Like that song, what is it?...

                         TRUMP
Bridge Over Troubled Water?

                                                      (CONTINUED)

                    CHRISTIE
Sexy and I Know It.

                    CONWAY
Hi Chris.

                         CHRISTIE sets out his deckchair
                         and sits.

                    CHRISTIE
Hey, Kellyanne. Wow, jeez, Mister Trump, it sure is nice of
you to invite me up here. I haven't been this high since
the time was left unattended with a glue stick in the
twelfth grade.

                    TRUMP
Chris Christie, could you please come here?

                    CHRISTIE
Oh definitely. Sure thing, Mister Trump.

                         He stands and moves to TRUMP.

                    CHRISTIE
Is this what you called me here for?

                         TRUMP holds out his foot.

                    TRUMP
Yes, it is. Now kiss.

                         CHRISTIE bends down and kisses
                         TRUMP's foot.

                    TRUMP
You can leave now.

                         TRUMP returns to his chair as
                         CHRISTIE folds up his deckchair
                         and goes to leave.

                                              (CONTINUED)
PERFORMANCE LICENSE EDITION   LICENSE # _ _ _ _ _ _ _ _

CONTINUED:

                          CHRISTIE
Thank you for this opportunity, Mister Trump. I'm really
grateful for it, sir, and jeez, Mister Trump, I won't let
you down.

                    CHRISTIE exits.

                          TRUMP
So, Kellyanne Conway, what was it that you were trying to
say?

                          CONWAY
I was just going to suggest that we tell Mike Pence about
everything that is going on with Russia.

                          TRUMP
That is actually a very good idea, Kellyanne Conway. Mike
Pence should know about everything going on, he is going to
need to know how Russia is helping us.

                          CONWAY
Do you want me to go talk to him right away, Mister Trump?

                          TRUMP
No. I have a much better idea. I want you to go and talk to
him right away.

                          CONWAY
Okay... I'll... go do that.

                              The DELIVERY DRIVER enters once
                              more, to hand TRUMP more food.

                          DELIVERY DRIVER
Another burger for you, Mister Trump.

                          TRUMP
Thank you.

                              The DELIVERY DRIVER exits a
                              final time.

                          TRUMP
This one is a midnight snack.

                                                    (CONTINUED)

                         CONWAY
But it isn't midnight.

                         TRUMP
It is in Moscow, Kellyanne Conway. It is in Moscow.

ACT I, SCENE FOUR | PENCE & PUTIN

                              PENCE'S OFFICE, TRUMP TOWER,
                              where PENCE sits reading at his
                              desk. Opposite is a door adorned
                              with a name plaque reading
                              "Mister Mother."

                         NARRATOR
                         (entering)
And so with a job to do, Kellyanne Conway ventures upstairs
to the floor above, where sat at his desk alone is Mic,
Donald J. Trump's vice-president pick. But while she comes
to talk to Pence, yet is she to learn that talking alone is
something that only makes him tense.

                              The NARRATOR exits as CONWAY
                              enters. After knocking on the
                              door, she approaches PENCE.

                         CONWAY
Mister Pence, sir.

                              PENCE glances, then immediately
                              runs offstage.

                         CONWAY
Mister Pence?

                              CONWAY moves back through the
                              door, and PENCE returns.

                              A moment later, she tries again.

                         CONWAY
Mike...

                                                      (CONTINUED)

                              PENCE runs offstage, and as
                              CONWAY moves back again, KUSHNER
                              enters.

                    CONWAY
Oh, hello, Jared.

                              KUSHNER takes a notebook and pen
                              from his pocket, writes, then
                              shows CONWAY.

                    CONWAY
                  (reading)
"Hello, Kellyanne."
                  (to KUSHNER)
Yes, hello. Look, Jared, could you help me out?

                              Again he writes then shows her.

                    CONWAY
                  (reading)
"What with?"
                  (to KUSHNER)
Well, I'm trying to talk to Mike, but he keeps running
away.

                              KUSHNER pauses then writes and
                              shows her.

                    CONWAY
                  (reading)
"Oh, don't worry about that. Mike is just scared of being
alone in the same room as a woman who isn't his wife."
                  (to KUSHNER)
Okay, so if you're not doing anything, can you come in with
me? Just so that he won't run away.

                              Again he writes then shows.

                    CONWAY
                  (reading)
"Of course, I'm not doing anything. I never do anything. I
don't serve any purpose here at all."
                    (MORE)

                                              (CONTINUED)

CONTINUED:

                                CONWAY (CONT'D)
                          (to KUSHNER)
Let's go in now then.

                                TRUMP enters behind them as
                                PENCE returns, this time with,
                                and in conversation with, PUTIN.

                                TRUMP
What is going on here?

                                CONWAY
Mister Trump, sir. I was trying to speak to Mike --

                                TRUMP
Who?

                                CONWAY
Mike Pence. But whenever I walk into his office he runs
away.

                                TRUMP
Okay, Kellyanne Conway. Clearly, this needs a real man, and
so I will come in with both of you.

                                All three go through the door
                                and approach PENCE and PUTIN.

                                CONWAY
Mister Pence, sir.

                                TRUMP
Mike Pence, and... Comrade Almighty One. What are you doing
here?

                                PUTIN
I came to fill in our Comrade about what Government of mine
are doing to help you with election win.

                                TRUMP
But how did you get in?

                                PUTIN
I have tunnel built from Trump Tower basement direct to
Kremlin. In it be fast loop.

                                     (CONTINUED)

                         TRUMP
But those things cost billions of zillions. How did you
afford it?

                         PUTIN
I make Mexico pay for it.

                         TRUMP
That is a good idea. Kellyanne Conway, note it down, we
should use that for the wall.

                         CONWAY
So does Mike know everything now?

                         PENCE
Yes, Kellyanne. Comrade Vladimir has told me all that I
need to know.

May I also apologize for earlier. I don't feel comfortable
being in a room alone with any woman who isn't my wife. You
know how men can be.

                         CONWAY
You think there's a risk of temptation?

                         PENCE
Well, I am an old white man, Kellyanne.

                         Beat.

                         TRUMP
Hey, Comrade Vladimir Putin, did you tell Mike Pence --

                              PENCE makes a cross on his chest
                              then hits the stage with a thud.

                         PUTIN
Did I tell Mike Pence that you start worshiping me over
Jesus? No. I not tell him.

                              They all look down as KUSHNER
                              kneels to check him.

                                        (CONTINUED)

                         TRUMP
Is he dead?

                              KUSHNER quickly writes on his
                              notepad and shows it to CONWAY.

                         CONWAY
                    (reading)
"No, he's just fainted."
                    (to all)
He's just fainted.

                         PUTIN
Donald, I leave you to clean up this mess.

                         TRUMP
Mike Pence is not a mess. Mike Pence is going to be the
reason my spirit lives on after I am impeached and
arrested.

                         PUTIN
Donald.

                         TRUMP
Sorry, Comrade Vladimir Putin, sir.

                         PUTIN
Better. Now, as I say, I leave you to clean up mess. Know
though, I never be far away... Good luck with campaign.

                              PUTIN leaves as the rest look
                              back to PENCE.

                         TRUMP
What are we going to do with Mike Pence?

                              KUSHNER writes, coughs, then
                              shows it to CONWAY.

                         CONWAY
                    (reading)
"I think we should move him."
                    (to all)
Jared Kushner thinks we should move him.

                                             (CONTINUED)

                          TRUMP
Okay. You two grab his legs, I will take his head.

                                   Between them, they lift PENCE
                                   and begin to carry him off.

ACT I, SCENE FIVE | THE CAMPAIGN TRAIL, PART ONE

                                   Various CAMPAIGN RALLIES across
                                   the country, but first, the
                                   NARRATOR enters.

                          NARRATOR
And so, with the help of Russia, the campaign could not
start any lusher. But the truth remains that it's hard to
rig every state to vote for the man who wears a wig. What
he needs to get his votes is his campaign notes filled with
quotable quotes. Something to rally the crowd, something
they can go and repeat for weeks to anyone nearby by
shouting it loud. But how can he get his message across to
convince the gullible to vote him the boss? He has to
journey to the land of the normal, for rallies that are
anything but formal.

                                   Lights up on the stage where
                                   TRUMP stands giving a speech
                                   while the ENSEMBLE (as VOTERS)
                                   stand cheering. All are wearing
                                   Dallas team shirts.

                          NARRATOR
Dallas, Texas.

                          TRUMP
We are going to lock her up...

                          ENSEMBLE
Lock her up! Lock her up! Lock her up!

                          TRUMP
We are going to build the wall...

                                                      (CONTINUED)

CONTINUED:

                    ENSEMBLE
Build the wall! Build the wall! Build the wall!

                    TRUMP
And we are going to make, this is so great, Mexico pay for
it!

                    ENSEMBLE
Who is Mexico? What is a Mexico? Where is Mexico?

                              They all remove their shirts to
                              reveal another underneath, this
                              time from a Little Rock sports
                              team.

                    NARRATOR
Little Rock, Arkansas.

                    TRUMP
Hillary Clinton is so crooked...

                    ENSEMBLE
Clinton is crooked! Clinton is crooked! Clinton is crooked!

                    TRUMP
She wants to spend money on healthcare...

                    ENSEMBLE
We're all going to die! We're all going to die! We're all
going to die!

                    TRUMP
She is such a nasty woman!

                    ENSEMBLE
What's a woman? I don't know any women! I've never touched
a woman!

                              They continue in silence,
                              changing their shirt every few
                              moments, as CONWAY and MILLER
                              enter to watch from the side.

                                                  (CONTINUED)

                         CONWAY
Why aren't there more people?

                         MILLER
I thought we were going to get thousands.

                         PUTIN enters next to them.

                         PUTIN
Do you not any idea how much it cost to convince person to
attend rally? Russia not be made of money.

                         MILLER
How come there's only one woman?

                         COHEN, wearing a torn suit,
                         enters next to them.

                         COHEN
I can only afford one.

                         The other three notice his suit.

                         MILLER
What happened to you?

                         COHEN
I can't afford a new suit. Being Trump's lawyer is
expensive.

                         CONWAY
We need more people. How can we get more?

                         MILLER
We could use children. Ivanka might lend us some of her
staff?

                         CONWAY
She pays them nearly a dollar a month. We're not paying
that much.

                                                   (CONTINUED)

CONTINUED:

                         PUTIN
I have idea.
                    (to COHEN and MILLER)
You, go.

                              Reluctantly, they follow his
                              instructions.

                         CONWAY
Do you want me to join them?

                         PUTIN
No. You stay here. We need people act as though they
support Donald convincingly.

                              The action returns to TRUMP and
                              the ENSEMBLE as they pull off
                              their final shirt and become
                              topless.

                         NARRATOR
Anchorage, Alaska.

                         TRUMP
We are going to win...

                    ENSEMBLE/ COHEN/ MILLER
We will win! We will win! We will win!

                         TRUMP
We are going to do so much winning...

                    ENSEMBLE/ COHEN/ MILLER
So much winning! So much winning! So much winning!

                         TRUMP
And now we all need to find our shirts and get out of here
before Sarah Palin turns up.

                    ENSEMBLE/ COHEN/ MILLER
No shirt! No shoes! No sophistication!

ACT I, SCENE SIX | THE RUSSIA MEETING

                        TRUMP TOWER, first in the
                        bedroom of TRUMP, where he sits
                        in bed, wearing suit and red tie
                        pajamas, trying to sleep over
                        the sound of Russian music.

                NARRATOR
               (entering)
It's the night before the first debate, and all throughout
Trump Tower, not a single campaign ass is plotting treason
to gain power. Or so Donald thinks, for no invite has he
seen, but downstairs on the floor below, music and dancing
are the scenes.

               The NARRATOR exits.

                TRUMP
Why can I, the great Donald J. Trump, hear music?

                        The volume grows, and TRUMP
                        looks around for the source,
                        after a moment he checks under
                        the bed.

                TRUMP
It sounds like it is coming from below.

                        He climbs out of bed and pulls
                        back the cover to reveal an
                        inflatable doll of himself.

                TRUMP
You wait here for me, inflatable Donald J. Trump. I need to
go turn that music off.

                        TRUMP exits as his bedroom goes
                        dark, and we move to the room
                        below where a party is going on.

                                      (CONTINUED)

CONTINUED:

> The music louder, JUNIOR stands talking to DMITRY and PETROV SUREFIRE (two Russian agents) while around them half of the ENSEMBLE (as RUSSIANS) are stood with drinks in hand.
>
> To the side of this main scene, the other half of the ENSEMBLE (as CANDIDATES) play musical chairs.

                    JUNIOR
It really is no trouble for us to set this up at all, comrades. As soon as I heard you had information on Hillary, it was my top priority.

                    PETROV
We are here to help, Comrade.

> They toast.

                    DMITRY
Comrades.

                    PETROV
To comrades.

                    JUNIOR
Comrades.

> TRUMP enters and looks around confused before he approaches JUNIOR, who is surprised to see him.

                    TRUMP
Donald Trump Junior.

                    JUNIOR
What are you doing here?

                                        (CONTINUED)

                         TRUMP
What is going on? I thought I told you to ask before you
invite friends over. I am trying to sleep, but all I can
hear is your music. Do you not know that it is the first
debate tomorrow?

                         JUNIOR
I'm sorry, dad. But that's what these people are here for.
They've got information on Hillary Clinton for us.

                         TRUMP
                  (pointing at the CANDIDATES)
What about all of them? They do not look Russian.

                         JUNIOR
Oh, they're not. They're Senate candidates. They're playing
musical chairs to see who gets to run. When the music
stops...

                              There's a pause in the music,
                              and the CANDIDATES fight for a
                              chair until one loses and exits
                              before the music starts again.

                         JUNIOR
They fight. By the end of the night, we'll have just one
person left, and they win the Senate seat. It's much
quicker than any primary.

                         TRUMP
But what if the public does not vote for them?

                         JUNIOR
Russia.

                              CONWAY enters, drink in hand,
                              and also looking surprised.

                         CONWAY
Mister Trump, sir. What are you doing here?

                         TRUMP
Hello, Kellyanne Conway.

                                             (CONTINUED)

CONTINUED:

                         CONWAY
                      (to JUNIOR)
     I thought we weren't inviting him?

                         JUNIOR
     I didn't. He just heard the music.

                         TRUMP
     Why was I not supposed to be invited?

                         JUNIOR
     Well, dad, you're a great guy and everything --

                              TRUMP pulls out his phone and
                              begins to type.

                         TRUMP
     Continue.

                         JUNIOR
     But we have to be subtle about the help we're getting, and
     well, often you're not.

                         TRUMP
                      (to himself, reading)
     "Just meeting with some very great people and finding out
     bad stuff about Crooked Hillary Clinton. More soon." And
     tweet.
                      (beat)
     What was that, Donald Trump Junior?

                         JUNIOR
     You know, it doesn't matter.

                              ERIC enters, a soda in hand.

                         ERIC
     Hey, I'm Eric. What's your name?

                         JUNIOR
     Calm down there, buddy. You don't want to be drinking too
     much of that soda now, it'll upset your stomach, and you
     don't want to be bringing up your alphabet pasta from
     earlier, do you?

                                                      (CONTINUED)

PERFORMANCE LICENSE EDITION   LICENSE # _ _ _ _ _ _ _ _

                          ERIC
But if I did, then I could eat it again for free.

                          JUNIOR
Just take it steady.

                              ERIC moves to the side, drinks
                              his soda in one, then begins to
                              dance.

                          TRUMP
So tell me, what have you found out about Crooked Hillary
Clinton?

                          JUNIOR
Well, we know that she's crooked. That's a start.

                          TRUMP
Anything else?

                          JUNIOR
No. We're not sure why she is crooked, when she was
crooked, or how she was crooked.

                              A phone rings out.

                          JUNIOR
Okay, so you know, that sounds like my phone.

                              He takes his phone from his
                              pocket to check it.

                          JUNIOR
I've just got a message from Julian Assange on Twitter. It
says...
                          (reading)
"I have just had my team hack the D-N-C email servers and
found this, I think it would help." And he's sent a
screenshot too. It looks as though it's an email from
Hillary to her campaign team.

                          CONWAY
What does it say?

                                                    (CONTINUED)

                         TRUMP
Can I read it, Donald Trump Junior?

                         JUNIOR
You don't know how to read, dad.

                         TRUMP
Good point. You read it then.

                         JUNIOR
                    (reading)
"Dear Subordinates. The pizzas will be delivered to the
office between six and seven P-M. Thank you for all that
you're doing."

                         TRUMP
Oh, my Comrade Putin.
                         (beat)
Wait, what does it mean?

                         JUNIOR
I think it means that she's ordered pizza.

                         TRUMP
Can we use that?

                         JUNIOR
Kellyanne, you're the campaign manager.

                         CONWAY
Well... I think it's clear. Hillary Clinton is obviously
choosing to feed her campaign team pizza over the
hardworking, patriotic American citizens of his country.

                         TRUMP
It is probably an illegal alien pizza too.

                         JUNIOR
That's it. She's feeding her campaign team Italian pizza
and taking away the jobs of American pizza. That will work,
won't it?

                         CONWAY
I think we might need something more.

                                              (CONTINUED)

                         JUNIOR
Well, we could always just edit the screenshot to make it
look like she's a trafficking people with the pizza guy?

                                   TRUMP begins typing on his phone
                                   again.

                         TRUMP
                    (to himself, reading)
"Just seen crooked email showing Hillary Clinton is very
crooked buying crooked pizza for her crooked team." Tweet.
                    (looking up)
Sorry, I missed that.

                         JUNIOR
Okay, so we're going with the pizza story then.

                         CONWAY
Pizza it is.

                                   ERIC approaches them again.

                         ERIC
I like pizza.

                         JUNIOR
That's right, you do like pizza, buddy. But you're not
having any tonight.

                         ERIC
Hey Junior, I feel sick.

                         JUNIOR
Well, just go slow, bud. You'll be okay.

                                   ERIC is sick in front of them,
                                   leaving a pile of alphabet pasta
                                   on the floor.

                         ERIC
Hey Junior, I was sick.

                                                      (CONTINUED)

                         JUNIOR
I think it might be time for bed. Come on, I'll tuck you
in.

                              JUNIOR begins to lead ERIC
                              offstage.

                         JUNIOR
Say goodnight to everyone.

                         ERIC
Goodnight to everyone.

                              They exit.

                         CONWAY
So...

                         TRUMP
We are alone, Kellyanne Conway.

                         CONWAY
Yes. Yes, we are.

                         TRUMP
We --

                         CONWAY
So have you thought of a campaign slogan yet?

                         TRUMP
No.

                              They both look down at the
                              alphabet spaghetti.

                         CONWAY
Maybe we could get some inspiration from this?
                    (looking closer)
Look, it says M-A-W-G.

                         TRUMP
M-A-W-G? How about, make America white again?

                                             (CONTINUED)

CONTINUED:

                         CONWAY
Maybe we should go for something a little less racist.

                         TRUMP
What are you suggesting?

                              CONWAY kneels and begins to
                              rearrange letters.

                         CONWAY
Well, let's change this W with... let's see, I know, an A.
M-A-G-A.

                         TRUMP
M-A-G-A? MAGA?

                         CONWAY
Make America great again.

                              TRUMP also kneels.

                         TRUMP
I have a better idea. I am going to switch this first A
here, with this letter --

                         CONWAY
An A, Mister Trump.

                         TRUMP
Correct. M-A-G-A. Make America great again.

                              Lights out.

                         TRUMP (IN DARKNESS)
Trademark.

ACT I, SCENE SEVEN | THE FIRST DEBATE

                              HOFSTRA UNIVERSITY, LONG ISLAND,
                              where a line of light runs from
                              the front of the stage to a desk
                              set further back.

                                             (CONTINUED)

                    NARRATOR
                    (entering)
September twenty-six and the scene is set. The first
debate, an event set to be so fierce the world just can't
wait. Hofstra University on Long Island, New York, is to be
the arena, and from N-B-C, Lester Holt is to be the judge.

                         LESTER HOLT enters and addresses
                         the audience.

                    HOLT
Good evening. I'm Lester Holt.

                         He goes to sit at the desk.

                    NARRATOR
And so it comes down to Kellyanne to take on the job of
getting old Donald to budge.

                         The stage lights up to reveal to
                         podiums flanking the desk, one
                         of them being approached by
                         CONWAY pushing TRUMP.

                    TRUMP
No, Kellyanne Conway, please do not do this to me.

                    CONWAY
Come on, Mister Trump. You need to debate.

                    TRUMP
But every time I go near a black man, I say something that
makes me look bad.

                    HOLT
And in the red corner, we have... DONALD J. TRUMP!

                    TRUMP
I do not feel comfortable.

                    HOLT
And in the blue corner, we have... HILLARY RODHAM CLINTON!

                                        (CONTINUED)

                              A CLINTON AIDE runs on stage in
                              a panic.

                    CLINTON AIDE
I don't know where she is.

                    HOLT
Do you mean to say that minutes before she's due to debate
live to the nation, Secretary Clinton still hasn't arrived?

                    CLINTON AIDE
That does appear to be the case.

                    HOLT
What's she doing? Taking the railroad here or something?

                    NARRATOR
You see, while Donald has arrived early, Hillary Clinton
will be late, or perhaps maybe, it's just that simply she
believes in fate?

                              A spotlight begins to search the
                              audience until it finds HILLARY
                              CLINTON watching from one of the
                              orchestra seats.

                    CLINTON
Oh, I'm not late. No, no, no. I've been here for hours. I'm
just watching from down here with my feet up because I'm
fairly sure I've got this one covered.

                              She turns to the person next to
                              her and pulls out her phone.

                    CLINTON
Hi, I'm Hillary Rodham Clinton, and it's nice to meet you.
I'm a relatable kind of person, as you can see. Let us take
a self-photograph together.

                              She brings her phone up but
                              quickly puts it down again.

                                                      (CONTINUED)

                          CLINTON
Oh, oops. My mistake there. Just an email that I forgot to
delete. I'll just sort it.

                    She clicks on her phone.

                          CLINTON
Now you didn't see anything that you shouldn't have seen
there, did you?
                    (frightful)
Otherwise, I'm going to have to make sure I delete you too.
                    (beat, then cheerful)

Hi, I'm Hillary Rodham Clinton.

                          HOLT
Secretary Clinton, may I please ask if you've got any
intentions of joining us up here on the stage?

                          CLINTON
                    (standing)
Well, I suppose I should, Lester. I need to at least be
sporting to Donald, but I'm telling you, I'm so ready to
knock this one out of the park today.

                                   CLINTON mimes a tennis shot
                                   before turning to another in the
                                   audience.

                          CLINTON
It's tennis.
                    (mimes again)
I play tennis. People play tennis. See? I'm a people. You
play tennis, don't you?
                    (beat, then reaches for a
                     handshake)
Nice to meet you, I'm Hillary Rodham Clinton.

                          HOLT
Madam Secretary, please can you join us so we can get his
underway?

                                             (CONTINUED)

                              CLINTON
I hear you, Lester. I'll be there in just a moment, just
have a quick matter I need to attend to first.

                                        She reaches under her seat to
                                        retrieve a pile of papers which
                                        she hands to another in the
                                        audience.

                              CLINTON
Would you mind disposing of these emails for me, please?

                                        On stage, DMITRY and PETROV
                                        enter and drag off the CLINTON
                                        AIDE. A moment later, they
                                        return with notes which they
                                        begin to show TRUMP.

                              CLINTON
I'll give you a dollar for your time.

                                        CLINTON pulls a dollar from her
                                        pocket and hands it over.

                              CLINTON
                          (shaking hands)
Hillary Rodham Clinton. Nice to meet you.

                               HOLT
Madam Secretary.

                              CLINTON
I'm coming, Lester.

                                        HOLT notices DMITRY and PETROV.

                               HOLT
Wait, Mister Trump, are you getting help from two Russians
right now?

                               TRUMP
Russians? I do not see anyone rushing. This is a debate,
Lester Holt, it is not a running race.
                              (MORE)

                                                          (CONTINUED)

CONTINUED:
                         TRUMP (CONT'D)
If it was a race, I would win, because I am athletic and I
am the best. I am a winner, everyone knows it.

                         HOLT
What the hell are you talking about?
                    (beat)
Mister Trump, there are two men standing in front of you
right this moment showing you notes.

                         TRUMP
I do not see anyone here.
                    (to PETROV and DMITRY)
What does that bit say?
                    (to HOLT)
There is no one else here, Lester Holt.
                    (to PETROV and DMITRY)
Does either of you see anyone else?

                              DMITRY and PETROV turn to HOLT,
                              shake their heads, then turn
                              back to TRUMP.

                         TRUMP
Do you see that, Lester Holt? These two nice Russian men
agree with me. There is no one else here.

                         HOLT
Mister Trump, those two nice Russian men, as you put it,
are them. They just spoke.

                         TRUMP
Stop persecuting me just because of the color of my skin.
It is not my fault that I am orange. I do not deserve to be
mistreated.

                         HOLT
Mister Trump, they are stood in front of you.

                              He stands and approaches.

                         HOLT
You are both clearly Russian agents from the Kremlin.

                                                  (CONTINUED)

                              PETROV
We're not Russian.

                              DMITRY
No. Definitely not Russian.

                              HOLT
But you're wearing the Russian flag on your shirts.

                              TRUMP
How are you speaking to ghosts, Lester Holt? I did not know
that the dead were here tonight. Steve Bannon said he was
watching from home.

                              PETROV
We're Dutch.

                              DMITRY
This is the Dutch flag.

                              HOLT
The Dutch flag goes red, white, and then blue, not white,
blue, and then red.

                              DMITRY
It's the alternative Dutch flag.

                                        CLINTON finally makes it to the
                                        stage.

                              CLINTON
I'm here, Lester. You can stop all your worrying now.

                                        HOLT turns to her as the DMITRY
                                        and PETROV exit quickly.

                              HOLT
Finally.

                                        He turns back to TRUMP.

                              HOLT
Wait, where have the Russians gone?

                                                            (CONTINUED)

                          TRUMP
There were no Russians. They were ghosts.

                          HOLT
Mister Trump, what are you talking about?

                          TRUMP
Woooooo. Woooooooo. Wooooooooo.
                    (beat)
Woo.

                         Shaking his head, HOLT returns
                         to his desk.

                          HOLT
Let's just get this over with.

                         CLINTON approaches the NARRATOR
                         to shake hands.

                          CLINTON
Hi. I'm Hillary Rodham Clinton, nice to meet you.

                          NARRATOR
Narrator.

                          CLINTON
Nice to meet you, Nar-ray-tor.

                         She laughs to herself.

                          NARRATOR
                    (forced)
Ha.

                          CLINTON
Did you see that? Did everyone see that? I made a joke, and
you laughed because it was a funny joke. Jokes are funny,
and jokes are relatable.
                    (beat)
I'm Hillary Rodham Clinton. I'm here for the next eight
years.
                         (MORE)

                                                 (CONTINUED)

CONTINUED:

                        CLINTON (CONT'D)
                    (putting her arm around the
                    NARRATOR)
You know, I think we're going to be the best of friends.

                        HOLT
Secretary Clinton, for the last time --

                        CLINTON
I'm taking my place, Lester. Keep your hair on, or you'll
end up looking like Donald.

                        HOLT
Touché.

                        CLINTON
Exactly, Lester.

                        CLINTON takes her place at her
                        podium as the NARRATOR goes to
                        kneel next to HOLT.

                        HOLT
                    (clears throat)
Hello, and welcome to the first Presidential debate of the
two thousand and sixteen election. I will be your moderator
for tonight's increasingly personal argument, Lester Holt.

                        CLINTON
Hi, Lester. I'm Hillary Rodham Clinton.

                        HOLT
Madam Secretary, I know who you are.

                        TRUMP
And I am...

                        HOLT
Mister Trump?

                        TRUMP
Hold on, Lester Holt.

                        He takes a drawing from his
                        pocket and unfolds it.

                                            (CONTINUED)
PERFORMANCE LICENSE EDITION   LICENSE # _ _ _ _ _ _ _ _

CONTINUED:

                          TRUMP
                        (reading)
"I am Eric."

                          HOLT
I'm sorry?

                          TRUMP
No, you are Lester Holt.

                          HOLT
Mister Trump, you're not Eric.

                          TRUMP
I was reading from a good luck picture that my son drew for
me.

                    He shows off the drawing.

                          TRUMP
He drew a bunny.

                          HOLT
Can we please just start this debate?

                          CLINTON
Of course, Lester. Let's get on with it.

                          HOLT
Thank you.
                        (beat)
And so onto this evening's first topic, achieving
prosperity. Secretary Clinton, you have the floor.

                          TRUMP
Does that mean I have the roof?

                          CLINTON
Thank you, Lester. I have a very clear position on this
subject. I think that for America to achieve prosperity and
be successful, we need to be investing in education.

                    She mimes a tennis shot.

                                              (CONTINUED)

                          TRUMP
I think that too, but I thought of it first. Clearly,
Crooked Hillary Clinton is just stealing my ideas on
controlling immigration.

                          HOLT
Mister Trump, this section isn't about controlling
immigration, it's about achieving prosperity.

                          TRUMP
Are they not the same thing?

                          HOLT
No, Mister Trump, they are not the same thing.

                              The NARRATOR raises their arm on
                              CLINTON's side.

                          NARRATOR
Fifteen-love.

                          HOLT
Madam Secretary, would you like to continue?

                          CLINTON
Certainly, Lester. So, you know, today happens to be my
little granddaughters second birthday. She's a sweet, small
and polite girl, although that will soon change when she
starts kindergarten, but it means that I know first hand
just how important it is to ensure we're able to offer a
high level of quality education to everyone from a young
age.

                              She mimes another tennis shot.

                          HOLT
Mister Trump, your response, please.

                          TRUMP
Well, I too know just how important education, and also one
million dollars from your father, is at a young age.

                          (MORE)

                                                    (CONTINUED)

                              TRUMP (CONT'D)
Not a lot of people know this, but I have a son, and his
name is Eric Trump, and he is still in kindergarten, but
soon, when we have worked out how to teach him potty, he
will be starting big boy school.

                              Beat, then the NARRATOR holds up
                              their arm again.

                         NARRATOR
Thirty-love.

                         HOLT
Secretary Clinton.

                         CLINTON
Oh, is it my turn again already? How exciting, I'm enjoying
this. Well, let me go on by telling you exactly how I will
help this to bring prosperity back to this country... I
will not do anything that Donald Trump would do.

                              She mimes another tennis shot.

                         TRUMP
What people need to know about this woman is that she is a
very crooked woman. Crooked Hillary Clinton. No one has
ever been more crooked than Hillary Clinton. I do not know
why or when she was crooked, but I have just here, in my
pocket --

                         HOLT
Mister Trump?

                              TRUMP pulls out another drawing.

                         TRUMP
I have here an email that Hillary Clinton sent to someone
on her campaign team, and it says, just here that... Oh,
no, this is just another picture Eric Trump drew for me.

                              He shows off the drawing of a
                              cat.

                         TRUMP
He drew a dog. Look, you can see its whiskers.

                                        (CONTINUED)

                         HOLT
Mister Trump, what is this email that you are on about?

                              TRUMP reaches under his podium
                              to pick up a giant tennis ball.

                         TRUMP
It is an email that Crooked Hillary Clinton sent to
someone, and it proves that she is a very bad and also a
very crooked person who orders crooked pizza for her
crooked team. It was sent to my campaign by a great man
called Julian Assange, who does great things, and he and
WikiLeaks, with the help of Russia, hacked her email.

                         HOLT
Wait, you're saying that Russia and WikiLeaks hacked
Secretary Clinton's email, and all they found was that she
ordered pizza?

                         TRUMP
Did I mention that it was a crooked pizza?

                              He attempts to throw the tennis
                              ball, but it bounces back at
                              him.

                              DMITRY and PETROV return to talk
                              to TRUMP.

                         HOLT
So now the Russians are back.

                              CLINTON exits the returns a
                              moment later with an automatic
                              tennis ball launcher as the
                              DMITRY and PETROV leave again.

                         TRUMP
They were not Russians, Lester Holt. I would also to change
what I just said. I do not have an email, I did not get it
from Julian Assange, he did not get it from WikiLeaks, and
they did not get help from Russia to hack the D-N-C. None
of that happened, so bless Comrade Vladimir Putin.

                                             (CONTINUED)

                              HOLT
That is an incredibly specific statement for you to make,
Mister Trump.

                              TRUMP
Wrong.

                              HOLT
Secretary Clinton, back to you.

                              CLINTON
Oh, yes, thank you, Lester. Well, you may have all seen
there how Donald attempted to distract everyone from his
misdeeds. Speaking of which, I'm wondering just how many of
them he's going to be bringing up tonight. Perhaps he might
mention his fake university that has been scamming the
vulnerable out of thousands of dollars?

                              She taps the top of the
                              launcher, and it fires a ball
                              towards TRUMP.

                              CLINTON
Or perhaps the time he was sued for refusing to rent out
his properties to minority communities because he is a
racist?
                    (another tap)
Or the numerous businesses he's caused the failure or
bankruptcy of? Trump Steaks.
                    (another tap)
Trump Vodka.
                    (another tap)
Trump Atlantic City.
                    (another tap)
Numerous Trump golf courses.
                    (multiple taps)
Trump Airlines.
                    (another tap)
Trump Ice.
                    (another tap)
The year two thousand Trump Presidential Election campaign.
                    (another tap)
And, of course, his greatest failure of all, Eric Trump.
                    (a final tap)

                                              (CONTINUED)

                         TRUMP
Wrong. That is just not fair. A lot of that is true, but I
cannot take responsibility for that kid. Have you actually
seen him? That level of stupidity only comes naturally.

                         HOLT
Is there anything else that you'd like to add, Secretary
Clinton?

                         CLINTON
No, I'm done, Lester.

                         HOLT
Okay, Mister --

                         CLINTON
Wait, I've remembered! Trumped-up trickle-down economics.

                              She opens her mouth, and
                              theatrical flames shoot across
                              the stage.

                         HOLT
You know, Mister Trump? You shouldn't have moved out the
way. You could have had eyes that match the rest of your
face.

                              CONWAY enters, burnt, and with a
                              tennis ball in her mouth. She
                              spits it out then exits.

                         HOLT
So, Mister Trump, would you like to respond at all?

                         TRUMP
                       (quietly)
My microphone is not working, Lester Holt. I did not hear
what she said.

                         HOLT
I'm sorry, Mister Trump, what was that? I couldn't hear
you.

                                              (CONTINUED)

                         TRUMP
                      (shouting)
I said that my microphone is not working, and because of
it, I could not hear what Crooked Hillary Clinton said.

                         HOLT
Okay, firstly, Mister Trump, it's clear to all of us that
you were just whispering. And, secondly, you don't listen
with a microphone.

                         TRUMP
Do you not?

                         HOLT
No, Mister Trump. You do not.

                         TRUMP
                      (quietly)
It is broken again.

                         HOLT
I'm sorry?

                         TRUMP
                      (shouting)
I said that it is broken again.

                         HOLT
Clearly, Mister Trump, it is not broken.

                         CLINTON
It's okay, Lester. I can fix it.

                         CLINTON walks over to TRUMP and
                         adjusts his microphone.

                         TRUMP
Thank you, Crooked Hillary Clinton.

                         CLINTON
Don't mention it, Donald.
                      (pointing suddenly up)
What's that up there?

                                              (CONTINUED)

CONTINUED:

                          TRUMP
Where?
                     (begins pointing)
I do not see anything.

                          CLINTON
                     (pointing down)
And down there.

                                    TRUMP begins to point down with
                                    his other hand as though in a
                                    dance pose.

                          CLINTON
Just hold that for a moment.

                                    She pulls out her phone, steps
                                    back, and takes a photo.

                          CLINTON
Got it.

                                    CLINTON hands her phone to the
                                    NARRATOR.

                          CLINTON
Would you mind sending that photo to the media for me? I'd
do it myself, but I'm not too good with emails.

                          NARRATOR
Okay.

                          CLINTON
Thanks. I'm Hillary Rodham Clinton, nice to meet you again.

                                    She returns to her podium as the
                                    NARRATOR lifts their arm again.

                          NARRATOR
Forty-love. Matchpoint.

                          HOLT
Can we get back to debating now?

                                                        (CONTINUED)

                          TRUMP
MAGA!

                          HOLT
What's MAGA?

                          TRUMP
Thank you, Lester Holt, for asking me about MAGA. MAGA is
MAGA.

                          HOLT
Yes, I got that bit.

                          TRUMP
It stands for Make America great again, and I am very glad
that you like it, Lester Holt.

                          HOLT
Wait a moment, I never said that I like it, Mister Trump.

                          TRUMP
MAGA!

                          HOLT
I'm sorry?

                          TRUMP
MAGA! MAGA!

                          HOLT
Secretary Clinton, do you have anything to say?

                          CLINTON
Yes, I do. On education --

                          TRUMP
MAGA!

                          CLINTON
Healthcare --

                          TRUMP
MAGA! MAGA!

                                              (CONTINUED)
PERFORMANCE LICENSE EDITION   LICENSE # _ _ _ _ _ _ _ _

                         CLINTON
National security --

                         TRUMP
MAGA! MAGA! MAGA!

                         CLINTON
The economy --

                         TRUMP
MAGA! MAGA! MAGA! MAGA!

                         CLINTON
Immigration --

                         TRUMP
Deport the children.

                         CLINTON
Infrastructure --

                         TRUMP
MAGA! MAGA! MAGA! MAGA! MAGA!

                              HOLT falls from his chair onto
                              the floor. The NARRATOR helps
                              him up, but he now has visibly
                              white hair.

                         HOLT
                       (exhausted)
That's --

                         TRUMP
MAGA!

                         HOLT
Time.

                         TRUMP approaches HOLT.

                         TRUMP
Lester Holt --

                                                        (CONTINUED)

>   CONWAY enters and with the
>   NARRATOR'S help, drags him
>   offstage.
>
>   CLINTON approaches HOLT as he
>   recomposes himself.

                    CLINTON
Good debate, hey Lester? Any chance of a friendly chat with
you?

                    HOLT
Oh, I would love to Secretary Clinton, but I'm already late
for my... Mongolian cookery class.

                    CLINTON
Well, okay then.
                    (to audience)
Hey everyone, I'm Hillary Rodham Clinton, and I'm going to
be your president.

>   Happy with herself, she exits
>   while performing a unique dance.

ACT I, SCENE EIGHT | THE VICE-PRESIDENTIAL DEBATE

>   LONGWOOD UNIVERSITY, FARMVILLE,
>   and the NARRATOR enters a
>   spotlight.

                    NARRATOR
And so with the first debate over the campaigns rage strong
with the anticipation for the second high, but the wait not
too long. But first, we journey to Longwood University in
Farmville, Virginia, for it's October fourth and the
running mates have opinions of their own to set forth.

>   TIM KAINE and PENCE enter from
>   opposite wings to flank the
>   NARRATOR.

                    KAINE
Hello. I'm Tim Kaine.

                                        (CONTINUED)

PENCE
And I'm Mike Pence. Hello.

NARRATOR
But no one really cared about their debate so we'll just move on.

PENCE
Goodbye.

KAINE
Well, bye now.

KAINE and PENCE exit.

ACT I, SCENE NINE | THE CAMPAIGN TRAIL, PART TWO

VARIOUS SETTINGS, but first the AMERICAN MIDWEST where CLINTON stands talking to a MIDWESTERN VOTER.

NARRATOR
And so to the trail we do return, where we join our friend Hillary still failing to learn. For in the Midwest, she's trying to relate to a voter, Bill Clinton with her to help try promote her.

CLINTON
Hi, I'm Hillary Rodham Clinton.

MIDWESTERN VOTER
Screw you, Hillary. Your husband cost me my job.

BILL CLINTON enters.

BILL
Can I help here, Hillary?

CLINTON
Go away, Bill.

(CONTINUED)

                         BILL
Okay, I'm going.

                              BILL, CLINTON, and the
                              MIDWESTERN VOTER exit.

                              CONWAY (in disguise), MILLER,
                              TRUMP, and the ENSEMBLE (as
                              VOTERS) enter.

                         NARRATOR
But it was not only for Clinton that things were going
wrong, for over on the East Coast, team Trump are also not
so strong. For now, we join them in Boston, where their
campaign manager stands in costume.

                         TRUMP
Hello Boston.

                         ENSEMBLE
BOO!

                         TRUMP
That is a Giuliani approval.

                         MILLER
Kellyanne, why are you wearing that disguise?

                         CONWAY
Oh, this? It's because some people in Massachusetts still
want to stick me on a dunk tank to see if I'll float.

ACT I, SCENE TEN | THE SECOND DEBATE

                              WASHINGTON UNIVERSITY, ST. LOUIS
                              where ANDERSON COOPER and MARTHA
                              RADDATZ sit at a desk flanked on
                              both sides by the ENSEMBLE (as
                              VOTERS). Among them, DMITRY,
                              ERIC, JUNIOR, and KUSHNER, all
                              in disguise.

                                             (CONTINUED)

                          NARRATOR
                     (entering)
And so we reach our second debate, a further ninety minutes
for the candidates to share the hate. But this second is to
be different from the first, and not only because it's
going to be the worst. This is the time to hear the views
of all, and so this debate is to be a town hall. Questions
asked by the undecided to earn every vote, questions
designed to gain answers that are only of note. Questions
like, how can so many people still be undecided?
                     (beat)
From C-N-N and A-B-C are our moderators for the night,
Anderson Cooper, and Martha Raddatz.

                          RADDATZ
Good evening.

                          COOPER
Hello.

                          NARRATOR
And so with the stage all set, all that's left --

                         The NARRATOR is interrupted by
                         COOPER beginning to laugh.

                          RADDATZ
Anderson, are you okay?

                          COOPER
It's just so stupid.

                          RADDATZ
Anderson?

                          COOPER
                     (laughing harder)
Why are we here?

                          RADDATZ
We're moderating the debate.

                                                    (CONTINUED)

CONTINUED:

                         COOPER
But why are we debating? It's so stupid to think that
Donald Trump actually has a chance.

                         RADDATZ
Pull yourself together. This is a presidential debate, the
world is watching us.

                              COOPER sighs then composes
                              himself.

                         COOPER
                    (to the NARRATOR)
Continue, please.

                         NARRATOR
And so with the stage all set, all that's left is to
introduce the candidates.

                              The NARRATOR exits.

                         RADDATZ
Are you okay now?

                         COOPER
I think so.

                         RADDATZ
Okay, let's do this.

                              Beat.

                         COOPER
Good evening, I'm Anderson Cooper.

                         RADDATZ
I'm Martha Raddatz.

                         COOPER
This is the second presidential debate.

                         RADDATZ
And it's time to meet the candidates. First up, it's
Hillary Rodham Clinton.

                                             (CONTINUED)

>   CLINTON enters, waves to the
>   audience, then takes the stool
>   that waits for her.

                              COOPER
And up against her, it's sexual offender --

>   RADDATZ coughs.

                              COOPER
Alleged sexual offender, Donald J. Trump.

>   TRUMP enters and confused,
>   circles his stool for a moment
>   before sitting.

                              RADDATZ
Good evening to you both.

                              CLINTON
Good evening subjects.

                              TRUMP
Yes, I think that I am the perfect role model for all young
people in America. Why would the young boys not want to all
grow up to be just like me, the great Donald J. Trump? I
can do whatever I want. I have money, I have a tower, I
have a plane, I used to have a TV show, and I can even brag
about assaulting women on camera and still be considered
for the presidency.

>   Beat.

                              COOPER
Okay, Mister Trump... Well, we're going to get started with
our first question of the night now, which comes from John
Johnson.

>   JUNIOR stands.

                                                    (CONTINUED)

                         JUNIOR
Good evening, I am John Johnson. My question is, do the
candidates think that they are a good role model for young
people in this country? Especially young boys, who, as we
all know, are the real future.

                    ERIC applauds.

                         ERIC
Go, Junior!

                         RADDATZ
Mister Trump, would you like to answer first?

                         TRUMP
I have already answered. Did you not hear my answer? I
answered just before he asked the question.

                         RADDATZ
                    (suspiciously)
Yes, Mister Trump, we noticed that.

                         COOPER
Let's move on to your answer then, Secretary Clinton.

                         CLINTON
Well obviously, of course, I think that I am a good role
model for young people. How could the country's first
female nominee of a major party and soon to be the first
women as president, not be a good role model? I do think
it's important to say though, all young people deserve a
role model, the young girls just as much as the young boys.

                         TRUMP
Well, I actually agree with all of that, except for all of
the bits that I do not agree with. I do not think that it
is important for you girls to have a role model. All that
young girls need to know is that they should marry rich.

                         COOPER
My god, Mister Trump.

                                             (CONTINUED)

                         TRUMP
No, Anderson Cooper, I am not your god. God lives, as we
all know, in a big red castle in Moscow.

                         COOPER
Secretary Clinton, do you have a response?

                         CLINTON
Oh, I... did he really just say that?

                         COOPER
I think he did, yes.

                         TRUMP
You hear me correctly, Crooked Hillary Clinton. I would
also like to add...

                              He pulls out notes and checks
                              them.

                         TRUMP
I think that it is very unfair that rich people should ever
have to pay for the healthcare of the poor. I worked very
hard to scam my way to becoming a fake billionaire.

                         RADDATZ
Mister Trump, I'm not sure what you were answering there,
so we're going to move onto our second question.

                         COOPER
Which tonight comes from a mister V ordinary American
voter. Mister American voter, what is your question?

                         DMITRY stands.

                         DMITRY
Yes, hello. I am ordinary American voter boy who likes
American things like baseball and cheese that not be made
of cheese. I am fourteen years of age.

                         RADDATZ
And what is your question?

                                             (CONTINUED)
PERFORMANCE LICENSE EDITION   LICENSE # _ _ _ _ _ _ _ _

                          DMITRY
My question is for Mister Donald Trump, do you think that
it is unfair for rich people to ever be expected to pay for
the healthcare of the poor?

                          RADDATZ
Mister Trump, didn't you also just answer that question
before it was asked too?

                          TRUMP
Yes, I did, Martha Raddatz. It is a great question, and I
gave a great answer.

                          RADDATZ
Okay, is there something going on here?

                          COOPER
Martha --

                          RADDATZ
                    (ignoring COOPER)
It's almost as though you've been colluding with the people
here tonight so that you can find out the questions before
we began.

                          COOPER
Please consider what you're actually accusing the Trump
campaign of.

                          RADDATZ
You're right, Anderson, none of them have the intelligence
to plan that.

                          COOPER
Let's just move onto the next question.

                          CLINTON
Oh, don't I get to say anything?

                          COOPER
You wanted to say something inspiring about how you've got
a plan to solve all the issues surrounding healthcare in
this country, Secretary Clinton?

                                              (CONTINUED)

                         CLINTON
No, I'll pass.

                         COOPER
We'll move on then.

                         RADDATZ
Our third question tonight comes from Mister Eric.

                    ERIC stands.

                         ERIC
Hey, I'm Eric.

                         RADDATZ
And what is your question, Mister Eric?

                         ERIC
I forgot.

                         DMITRY
                    (to JUNIOR)
Why did we have to bring him again?

                         JUNIOR
I had no choice but to bring him along. His wife said she
wanted a night off.

                         RADDATZ
Well, I guess if we haven't got a question, then we have no
choice but to move on.

                         COOPER
And it's our final question of the night which comes from
John Johnson Junior.

                         DMITRY
                    (to KUSHNER)
Could you not think of anything more original?

                         TRUMP
I like this question.

                                                        (CONTINUED)

                              KUSHNER stands with a number of
                              cue cards.

                    COOPER
                 (reading)
"John Johnson Junior."
                 (KUSHNER drops a card)
"My question is."
                 (KUSHNER drops a card)
"Hello, my name is."
                 (KUSHNER drops a card)
"It's nice to be here."
                 (KUSHNER drops a card)
"Crooked Hillary Clinton is Crooked."
                 (KUSHNER drops a card)
"But, what are you going."
                 (KUSHNER drops a card)
"We all know that."
                 (KUSHNER drops a card)
"To do about it?"

                         Beat.

                    COOPER
I think that you might have your cue cards in the wrong
order, Mister Johnson Junior.

                    DMITRY
I think what my friend is trying to ask here is what is
Mister Trump going to do about Hillary Clinton being
crooked?
                 (to KUSHNER)
Is that not correct?

                         KUSHNER nods.

                    DMITRY
                 (to COOPER)
You see?

                    RADDATZ
Okay, I'm sorry, but there is definitely something strange
going on here.

                                        (CONTINUED)

COOPER

I have to agree. The punctuation on those cue cards is
terrible.

CLINTON

You know, Anderson, I think Martha has a point. Donald has
clearly found out what the questions will be before the
debate, and I would go so far as to say he chose a few of
them too.

COOPER

That is a serious allegation, Secretary Clinton, but I can
see your point.

RADDATZ

There's certainly circumstantial evidence.

COOPER

Quite right.
                         (to CLINTON)
Well, we could stop this debate, choose new voters with new
questions, and start again. Would you like us to do that,
Secretary Clinton?

CLINTON

I think that is the only --

COOPER

I would also like to take this chance to remind you that
you're ahead in all polls and there is a free minibar in
your hotel room.

CLINTON

I think we can just let Donald answer this question.

COOPER

Mister Trump, your answer.

TRUMP

I am going to lock her up.

RADDATZ

Is that it?

                                                    (CONTINUED)

TRUMP

My supporters cannot remember more than three words at one
time.

COOPER

And with that, we have reached the end of our questions for
tonight's debate. Before we finish, though, while this is
not customary for a moderator, there is one subject that I
would like to bring up myself. Mister Trump, as I'm sure
you're aware, a few days ago, footage was leaked of you
bragging about sexually assaulting a woman.

RADDATZ

Yes, thank you for mentioning it, Anderson. I would like to
ask some questions about that tape if you don't mind. What
were you thinking? And do you not have even the smallest
amount of respect for women?

TRUMP

Firstly, it was just locker room talk, nothing more. And
secondly, correct.

RADDATZ

I think that a lot of people across the country would have
found it difficult to watch that footage or read about the
comments you made, and in some cases, I am sure that it
would have brought back memories of events some women would
rather forget. Do you not feel any remorse at all, Mister
Trump?

TRUMP

No, next question.

RADDATZ

Well, I think that the comments you made on that tape are
truly disgusting, Mister Trump. I've got to say it.

TRUMP

Thank you. But I do not think that you can have a fair
opinion because you are clearly biased. Not only are you a
woman, but you are also only a six out of ten.

(CONTINUED)

                          COOPER
Mister Trump, I am not a woman, and I also think that what
you said was disgusting.

                          TRUMP
Well, that is because you look like a little old lady.

                          CLINTON
Anderson, if I could comment?

                          COOPER
Go ahead, Secretary Clinton.

                          CLINTON
I, like a lot of people, watched the footage of Donald that
was leaked earlier this week with a feeling of sickness in
my stomach. At one point, I did, in fact, feel so sick that
I thought I was going to be, but thankfully I was able to
wash it all down with a bottle of champagne.

                          RADDATZ
Mister Trump, is there anything at all that you would like
to say in response to Secretary Clinton or the leaking of
this tape?

                          TRUMP
Yes, I would like to say, live from New York --

                          COOPER
Wrong show, Mister Trump. Your response, please.

                          TRUMP
                   (pointing into the audience)
What is that?

                              As they all turn to look where
                              he's pointing, TRUMP makes a run
                              for it and exits.

                          COOPER
I don't see anything, Mister --

                          RADDATZ
Where did he go?

                                                   (CONTINUED)

                          CLINTON
I didn't see anything.

                          RADDATZ
Well, if he's not here, then we can't really carry on, so
we're going to have to wrap up this debate and declare
Hillary Clinton winner by default.

                          COOPER
Our thanks to Secretary Clinton this evening and to all of
you for watching. I've been Anderson Cooper.

                          RADDATZ
I've been Martha Raddatz.

                          COOPER
And this has been the second presidential debate. Goodnight
to you all.

                          RADDATZ
Goodnight.

                                    Beat, and then CLINTON walks
                                    over to them.

                          CLINTON
Hey, Anderson, Martha --

                          COOPER
I would love to stay and catch up, Secretary Clinton, but I
have my... cross country skiing lesson to attend.

                          RADDATZ
And I said I'd give him a lift.

                                    COOPER and RADDATZ exit in a
                                    hurry.

                          CLINTON
Oh, well, okay then. Maybe next time.

ACT I, SCENE ELEVEN | THE ENDORSEMENTS

> NO SPECIFIC SETTING, but the
> NARRATOR stands center stage.

NARRATOR

And so with two debates down and just one to go, the war
rages stronger than ever, and the opinion of both sides
that the other could win? Never.

But just as in any battle, there are secret weapons known
to very few, or at least on team Trump, that is certainly
true. For there are statements of endorsements from the
famous kind, and for Clinton, they came in their hundreds,
while from Trump how there was any, one only wonders.

> Inspiring sounding music begins
> to play.

NARRATOR

And on team Clinton, we have...

> As the NARRATOR exits, a
> spotlight finds BILL.

BILL

This election day, I'm endorsing my wife, Hillary Clinton.
> (beat)
Hillary, can I have my medication back now?

> This time the spotlight finds
> BARACK OBAMA and MICHELLE OBAMA.

OBAMA

Well, hello to all of you... Barack Obama here, that's
President Barack Obama... I'm here today with my lovely
wife Michelle, who I love very much... and who I am married
to, we also have two beautiful children... we're a family.

(CONTINUED)

MICHELLE

We just wanted to take the time to visit this theatrical venue for the creative arts, something that both me and Barack view as such a vital part of everyday life and a place where families like ours come together for enlightenment and entertainment brought to us by the very talented performers on the stage, to endorse for the forty-fifth Presidency of these United States --

OBAMA

That is the forty-fifth since our founding father George Washington was our first.

MICHELLE

Both mine and Barack's good friend, Hillary Rodham Clinton.

OBAMA

Because we're stronger... together.
                    (beat, then to MICHELLE)
That should stop her from calling us every night.

                              Moving again, the spotlight
                              finds BERNIE SANDERS.

SANDERS

A recount, I would like to request a recount. What? I was told this was the line to request recounts. The Hillary Clinton endorsement line? No, no. That would be like your flight being thirty minutes late and then going and writing the airline a five-star review on Yelp. I want to request a recount.

                              This time, it finds JOHN OLIVER.

OLIVER

Well, hello and welcome, America. There's just time for a quick round-up of this shit show so far, and well basically America, here we are, we're either screwed, or we're slightly less screwed.

(MORE)

                                                    (CONTINUED)

CONTINUED:

                          OLIVER (CONT'D)
I'm British, and so it would be wrong of me to make any
endorsement right now, but please, America, we've been
through a lot together, don't mess it up now by this
bargain-basement liberty torching day of democracy fiddling
voting for Donald Trump. The man looks like a baboon's anus
experiencing difficulties after the baboon ate a
particularly large tangerine. **Bad baboon, don't eat that
particularly large tangerine, baboon.**
                    (beat)
And now, this...

                                   The music changes to that of a
                                   comical nature as the spotlight
                                   finds MIKE HUCKABEE.

                          HUCKABEE
Did y'all hear the one about the chicken crossin' the road?
It was running away from Hillary Clinton folks. Well
anyway, vote Donal' Trump, 'cause at least he comes with a
penis.

                                   This time, it finds SARAH PALIN.

                          PALIN
Well, I gotta' say, it sure is nice of you all to silence
the applause quickly so you can hear my thoughts on a few
matters. You know, usually, to speak to an audience this
big I have to run into a town hall meeting and scream help,
there's a polar bear chasing me.

                          NARRATOR
Are you okay, Sarah?

                          PALIN
Oh, me? I'm fine. It's sweet of you to ask, though. It's
pretty sweet to be here too. Who would have thought that I
would ever be relevant again?
                    (laughs to herself)
I thought about it for a while, though. I said to myself,
Sarah, you've been relevant before and it could come back,
you know. Well, I guess you're all thinking I'm not so bad
right now, aren't you? --

                                             (CONTINUED)

                         NARRATOR
                         (coughing)
Sarah, if you could, please get on with it.

                         PALIN
Oh right. I'm sorry. Sometimes I just let myself get
carried away, and it's like, Sarah, what are you doing?
Anyway, I'd like to endorse the white guy.

                         NARRATOR
Thank you.

                         PALIN
Oh, can I say something else? I was really hoping I could
plug my Soundcloud while I'm here. On it, you can find all
of your favorite gay anthems but rewritten for us good old
law-abiding religious folk who think the only thing that
should go near a vagina is a penis and vacuum cleaner once
a month to tidy it all up real good for date night. As a
special bonus, if you go there now, you'll also find Palin
does the Village People, featuring Trey Gowdy as the cowboy
and Mike Pence as the police officer. I'm the construction
worker.

                                   Moving for a final time, the
                                   spotlight finds TRUMP wearing
                                   glasses.

                         TRUMP
I am David Dennison, and I am an ordinary American voter
from the state of East Dakota. I would like to endorse the
very great, trust me, no one is greater, Donald J. Trump,
to make America great again.

ACT I, SCENE TWELVE | THE THIRD DEBATE

                                   The UNIVERSITY OF NEVADA, LAS
                                   VEGAS, where the NARRATOR stands
                                   front center while behind them,
                                   CLINTON and TRUMP stand at
                                   podiums opposite sides of CHRIS
                                   WALLACE who sits at a desk.

                                                       (CONTINUED)

NARRATOR

And so we reach our third debate, the final, the last, the one to decide the world's fate. Fox News is this time to host, the channel which we feel we can joke the most... only we're not sure they've got a sense of humor, and we don't want to be sued.

The NARRATOR exits.

WALLACE

Good evening to you all and welcome to the third presidential debate. That's right, third because apparently this election hasn't been embarrassing enough yet. I will be your moderator for this evening, Chris Wallace. Now, let's meet our candidates, and first up it's --

CLINTON

President Hillary Clinton.

WALLACE

I'm sorry, Secretary Clinton?

CLINTON

President Hillary Clinton, nice to meet you.

WALLACE

President? You do know that the election isn't until next week?

CLINTON

Yes, I do know that, Chris. But I think that I'm going to be okay. I've already had President Clinton printed on those little pens they give out to visitors to the White House. Bill had some left, but I wanted new ones that write in red ink, it's the color of blood.

WALLACE

That is an awful lot of confidence you've got, Secretary Clinton.

CLINTON

Well, Chris, I can have that level of confidence. I mean, it's not like someone, let us say, F-B-I director, James Comey, is going to murder my campaign.
(MORE)

(CONTINUED)

CONTINUED:

                          CLINTON (CONT'D)
No one would be that desperate for attention that they'd
risk all of our democracy and nuclear war. Knocking on
wood, of course.

                                        CLINTON taps the top of her
                                        podium.

                          WALLACE
Secretary Clinton, I believe those podiums are actually
made from imitation wood.

                          CLINTON
Well, gosh dang.

                              Beat.

                          WALLACE
Okay, well, can everyone please give a hand to our first
candidate, Secretary Hillary Clinton.

                          CLINTON
Nice to meet you all.

                          WALLACE
And now, please give the finger to our second candidate,
Donald J. Trump.

                          TRUMP
Does anyone know how long this will be? Only, I have left
Eric Trump in the parking lot, and I forgot to open a
window.

                          WALLACE
The debate is ninety minutes, Mister Trump, but let's not
waste any time as we move to the first question. Mister
Trump, what is your opinion on birth control?

                          TRUMP
I like birth control. I mean, look at me, no one likes
birth control more than I do. I am a walking advertisement
for birth control.

                          WALLACE
Secretary Clinton, the same question to you.

                                                    (CONTINUED)

                        CLINTON
Well, I am quite clear on this subject. I believe that all
women should have access to birth control at no cost and
without the judgment or interference of anyone else,
especially men. Why do I think this? I'm simply just not an
asshole --

                        TRUMP
Wrong.

                        WALLACE
I'm sorry, what was that, Mister Trump? You think that
Secretary Clinton is an asshole?

                        CLINTON
It's okay, Chris. It takes one to know one, and Donald
certainly is one.

                        WALLACE
Okay, we'll move on to another question now, this time for
you, Secretary Clinton.

                        CLINTON
Ask away, Chris. Anything you like, I'm happy to give you a
clear answer.

                        WALLACE
Thank you. About your emails…

                        Beat.

                        CLINTON
I would like to retract my previous statement.

                        WALLACE
Secretary Clinton, I'm sure that you're aware by now that
there are a lot of questions being raised about your emails
in the past week.

                        CLINTON
Yes, well about those...

                              CLINTON makes her way into the
                              audience.

                                        (CONTINUED)

                          WALLACE
Secretary Clinton, where are you going?

                          CLINTON
I won't be a moment, Chris.

                          WALLACE
Please don't leave me alone with Donald.

                                        CLINTON approaches the audience
                                        member who she gave her earlier
                                        emails to.

                          CLINTON
I thought I told you to destroy those emails I gave you.
Why did you leak them to the press?
                              (beat)
Anyway, I'm in a tight spot, and I need to get rid of some
more.

                          WALLACE
                       (shouting out)
He's looking at me.

                                        CLINTON pulls more emails from
                                        her pocket and hands them over.

                          CLINTON
I'll pay you later.

                                        CLINTON returns to the stage.

                          CLINTON
Now, where were we?

                          WALLACE
Your emails.

                          CLINTON
That's right, the Access Hollywood tape.

                          WALLACE
Secretary Clinton --

                                                      (CONTINUED)

CONTINUED:

                         CLINTON
I would be happy to clarify my position on that tape. As
I've said before, I find the words that my opponent used
absolutely horrifying, yet also in a strange way, very
beautiful.

                         TRUMP
Wrong.

                         WALLACE
Mister Trump.

                         TRUMP
It was just locker room talk. I know because I am the best
person in the world at locker room talk. I am actually so
great at locker room talk that I will soon be releasing a
new book --

                         WALLACE
Mister Trump, please --

                              TRUMP reaches for a giant book
                              from under his podium and holds
                              it up, the cover reading "Locker
                              Room Talk by Donald J. Trump."

                         TRUMP
Called Locker Room Talk. It is a picture book, and it will
have pictures in it. It is going to have pictures of…

                              He turns to a page to reveal a
                              picture of a cat.

                         TRUMP
Cats.
                    (beat)
Why does it have a cat in it? I knew I should not have left
Eric Trump to put this together. What is on this page?

                              Turning the page, there's a
                              diagram of a vagina labeled
                              "Mrs. Eric."

                                                    (CONTINUED)

                         TRUMP
A missus Eric. And what about this page?

                              Turning again, there's a photo
                              of himself.

                         TRUMP
Me.

                              Beat, and then he puts the book
                              away.

                         TRUMP
I think we should move on, Mister Christopher Wallace.

                         WALLACE
I agree, Mister Trump. Let's move on now to our final
question of the night --

                         CLINTON
Oh, one moment. I just need a drink of water.

                              She brings a small glass of
                              water from under her podium and
                              drinks from it.

                         TRUMP
I too also need water.

                              TRUMP brings up his own,
                              slightly bigger glass, and
                              drinks using both hands.

                         TRUMP
I only drink the best and wettest water.

                              CLINTON reaches for a still
                              bigger glass and drinks.

                              TRUMP watches for a moment then
                              reaches for an even bigger
                              glass. As he drinks, his hands
                              shake.

                                              (CONTINUED)

                    WALLACE
Mister Trump, what are you doing?

                                        CLINTON reaches for yet another
                                        bigger glass and drinks.

                                        Refusing to give in, TRUMP
                                        reaches for a bucket of water,
                                        brings it to his face, his hands
                                        shaking, and attempts to drink
                                        but ends up pouring it down
                                        himself.

                    TRUMP
I need a towel.

                    WALLACE
I don't have a towel, Mister Trump.

                    CLINTON
Don't worry, Donald, I've got one you can have. I thought
we might need one tonight, we all know how old men like you
can be at times.

                                        CLINTON reaches for a towel and
                                        throws it to TRUMP. He opens it,
                                        and without noticing the "I'm
                                        With Her" slogan on the other
                                        side, dries himself and throws
                                        the towel offstage.

                    WALLACE
Am I able to continue with the question now, or would you
like to go for a paddle, Mister Trump?

                    CLINTON
                 (laughing hard)
Ha! That's a really funny joke.

                    TRUMP
I do not get it.

                                                              (CONTINUED)

                         WALLACE
And so our final question of the evening, what qualities do
you think you each have that make you suitable for the role
of President of the United States?
                         (a pause)
And so that concludes tonight's debate, thank you to --

                         CLINTON
Wait! I've got one.

                         WALLACE
Well, do enlighten us, Secretary Clinton.

                         CLINTON
I am not Donald Trump.

                         WALLACE
Is that all you've got, Secretary Clinton?

                         TRUMP
Oh, no.

                         CLINTON
                       (smiling)
I could instead tell you about all of my achievements,
including those while I was First Lady, or my response on
nine eleven as a New York Senator, or those while I was
this great nation's Secretary of State. Did you know that I
played a part in ridding the world of Osama Bin Laden?
Right after it happened, I got the very eighth fist bump
with Barack Obama as we celebrated. But why do I need to
mention any of those? Is not being a balding old orange
racist who clearly volunteers as the mop for a local dog
grooming salon, not enough?

                         WALLACE
Well, that is for the voters to decide, Secretary Clinton.
Mister Trump, do you have anything to say? What qualities
do you have that make you suitable to be president?

                         TRUMP
Can I phone a friend?

                                                   (CONTINUED)

                        WALLACE
We've already told you, Mister Trump, it costs three
dollars a minute to call Moscow.

                        TRUMP
Can I call a local friend?

                        WALLACE
It's not customary in a presidential debate, but if you
promise to be quick, we'll make an exception.

                              CONWAY enters holding a large
                              toy phone.

                        CONWAY
What's the number, sir?

                              As he speaks, TRUMP holds up the
                              wrong number on his hand each
                              time.

                        TRUMP
Two-one-two-eight-three-six-three-two-four-nine.

                              CONWAY dials, and the phone
                              rings out.

                        RECORDED VOICE (OFF)
                        (in Russian accent)
Hello, you're through to the Trump Grill at Trump Tower.
Visit now and ask for our special, the triple nothing
burger with treasoning. We promise Eric hasn't touched it.

Here at the Trump Grill, we now accept roubles.
                        (beat)
Press one to make a reservation. Press two to inquire about
our menu. Press three if you are a foreign dictator and
wish to pay your deposit to secure a meeting with Donald
Trump. Press four if you have dirt on Hillary Clinton.
Press five to speak to the manager.

                        TRUMP
Press five.

                                                    (CONTINUED)

                         CONWAY presses, and it continues
                         to ring until JUNIOR answers.

                    JUNIOR (OFF)
Hello, you're through to the manager of the Trump Grill at
Trump Tower... What are you wearing?

                    TRUMP
                  (on phone)
Donald Trump Junior, I am just one question away from
making myself billions --

                    JUNIOR (OFF)
I thought we were both going to be rich when you become
president?

                    TRUMP
                  (on phone)
That is right, making us billions.

                    JUNIOR (OFF)
Okay, what's the question? I'll try to help.

                    TRUMP
                  (on phone)
What qualities do I, Donald J. Trump, have that make me
suitable to be president?

                    JUNIOR (OFF)
Is it multiple choice?

                    TRUMP
                  (to WALLACE)
Is it multiple choice, Christopher Wallace?

                    WALLACE
No, Mister Trump, it is not multiple choice.

                    TRUMP
                  (on phone)
No, it is not multiple choice.

                    JUNIOR (OFF)
Well, can you ask the audience?

                                              (CONTINUED)

                         TRUMP
                       (on phone)
We are in Las Vegas, this is not my crowd. Here they prefer
casino owners who do not go bankrupt.

                         JUNIOR (OFF)
Here's what I think you should do. Ignore the question and
just say something outrageous.

                         TRUMP
                       (on phone)
I'll try it.

                         The call ends, and CONWAY exits.

                         TRUMP
He said I should just be myself.
                       (beat)
Crooked Hillary Clinton is a nasty woman, and I would only
give her a three.

                         CLINTON
This is just typical Donald Trump, isn't it? But as my
friend Michelle Obama says, when he goes low, we should go
high, and personally, I'd give Donald ten.

                         WALLACE
You would give him ten, Secretary Clinton?

                         TRUMP
I did not know you thought I looked that good.

                         CLINTON
Looks? I didn't know we were talking about looks. I thought
we were on about electoral votes.

                         A gong sounds.

                         WALLACE
Oh, and that is our indication that we have run out of time
for this debate.

                                                    (CONTINUED)

                              CLINTON
Well, I'm off to the White House. I've got to measure the
curtains.

ACT I, SCENE THIRTEEN | CLINTON & OBAMA

                              A WHITE HOUSE OFFICE where
                              CLINTON and OBAMA sit talking.

                              NARRATOR
                          (entering)
With the three debates over it's three-zero to team blue
and a reputation of terror sticking to Trump like a
particularly strong glue.

For Clinton, what can go wrong? Nobody knows. Her
Presidency is a certainty with a percentage that only
grows.

The campaigns have been long, but there are still some days
for both to go. But first, for Hillary, there's time for a
meeting not for sorrow or show, but with a man who is now
her mentor and friend, and no longer a foe.

                              The NARRATOR exits.

                              CLINTON
And then, you'll never believe this, Barack, he said that
no one respects women more than him.

                              OBAMA
In fact, Hillary, as it so happens, I did actually see him
making the comment that you are referring to there... I was
watching that rally of his on my electrical television set
over in the White House Residence... It's just out of this
door, through another, outside, left and then straight on
past the bush that looks suspiciously like a Russian spy
wearing camouflage... But despite having witnessed Donald
Trump making the claim that you have just reported in your
own words... I do still find it hard to believe, which, as
you know, is an unusual thing for me... because always in
my administration I have strived to see... the best in
people.

                                                  (CONTINUED)

CLINTON
Yes, yes, but do you know what else he said?

OBAMA
Yes, Hillary, I do know... but in order to avoid a social
conflict or any form of tension... how about you remind me
in words that are rendered from your own free thought?

CLINTON
He said that he would be the most qualified president ever.

OBAMA
Now that really is quite funny... it's like a joke. A funny
joke.

                         As they laugh, the NARRATOR
                         enters, takes a photo of them,
                         then exits.

CLINTON
What was that? They had a camera. Why is there someone with
a camera?

OBAMA
That was a photographer that I arranged... I thought it
would be a good idea if we could put out a photo of you
laughing... and looking human.

CLINTON
Why? Don't I normally look human? I'm a human. I look
human. People think I'm human.
                    (beat)
Hey, Barack, would you mind putting out a formal statement
confirming that I'm human?

OBAMA
Putting out a statement of words from our English
language... that achieve such a purpose is certainly
something that I would be willing... to look at doing for
you.

CLINTON
Thanks, Barack. Where would I be without you?

                                              (CONTINUED)

CONTINUED:

                    OBAMA
You would have been president eight years ago.

                              COOPER enters on a moving desk.

                    COOPER
Hello, you're watching C-N-N, and I'm Anderson Cooper here
with breaking news.

                    OBAMA
                 (waving)
Well good post afternoon to you, Anderson.

                    COOPER
                 (waving back)
President Obama, sir.
                 (to audience)
This just in. F-B-I director, James Comey, has today
written to Congress to inform them that he is re-opening
the investigation into the use of private emails by Hillary
Clinton.

                    Beat.

                    CLINTON
I'm sorry. I'm not sure I heard that.

                    COOPER
In a letter that was addressed to the Chair of the House
Intelligence Committee, Mister Comey confirmed the F-B-I
has uncovered new emails that were not included as part of
the first investigation, which later concluded after
finding no wrongdoing from the former Secretary of State.
While it is not known the extent of the new evidence these
new emails contain, it will surely have a negative impact
on the Clinton campaign just a few days out from the
election.
                 (beat)
Duck.

                              He ducks and is narrowly missed
                              an object thrown by CLINTON.

                                        (CONTINUED)
PERFORMANCE LICENSE EDITION   LICENSE # _ _ _ _ _ _ _ _

CONTINUED:

                         COOPER
That's all from me for now.

                    COOPER and his desk exit.

                         OBAMA
Hillary, are you okay? That news there... it didn't sound
as though it would please a person such as yourself... at
the present time.

                    A pause.

                         CLINTON
I... I just need a moment. I need a moment, Barack.

                    CLINTON exits, screams, and then
                    returns to the stage.

                         OBAMA
Hillary?

                         CLINTON
This is --

                         OBAMA
Hillary?

                         CLINTON
Going to be okay.

                         OBAMA
Are you sure that there is truth in the words you are
using?

                         CLINTON
This is going to be okay. I can still win. America isn't
stupid. I can win this. I can do this.

                         OBAMA
What if you don't?

                                                        (CONTINUED)

                         CLINTON
If I don't?
                    (beat)
Then I will personally see to it that I get revenge.

ACT I, SCENE FOURTEEN | ELECTION DAY

                         First, a NEW YORK POLLING
                         STATION where TRUMP and
                         CARDBOARD MELANIA TRUMP are
                         voting. Nearby, CONWAY (in
                         disguise), and an ELECTION
                         OFFICIAL.

                         NARRATOR
                    (entering)
The eighth day of November, one to go down in history, for
today is the day America elects its first woman as
president or the day it elects it by a landslide. No matter
the news of emails, the voters don't care, or so the polls
say. The result of the vote's expected to go only one way.
So what will go wrong? That is the question as we reach the
start of the day that is America's General Election.

                         COOPER enters.

                         COOPER
Thank you, Narrator. I can take it from here.

                         The NARRATOR exits.

                         COOPER
Good morning to all of you, it's November eighth, I'm
Anderson Cooper reporting here for C-N-N, and I can tell
you all, I'm looking forward to getting my sticker later
today.

                         HOLT enters.

                         HOLT
Hello America. Lester Holt here for N-B-C on what is set to
be a historic day for the country.
                         (MORE)

                                        (CONTINUED)

CONTINUED:
                        HOLT (CONT'D)
Are we getting our first president who is a woman, or are
we getting our first who is a high contrast sitcom
character?

                        RADDATZ enters.

                        RADDATZ
Martha Raddatz here for A-B-C, good morning America. Well,
it's election day again, don't forget to get out and vote.

                        STEVE DOOCY, AINSLEY EARHARDT,
                        and BRIAN KILMEADE all enter.

                        DOOCY
Good morning, Steve Doocy here.

                        EARHARDT
I heard that it's a good morning too, Steve. I'm Ainsley
Earhardt.

                        KILMEADE
I'm Brian Kilmeade, and last night, I had to go to the
emergency room because when I tried to pick my nose, my
finger got stuck.

                        EARHARDT
That's a funny story, Brian. Welcome to Fox and Friends,
everyone.

                        KILMEADE
I don't have any friends, Ainsley.

                        DOOCY
What beautiful weather we have this election day, certainly
here in New York City where we're joining Republican
candidate, Donald J. Trump as he casts his own vote. I
wonder who he voted for?

                        EARHARDT
You know, Steve? I'm wondering that too. Ahaha.

                                                (CONTINUED)

CONTINUED:

                        KILMEADE
I voted earlier, but I don't want anyone to know that I
voted for Donald Trump, so I kept my ballot paper in my
pocket.

                        COOPER
I'm in New York City this morning, just a few blocks away
from where stands the Fifth Avenue tower that Donald Trump
calls home. Will he still be calling it home after today?
The polls certainly say so.

                        HOLT
The Republican nominee and his wife are here about to cast
their own votes in this historic election.

                        RADDATZ
I'm sure we need no panel of experts to discuss how they
will be doing so.

                                TRUMP looks across to see who
                                CARDBOARD MELANIA is voting for.

                        TRUMP
Oh good. You're voting the same as me.

                                TRUMP takes his ballot and
                                places it in the box.

                        DOOCY
You know guys, I wonder if Mister Trump would be willing to
talk to us quickly?

                        EARHARDT
I'm wondering that too, Steve. What do you think, Brian?

                        KILMEADE
I don't think, Ainsley.

                                All three wave at TRUMP.

                        DOOCY
Hey, Mister Trump.

                                                (CONTINUED)

PERFORMANCE LICENSE EDITION   LICENSE # _ _ _ _ _ _ _ _

CONTINUED:

                    EARHARDT
I also say hello to Mister Trump, Steve.

                    KILMEADE
Ahoy-hoy.

                         TRUMP walks to them while
                         behind, CARDBOARD MELANIA "runs
                         off."

                    TRUMP
Hello Steve Doocy, Ainsley Earhardt and, sorry, I forgot
your name.

                    KILMEADE
I'm Donald Trump. It's good to see you today, Brian
Kilmeade.

                    TRUMP
It is great to be here, Donald Trump.

                    RADDATZ
First on A-B-C --

                    HOLT
Breaking news just in --

                    COOPER
Dang it.

                    HOLT
Too slow, Anderson.

                    COOPER
Third on C-N-N, Hillary Clinton has arrived to cast her own
vote.

                         CLINTON enters.

                    CLINTON
Hello everyone. It's Hillary Rodham Clinton here.

                         COOPER, HOLT, and RADDATZ rush
                         to her.

                                                    (CONTINUED)

                              HOLT
Secretary Clinton.

                             CLINTON
Hello, Lester, Martha, good to see you both again. Oh, and
we have Anderson here too.

                              HOLT
Last again, Cooper.

                             COOPER
We'll see who's last when the ratings come in, Holt.

                             TRUMP
Ratings? Did someone mention ratings?

                             DOOCY
So, Mister Trump, can you tell us who you voted for today?

                             TRUMP
Steve Doocy, let me tell you who I did not vote for. I did
not vote for that woman over there.
                    (pointing at CLINTON)
That woman, not a lot of people know this, is my opponent,
Hillary Clinton, okay. Unlike me, she is not so great. She
is bad and evil and nasty and crooked and a woman. I would
never vote for her. In fact, I would never vote for her so
much that so show it, I put a big cross, like a huge no, in
the box next to her name on my ballot paper, and I
encourage all of my supporters to do the same.
                    (turning back)
And my wife, who is just here -- Wait, where did she go?

                             CLINTON
Hey, Donald, you know that by putting a cross next to my
name, you actually voted for me?

                             TRUMP
What?

                             DOOCY
I think she might be right, Mister Trump.

                                              (CONTINUED)

CONTINUED:

                         EARHARDT
I think so too, Steve, which is unusual because Hillary is
a woman and we all know what we think about that here on
Fox and Friends...

                         KILMEADE
I drew a picture of a bumblebee in the box to cast my vote.

                         EARHARDT
No, Brian. That is not what we all think.

                              TRUMP approaches the ELECTION
                              OFFICIAL.

                         TRUMP
Hello, election people. I hereby demand that I get to vote
again. I voted for the wrong person.

                    ELECTION OFFICIAL
I'm sorry, Mister Trump, but I can't allow that. There's no
way for us to know which ballot you put in the box.

                         TRUMP
It is the one marked in crayon.

                    ELECTION OFFICIAL
I can't help you, sir.

                         TRUMP
This is rigged. This whole election is rigged.

                         CONWAY
                    (removing her disguise)
Yes, it is, Mister Trump. But we're not supposed to let
everyone know.

                              As she puts her disguise back
                              on, the NARRATOR enters.

                         NARRATOR
Six hours until the polls close.

                                             (CONTINUED)

CONTINUED:

                         The NARRATOR exits with CLINTON,
                         CONWAY, and TRUMP, and the
                         action moves to a WISCONSIN
                         POLLING STATION.

                    COOPER
It's been an eventful election day so far as millions have
turned out across the country to have their say.

                    HOLT
But as we all know, it's the swing states that really
matter on days like this. States like Florida.

                    COOPER
Once every four years isn't bad.

                    RADDATZ
To bring you the latest coverage on the way the country is
swinging, I'm at a polling station in the swing state of
Wisconsin.

                         A WISCONSIN VOTER enters and
                         HOLT approaches.

                    HOLT
Lester Holt from N-B-C. Can I ask you how you voted today?

                    WISCONSIN VOTER
Yes, you can ask me.

                    HOLT
Thank you. How did you vote today?

                    WISCONSIN VOTER
I voted for Hillary Clinton.

                    HOLT
And can you talk about why you voted that way?

                    WISCONSIN VOTER
She didn't visit us that much, and if she's considerate
enough not to make us listen to her, she gets my vote.

                         HOLT bows towards COOPER.

                                        (CONTINUED)

                              HOLT
Exclusive insight, only on N-B-C.

                            EARHARDT
Guys, what are we doing here in Wisconsin?

                            KILMEADE
I've been to Wisconsin once before. It's just like Michigan
except it's not Michigan, it's Wisconsin.

                             DOOCY
Well, Ainsley, we were here to talk to Paul Ryan, but did
you know he wasn't able to cast his vote today?

                            EARHARDT
I did know that, Steve. But do you know why he wasn't able
to vote?

                             DOOCY
Yes, I do know, Ainsley. It's because a voter decided to
ask him a question about healthcare on his way to vote and
so he was forced to run away.

                            EARHARDT
It's so inconsiderate of the voter. How dare they ask the
Speaker of the House for his views on a major topic.

                             DOOCY
Especially on election day.

                            EARHARDT
Especially on election day, Steve.

                            KILMEADE
I don't think there's anything wrong with healthcare in
this country. Whenever I go to the doctor, they always give
me a sticker for not crying.

                                   COOPER pulls out and begins
                                   looking on his phone.

                             COOPER
                          (looking up)
I bet you haven't got this one, Holt.
                            (MORE)
                                                  (CONTINUED)

CONTINUED:

                              COOPER (CONT'D)
                         (beat)
Breaking news on C-N-N...

                         HOLT
A dog in San Diego has learned how to jet ski. An exclusive
first on N-B-C.

                         COOPER
Oh, come on!

                              HOLT begins to point into the
                              wings.

                         HOLT
Look, Anderson. There's a breaking story in the distance.

                              COOPER begins to look.

                         COOPER
Where?

                              COOPER exits into the wings.

                         DOOCY
So what do you guys think about voters requiring a form of
photo I-D to be allowed to vote?

                         EARHARDT
I think that it's a good idea, Steve. We don't want all
those nasty illegals making no difference by all voting in
a state Hillary Clinton is already guaranteed to win.

                         DOOCY
That's right, Ainsley.

                         KILMEADE
I heard they can't take voter's photos in Pennsylvania
because everyone there is a vampire.

                         EARHARDT
That's Transylvania, Brian, not Pennsylvania.

                                                        (CONTINUED)

PERFORMANCE LICENSE EDITION   LICENSE # _ _ _ _ _ _ _ _

CONTINUED:

>   A badly disguised PUTIN enters
>   and approaches the ELECTION
>   OFFICIAL.

                    PUTIN
Hello. I be here to vote.

                    ELECTION OFFICIAL
Can I take your name?

                    PUTIN
Mister A person.

                    ELECTION OFFICIAL
Here's your ballot.

>   PUTIN takes the ballot, marks
>   it, places it in the box then
>   moves to center stage.

                    PUTIN
I'm ready.

>   DMITRY and PETROV run on stage
>   with a screen to block him from
>   view.
>
>   There is a pause while he
>   changes.

                    PUTIN
I'm done.

>   DMITRY and PETROV exit to reveal
>   PUTIN now dressed as a farmer.
>   He approaches the ELECTION
>   OFFICIAL.

                    PUTIN
Well, howdy there partners. I'm be here to cast my olde
vote.

                    ELECTION OFFICIAL
Can I take your name?

                                        (CONTINUED)

                    PUTIN
Mister A farmer.

                    ELECTION OFFICIAL
Here's your ballot.

                              PUTIN takes the ballot, marks
                              it, and places it in the box.

                              The NARRATOR enters.

                    NARRATOR
Polls closed.

                              The NARRATOR exits.

                    RADDATZ
And that is it, the voting is over. All we can do now is
wait for the results as they come in.

                    HOLT
And those results will be coming in on N-B-C all night
long.

ACT I, SCENE FIFTEEN | THE RESULTS

                              And those results will be coming
                              in on N-B-C all night long.

                    NARRATOR
                    (entering)
While the polls may have closed, it's still early in the
night, and both sides remain more than ready and up to
continue their fight. For as all across the country, the
counting begins, both team red and team blue wait up to see
who wins.

                    CLINTON
Oh, I'm so nervous. What if I only win by two hundred
electoral votes?

                    BILL
Then we'll be drug testing the entire population of Texas.

                                                  (CONTINUED)

                              NARRATOR
And so as we journey forth to find out who has won the
states in the south and those in the north, who better to
set our course than Anderson Cooper, C-N-N's number one
anchor, and from Fox News, their number one --
                              (beat)
Sean Hannity.

                    COOPER and SEAN HANNITY enter
                    and flank the NARRATOR.

                              COOPER
Good evening. I'm Anderson Cooper, and no, I do not know
how Lester Holt ended up on a non-stop to South America.

                              HANNITY
You're watching Hannity with me, Sean Hannity. Tonight, is
the grass really green, or is it just a liberal conspiracy?
That coming up later, but first, it's going to be a long
night, no worry for me, of course, I've got my trusty
Keurig coffee in hand, those guys will never let me down.
It's the two thousand and sixteen election.

                              NARRATOR
Delaware.

                              COOPER
And that's it, we're off with the first result of the
night, and it's a win for Hillary Clifton in Delaware as
she takes the lead in the electoral college.

                              HANNITY
The election will have to wait though as we kick off with
our top story of the night. And we're going to San Diego
where a dog has, get this, learned to jet ski. Is it just a
smart Republican dog? Or is Hillary Clinton training up an
army of animals to go against the American people?

                              NARRATOR
Indiana.

                              COOPER
And with the second result in, it's ten votes from Indiana
to Trump, putting him in the lead.

                                              (CONTINUED)

                         HANNITY
I guess we'll just have to wait and see because right now
we've just heard that Donald J. Trump has taken the lead in
the electoral college with a win in his running mate, Mike
Pence's home state.

                         NARRATOR
New York.

                         COOPER
With a win in both her and her opponent's home state,
Hillary Clinton has taken the lead.

                         HANNITY
We now return to San Diego.

                         NARRATOR
Texas.

                         COOPER
And with Texas in it's now a narrow lead for Donald Trump.

                         HANNITY
Breaking news, Hillary Clinton is a loser.

                         NARRATOR
California.

                         COOPER
As expected, a big boost for Hillary Clinton here.

                         HANNITY
Well, screw the dog in San Diego. Let's admire this video
of Ted Cruz cooking bacon on a gun instead.

                         NARRATOR
Wisconsin.

                         COOPER
They've previously elected Paul Ryan, and clearly, they
never learn. It's a boost for Trump here, but Clinton still
leads.

                                              (CONTINUED)

                    HANNITY
That really is some beautiful bacon.

                    NARRATOR
Alabama and Oklahoma.

                    HANNITY
Two great placed both voting red, that's sixteen electoral
votes for Donald J. Trump.

                    COOPER
A number which some of them, thanks to their unique
genetics, are able to count on their sixteen fingers across
both of their three hands.

                    NARRATOR
D-C, Nevada, Washington, Vermont, New Jersey.

                    COOPER
And Secretary Clinton is still in the lead.

                    HANNITY
I want to now spend some time discussing one of the major
issues that old white men face in the office. Do you draft
the non-disclosure agreement before or after?

                    NARRATOR
Alaska, Kentucky, North Dakota, Ohio, West Virginia,
Tennessee, Michigan, Utah, Montana, and Louisiana.

                    HANNITY
Staying on that subject, Donald Trump has retaken the lead
in the electoral college.

                    NARRATOR
Maryland, Colorado, Connecticut, New Mexico, Oregon, Rhode
Island, Nebraska, Virginia.

                    COOPER
We're calling all of these for Clinton on C-N-N.

                    HANNITY
We're calling all of these traitors on Fox News.

                                           (CONTINUED)

                         NARRATOR
Maine.

                         COOPER
One vote to Trump and three to Clinton here.

                         NARRATOR
Arizona, South Carolina, North Carolina.

                         COOPER
Called for Donald Trump.

                         HANNITY
Called for Donald Trump.

                         NARRATOR
Georgia, Idaho, Kansas, Iowa, South Dakota.

                         HANNITY
Get this, Trump is leading the electoral college.

                         NARRATOR
Illinois, Minnesota, New Hampshire.

                         COOPER
We're calling these three for Hillary Clinton, but she
still trails behind. If she can just win in Missouri,
Arkansas, Mississippi, and Wyoming, she'll take the lead
again.

                         NARRATOR
Missouri.

                         HANNITY
Called for Donald Trump.

                         NARRATOR
Arkansas.

                         HANNITY
Donald Trump.

                         NARRATOR
Mississippi.

                                                    (CONTINUED)

PERFORMANCE LICENSE EDITION   LICENSE # _ _ _ _ _ _ _ _

                         HANNITY
It's Donald Trump.

                         NARRATOR
Wyoming.

                         HANNITY
Again, we're calling it for Donald Trump.

                         COOPER
I need to call for a change of pants.

                         NARRATOR
Pennsylvania.

                         COOPER
Called for Donald Trump.

                              All on stage stop and stare at
                              COOPER.

                         HANNITY
What?

                         NARRATOR
What?

                         CLINTON
What?

                         OBAMA
Now, what is going on there? That result makes no sense...
It's like an onion in a fruit salad.

                         TRUMP
Losers. Pennsylvania is just full of losers.

                         JUNIOR
Dad, you won the state.

                         TRUMP
Wait, what?

                                                        (CONTINUED)

                          NARRATOR

Florida.

                          COOPER

It's the final result of the night, and it's just come in.
Florida is this year swinging red.

                          OBAMA
                         (standing)

Oh...

                          COOPER

C-N-N is calling it. With Clinton at two hundred and twenty-
seven votes...

                          OBAMA

My...

                          COOPER

Donald J. Trump is going to be the forty-fifth President of
the United States.

                          OBAMA

GOD!

                    Lights out.

                  <u>END OF ACT I</u>

                                              (CONTINUED)

ACT II : "THE FIRST YEAR"

ACT II, SCENE ONE | ACT II OPENING

> With the audience seated once
> again, the lights across the
> auditorium go down, and the
> anticipation is allowed to build
> on the empty stage before a
> single spotlight shines, and the
> music begins.

                    NARRATOR
                  (entering)
/YOU MIGHT BE THINKING YOU'RE IN THR WRONG SHOW, BUT NO
NEED TO WORRY, FOR THIS IS JUST A PARODY SONG, WHICH JUST
LIKE THIS PARODY PRESIDENT SHOULDN'T LAST LONG.

A TREASONOUS RACIST, MISOGYNIST, ALL TOGETHER HATED MAN IN
THE WHITE HOUSE, WHAT - THE - HELL'S - HE - TWEETED - NOW?/

> A light goes up on CLINTON, who
> stands drinking from a bottle of
> wine.

                    CLINTON
/CAN WE ALL SCREAM NOW?/

                    NARRATOR
                (gesturing at the bottle)
Please?

> The NARRATOR takes the bottle,
> drinks from it, and then hands
> it back before she exits.

                    NARRATOR
/YOU CAN'T BELIEVE IT YET, YOU HAVEN'T HAD THE CHANCE, HIS
WHOLE VOTER BASE IS CLEARLY IN A TRANCE, AND SOMEHOW HE
CAN'T EVEN FIND TO WEAR, CORRECTLY - FITTING - PANTS./

> The stage fills with light as
> the ENSEMBLE stand in a line.

                                        (CONTINUED)

CONTINUED:

>   In front of them, TRUMP, his
>   pants clearly too tight.

                         ENSEMBLE
/DONALD TRUMP IS AN ORANGE MAN (WITH VERY TINY HANDS), AND
HE HAS RACIST FANS --/

                         TRUMP
WAIT!

>   The music stops, and the
>   ENSEMBLE clear the stage.

                         TRUMP
I do not like this song. This song is from a show I do not
like, which I hear is highly overrated and also not so
great. The cast was also very mean to Mike Pence, and Mike
Pence deserves better. He has had a very tough life
because, for the last fifty-seven years, he has had to live
as Mike Pence.

                         NARRATOR
Mister President-Elect --

                         TRUMP
No one, except the audience of this show perhaps, has ever
had a tougher time in a theater than Mike Pence. Especially
no politician.

                         NARRATOR
What about President Abraham Lincoln?

>   Beat.

                         CLINTON
                    (leaning on stage)
I just want to say, I like that show. I'm down with that
relatable stuff. I love rap, it's what Bill and I order as
a sandwich when we feel adventurous.

                         TRUMP
Go away, Crooked Hillary Clinton.

>   CLINTON exits.

                                        (CONTINUED)

                         TRUMP
Can we sing something different?

                         NARRATOR
Sure, I've got another.

                         The NARRATOR stamps their foot.

                         The music begins, and the
                         ENSEMBLE enters wearing TRUMP
                         masks.

                         ENSEMBLE
/TRUMPY LUMPY TRUMPETY DOO, HE...
                    (pointing at TRUMP)
DOESN'T GIVE A DAMN ABOUT YOU.
                    (pointing at the audience)
TRUMPY LUMPY TRUMPETY DEE.../

                         Stepping forward and removing
                         their mask, one of the ENSEMBLE
                         reveal themselves as PUTIN.

                         PUTIN
                    (bringing a tape from his
                     pocket)
/I HAVE TAPE WHERE HE BE COVERED IN PEE./

                         The music stops, and the
                         ENSEMBLE clear to leave the
                         NARRATOR, PUTIN, and TRUMP.

                         TRUMP
What tape?

                         PUTIN
Well, Donald, that tape.

                         TRUMP
But you cannot have that tape. It does not exist.

                         PUTIN
                    (holding the tape up)
It exist. I have tape here. It show you covered in pee-pee.

                                             (CONTINUED)

                         TRUMP
I do not remember that happening.

                         PUTIN
Really, do you not? What about in Moscow?

                         TRUMP
I do not remember being in Moscow.

                         PUTIN
In Ritz Carlton hotel?

                         TRUMP
I do not remember staying at the Ritz Carlton hotel.

                         PUTIN
In presidential suite?

                         TRUMP
I do not remember staying in the presidential suite.

                         PUTIN
Their names be Dominika and Kristina.

                    Beat.

                         TRUMP
I remember.
                    (moving closer)
Do you have the bit where?

                         PUTIN
Yes.

                         TRUMP
What about the bit where they --

                         PUTIN
Yes.

                         TRUMP
How about the bit where --

                                        (CONTINUED)

                         PUTIN
I have all of it, Donald.

                         TRUMP
Even the bit where...

                                   TRUMP whispers into PUTIN'S ear,
                                   and PUTIN's expression turns to
                                   one of disgust.

                         PUTIN
No. I not know you did that.
                         (beat)
You are it after?

                                   PUTIN notices the NARRATOR stood
                                   watching them.

                         PUTIN
Hello, Narrator. May I ask you, would you care to see
people you know ever again?

                         NARRATOR
Yes, I would.

                         PUTIN
Then listen to me. You need to help out old Uncle Putin, do
you understand?

                         NARRATOR
Yes.

                         PUTIN
Good, then I need you, as I believe you put it in west...
go away and tell no one about what you just heard. Do you
still understand me?

                         NARRATOR
I think so.

                         PUTIN
Good. Then go away.

                                   The NARRATOR exits.

                                                  (CONTINUED)

                        PUTIN
Now then, Donald.

                        TRUMP
Yes, Comrade Vladimir Putin, sir.

                        PUTIN
We need to talk.

                        TRUMP
Are you breaking up with America?

                        PUTIN
No. Why would I break up with America? It take big effort
to rig election?
                    (beat)
But there be things that I need to make sure you understand
now that you be President of United States.

                        TRUMP
Yes, Comrade, sir.

                        PUTIN
Number one. You belong to Putin.

                    Beat.

                        TRUMP
What is number two?

                        PUTIN
There be no number two. Putin not want to confuse you with
big numbers.

                        TRUMP
Thank you, Comrade Vladimir Putin, sir.

                        PUTIN
I own you now, Donald. You do Putin say when Putin tell
you. Do you understand me?

                        TRUMP
Yes, sir.

                                            (CONTINUED)

PUTIN
And should you fail to obey, this tape of golden moment of become public.

TRUMP
I will do whatever you say.

PUTIN
Very good. I see message has gotten across. Kneel.

TRUMP
What?

PUTIN
I said kneel.

TRUMP kneels before him.

PUTIN
Now crawl offstage.

TRUMP does as he's told.

PUTIN
(to audience)
I know where all of you live also.

PUTIN exits.

ACT II, SCENE TWO | TRUMP MEETS WITH OBAMA

At first, a dark and empty stage.

NARRATOR
(entering)
Well, I think we can all agree that got weird.
(beat)
And so it is that with the election over, the world sits in shock, for America has elected to get a new president who all expect to run amok.
(MORE)

(CONTINUED)

CONTINUED:
                          NARRATOR (CONT'D)
But before we can reach the day of his inauguration, a day
which many feel can never come too late, the new President-
Elect is off to meet with the man who previously, he had
feelings toward of nothing but hate.

                              As the NARRATOR exits, lights go
                              up on the OVAL OFFICE, where the
                              ENSEMBLE (as PRESS) sit in front
                              of TRUMP, who himself is sat
                              waiting next to an empty chair.

                          TRUMP
Do any of you know where he is? I thought he would be here
by now. He said he would be here ten minutes ago. I know
some people would call this late. I would never say that,
but some people would. I guess we do have to let him off,
right? He does have a long commute. Did you know that the
guy flies in from Kenya every morning?

                              A spotlight finds OBAMA at the
                              other side of the stage drinking
                              shots. After a moment, he slaps
                              himself on the face and then
                              walks over to TRUMP.

                          TRUMP
                          (standing)
Oh, here is he. He has made it. Mister President, it is
good to see you.

                          OBAMA
Oh... my... god...

                              They both sit.

                          PRESS #1
Mister President, Mister President-Elect, how are you both
feeling about last night's result?

                          TRUMP
                          (to OBAMA)
Would you like to start?

                                              (CONTINUED)
PERFORMANCE LICENSE EDITION   LICENSE # _ _ _ _ _ _ _ _

                          OBAMA

Oh... my... god...

                          TRUMP

I guess I am starting then. Well, press journalist person,
I do not know your name --

                          PRESS #1

It's Rachel, I'm from C-N-N --

                          TRUMP

Fake news. You are fake news. I do not care about your
name, but I do care that I am very pleased about the result
last night. It was great, it could not have gone any more
great, it was just fantastic.

                              OBAMA lets out an audible groan.

                          TRUMP
                        (to OBAMA)
Would you like to say anything?

                          OBAMA

Oh... my... god...

                          TRUMP

I think we are ready for the next question.

                          PRESS #2

Mister President-Elect, you've made quite a few strongly-
worded statements over the years about the President, often
criticizing his judgments and actions. So will you be
calling on him for advice as you enter office yourself?

                          TRUMP

That is fake news. I have never said anything bad about
this man.

                          OBAMA

Oh... my... god...

                        PRESS #2
Mister Trump, that simply isn't true. In the past you have
spent years leading a moment questioning where the
President was born, you have accused him of being the
founder of ISIS, and you have said multiple times that you
feel he is the worse leader that America has ever had.

                        TRUMP
Correct. Fake news. Next question.

                        PRESS #3
President Obama, have you had the chance to speak to
Secretary Clinton this morning? Do you know if she's doing
okay?

                                    A scream comes from somewhere
                                    backstage.

                        OBAMA
Oh... my... god...

                        CLINTON (OFF)
Nearly three million votes. Three million.

                                    OBAMA points towards the wings
                                    and stands.

                        PRESS #4
Mister President, do you need to attend to that?

                                    OBAMA begins to nod then slowly
                                    begins shaking his head.

                        OBAMA
Oh... my... god...

                        PRESS #4
We understand, sir.

                                    OBAMA exits.

                        TRUMP
Wait, where is he going? He is being very rude toward me.

PERFORMANCE LICENSE EDITION   LICENSE # _ _ _ _ _ _ _ _

ACT II, SCENE THREE | TRUMP PICKS HIS CABINET

>   TRUMP'S OFFICE on another day
>   where CONWAY and TRUMP are mid-
>   conversation.

                    CONWAY
I agree that celebrating is important, Mister Trump. But
you also need to start choosing cabinet positions, sir.

                    TRUMP
How many do I get to choose, Kellyanne Conway?

                    CONWAY
You have to choose twenty-two, sir.

                    TRUMP
I want them all to be made out of solid gold and mounted on
the wall of the Oval Office.

                    CONWAY
Sir?

                    TRUMP
One of them also needs to be really bigly so that I can fit
all of my awards in it. Did you know last year I won the
Trump Organization employee of the month thirteen times?

                    CONWAY
Mister Trump, sir, I'm talking about your government
cabinet, not... cabinets.

                    TRUMP
I do not understand.

                    CONWAY
Well, the cabinet is made up of the heads of federal
executive departments and a few other top advisors.

                    TRUMP
Like Eric Trump?

                    CONWAY
No, sir, that's feral.

                                        (CONTINUED)

                         TRUMP
Okay, I want to pick Ivanka Trump, Donald Trump Junior,
Steve Bannon, and Vladimir Putin.

                         CONWAY
I'm not sure that would be appropriate. We don't want to
make it look as though you're only appointing people you
like.

                         TRUMP
What about Jeff Sessions? No one could ever believe that
someone likes Jeff Sessions?

                         CONWAY
Jeff Sessions is good. How about Ben Carlson?

                         TRUMP
It would stop him calling me asking for a job. And we
should try to look diverse.

                         CONWAY
What about Betsy DeVos too? It might be good to get a woman
in there.

                         TRUMP
I like your thinking, Kellyanne Conway.

                         CHRISTIE enters unnoticed.

                         TRUMP
I have to attend an important meeting with Kanye West right
now, can I leave the rest of the decisions to you?

                         TRUMP turns to notice CHRISTIE.

                         CHRISTIE
Hey, Mister Trump.

                         TRUMP
Chris Christie.

                         CHRISTIE
Yes, Mister Trump.

                                                        (CONTINUED)

                    TRUMP
I am not choosing you. I know I said we should try to look
diverse, but we do not need to look that diverse.

                    CHRISTIE
Wow, jeez, sir. That really hurts.

ACT II, SCENE FOUR | THE PRESS CONFERENCE

                              A room in TRUMP TOWER where
                              TRUMP is stood behind a podium
                              with CONWAY next to him. In
                              front of them, the ENSEMBLE (as
                              PRESS) sit waiting.

                              At the side of the podium is a
                              table topped with papers and a
                              box.

                    TRUMP
Okay, everyone, I have called this press conference today
to tell you all about the great things I have been doing
since the election and all of the great things that I will
be doing after I am inaugurated next week.
                    (beat)
I will take questions now.

                    PRESS #1
Mister President-Elect, it's been two months since the
election, and this is the first press conference that
you've held. Can you tell us what you've been doing since
November?

                    TRUMP
No, next question.

                    PRESS #5
Mister Trump, could you tell us more about the plans for
your inauguration day? What can we expect to see?

                    TRUMP
Thank you for that question Fox News. I would be happy to
talk about all of the great things that will be happening.
                    (MORE)
                                        (CONTINUED)

CONTINUED:

                          TRUMP (CONT'D)
You can expect to see so many great things that your mind
will be blown. In the evening more great things will be
happening, and it will be so great and so fantastic. We are
even going to have some fireworks, which will be great, and
do not worry, I have checked the immigration papers of all
of the fire before they started working, okay.

Also, after everyone has left, Paul Ryan, Mitch McConnell,
and Donald J. Trump are going to dismantle all rights for
women using executive orders.

                          PRESS #2
Mister Trump, can I ask you about the pee-pee tape?

                          TRUMP
How do you know about that?

                          PRESS #2
It was mentioned in a leaked dossier that also alleges
Russia helped you to win the election.

                          TRUMP
Neither of those things is true, okay. There is no pee-pee
tape, and Russia did not help me win the election. It is
fake news.

                          PRESS #2
Are you sure, Mister Trump? Because we all got emailed a
link to a password protected movie titled "Trump's Golden
Moments."

                          PRESS #3
It also came with the note, "from Russia with love."

                          PRESS #4
Mister Trump, is this pee-pee tape going to be your
Watergate?

                          PRESS #2
It's going to be his broken-Watergate.

                              The ENSEMBLE laugh as CONWAY
                              whispers to TRUMP.

                                              (CONTINUED)
PERFORMANCE LICENSE EDITION   LICENSE # _ _ _ _ _ _ _ _ _

CONTINUED:

                         TRUMP
Okay, I want all of you to listen because we need to get
some things clear. You are all fake news losers, apart from
you, Breitbart, Fox News and Russia Today, you are all
great and you are doing a fantastic job. But from the rest
of you, I am not going to put up with your fake mainstream
media news. Let me show you something...
                    (choosing someone)
You. Where are you from?

                         PRESS #6
San Fransisco.

                         TRUMP
Then you must be a liberal from M-S-N-B-C?

                         PRESS #6
That's right.

                         TRUMP
Come up here.

                              PRESS #6 stands and moves over
                              to TRUMP.

                         TRUMP
Let us get something clear, okay. You are going to report
as I want you to, and the first thing you are going to
report on is how much work I have been doing. Do you see
all of these papers? You are going to tell everyone that
this is all work and that it is great.

                         PRESS #6
                    (checking the papers)
Mister President-Elect, these are all just blank pieces of
paper. And this box, this is probably empty...
                    (checking inside the box)
There's a horse's head in this box.

                         TRUMP
Casino?... I mean, capiche?

                         PRESS #3
Mister Trump, are you threatening us right now?

                                             (CONTINUED)

PERFORMANCE LICENSE EDITION   LICENSE # _ _ _ _ _ _ _ _

                          TRUMP
I could kidnap all of your families if that would help?

                          PRESS #1
You do know this press conference is being broadcast live,
don't you?

                          TRUMP
Is it?

                          PRESS #1
Yes, Mister Trump, it is.

                          TRUMP
                     (to CONWAY)
Kellyanne Conway, we are going to need more horse's heads.

                          CONWAY
We don't have anymore, Mister Trump, sir. Don't you
remember? You used the rest of your horses in Trump Steaks.
Does your daughter have any?

                          TRUMP
She prefers goats, that is why she married Jared Kushner.

ACT II, SCENE FIVE | AT THE CLINTON'S

                              The CLINTON RESIDENCE, where
                              CLINTON is mid-conversation on
                              the phone.

                          NARRATOR
                     (entering)
And so it is that on the night before the inauguration,
many are feeling sick, scared, and uncomfortable right
across the nation. But for some time is scarce to worry,
for protests in a flurry are already planned to take place
tomorrow right across the land. Meanwhile, in New York's
Chappaqua, a small and homely hamlet, Hillary Clinton is
wondering why to get out of the inauguration nobody has a
plan yet.

                              The NARRATOR exits.

                                            (CONTINUED)

                           CLINTON
                         (on phone)
No, I got you, Jimmy. I know it's supposed to be a
tradition for all of us to go, but you know, I've spoken to
W, and he says the seniors are in hospital and being forced
to miss it. Well, we're all old, I'm sure we can catch a
cold or break a leg for the weekend... Oh, you've already
packed the Xanax? I must remember to get some of that.
                         (shouting out)
Hey, Bill, do we have any Xanax?
                         (on phone)
Hey, Jimmy, would it be okay if I was to borrow some of
yours? I'm all out. I'm sure I can bring you something in
return. How about earplugs? Oh, W's sorted those. Alcohol?
No, Barack's on that is he?

                           BILL (OFF)
Hillary.

                           CLINTON
                         (on phone)
I'll work something out. I've got to go now though, Bill's
calling me. We'll catch up properly tomorrow.

                               CLINTON ends her call as BILL
                               enters, looking excited.

                           BILL
Oh, this is going to be the best inauguration day ever.

                           CLINTON
                         (standing)
If you say that again, we're getting a divorce.

                           BILL
But Hillary, it will be. I've found it.

                           CLINTON
Found what? What have you found? Is it a hundred thousand
votes in Michigan?

                               BILL pulls a key from his
                               pocket.

                                                  (CONTINUED)

                          BILL
This is better. It's my spare key to the White House.

                          Beat.

                          CLINTON
Hey, Bill, do you still have any of those whoopee cushions
left over from the time the D-N-C leadership came over for
dinner?

                                   BILL pulls a whoopee cushion
                                   from his pocket.

                          BILL
That I do, Hillary. That I do. And I've got a whole pile of
photos of us with the Obamas and some strong glue too.

                          CLINTON
I don't say this to you often enough, but William Jefferson
Clinton, I really like you sometimes.

ACT II, SCENE SIX | THE INAUGURATION

                                   THE CAPITOL, Washington, where
                                   the ENSEMBLE (as SPECTATORS) are
                                   gathered for the inauguration of
                                   Donald Trump. Sat among them,
                                   CONWAY, ERIC, IVANKA, JUNIOR,
                                   and SEAN SPICER.

                                   The NARRATOR enters to stand at
                                   the glass podium front center.

                          NARRATOR
The twentieth day of the year's first month, a day which
many in the world hopes will end shortly before lunch. For
today is the day that judgment will fall. Today is the day
that parents will call to tell their children they love
them all.

On Capitol Hill in Washington DC, a breeze blows slowly
over all that's to be.
                          (MORE)

                                                        (CONTINUED)

CONTINUED:
                        NARRATOR (CONT'D)
And as he prepares to take his spot among those who before
him's legacies he'll soon work to rot, friends of his
gather among those foes who still matter. While out in the
crowds, thousands now stand to shout to him cheers, while
walking the streets millions more prepare to scream leers.
Three million votes behind, but that's never a fact his
supporters will mind, for all they want to see is their new
president claiming to be making them free.

Celebration will follow for all those who for Donald they
did vote, while a drive to inspire change will fill many
more of those who begin to take note.

An inauguration of unity is what many will claim, but days
will follow where Barack Obama is still given the blame.

And so as Trump and Pence to this spot they make their way,
it's time to begin the ceremony that will keep decency at
bay.

                        MICHELLE (OFF)
Barack, hurry up. You don't want to miss it.

                        BILL, CLINTON, and MICHELLE
                        enter.

                        CLINTON
I wouldn't be so sure about that.

                        MICHELLE
Barack.

                        OBAMA enters and joins them.

                        OBAMA
Oh... my... god...

                        CLINTON
Hey, where are the Carters?

                        MICHELLE
They called this morning and said their train has been
canceled.

                                                    (CONTINUED)

CONTINUED:

                    CLINTON
Dang it. Why didn't we think of that?

                    BILL
What about the Bushes? I was hoping to catch up with W.

                    MICHELLE
He accidentally booked his flights to the wrong Washington.

                    OBAMA
Oh... my... god...

               The four of them take their
               seats among the crowd.

                    NARRATOR
And now, please find something to hold on to as we welcome
President-Elect, Donald Trump, and Vice-President-Elect,
Mike Pence.

               PENCE and TRUMP enter.

                    TRUMP
Mike Pence, why is your wife not here to watch you today?

                    PENCE
Oh, Mother said she had an appointment with her doctor
scheduled for today.

                    TRUMP
What a coincidence. Mary said the same thing to me.

                    PENCE
Who is Mary, sir?

                    TRUMP
Number three.

               Together, they make their way
               towards the podium and shake
               hands with the NARRATOR.

                                        (CONTINUED)

> CLINTON hands the NARRATOR a
> bottle of hand sanitizer.

                    CLINTON
Here, take this.

> The NARRATOR cleans their hands
> then hands the bottle back.

                    NARRATOR
Thank you.

                    CLINTON
No problem. Just remember to vote for me in four years. Or
just remember me... please remember me.

                    NARRATOR
                (to PENCE and TRUMP)
Mister Trump. Mister Pence. If you're both ready, we'll get
started.

                    TRUMP
Before we begin, I do not like the Bible. I prefer people
named Jesus who do not get crucified, and so I have a
different book to swear on.

> He brings a book from his pocket
> and shows it to the audience.

                    TRUMP
It is a great book. Such a fantastic read. It is called --

                    NARRATOR
The Art of the Deal by Donald J. Trump.

                    TRUMP
Available now from the failing Amazon dot com, which I hear
is owned by the failing Washington Post loser.

                    PENCE
Such a strong statement, sir.

                    TRUMP
Thank you, Mike Pence.

                                           (CONTINUED)

                              The NARRATOR gestures towards
                              the book.

                         NARRATOR
Mister Pence, would you mind?

                              PENCE takes the book and holds
                              it for TRUMP to place his hand
                              upon.

                         NARRATOR
                         (to audience)
Ladies, gentlemen, and Bill Clinton. We are gathered here
today to mourn the loss of democracy, compassion, decency,
and, most importantly of all, style in the White House.

                         TRUMP
It is going to be so great.

                         NARRATOR
We'll begin with the President-Elect.
                         (to TRUMP)
Donald Jenius Trump, do you solemnly swear that you will
faithlessly embarrass your country on the world stage,
insult and alienate allies, and to the best of your
ability, completely ignore the Constitution of the United
States?

                         TRUMP
So help me, Comrade Vladimir Putin.

                         NARRATOR
Then if nobody has any objections...

                              CLINTON stands, but BILL pulls
                              her down.

                         CLINTON
I've got a few.

                         NARRATOR
Then I do now declare you to be...

                                                    (CONTINUED)

TRUMPED: AN ALTERNATIVE MUSICAL
PART ONE & TWO
CONTINUED:

                         OBAMA
Oh... my... god...

                         NARRATOR
The President of the United States.

                         OBAMA
Wait.

                    Everyone on stage watches as
                    OBAMA stands and makes his way
                    to the podium.

                         OBAMA
If you wouldn't mind, Narrator, I would like to say...
something.

                         NARRATOR
Please go ahead.

                         OBAMA
Thank you.

                    The NARRATOR steps to the side
                    as OBAMA begins to address the
                    audience.

                         OBAMA
Now a lot of people have asked me, ever since the election,
about what I think of the fact that this suntanned turd...
is going to become the President of the United States... I
have not given an answer to that inquiry before, but today,
I am going to give you one... Because the answer is really
quite simple... Let me tell you now that the answer is
yes... yes I do like piña coladas, and I also enjoy...
getting caught in the rain.

                    He rips off his pants to reveal
                    a pair of Hawaiian shorts.

                         OBAMA
                    (to the NARRATOR)
Narrator, my sunglasses if you please.

                                             (CONTINUED)
PERFORMANCE LICENSE EDITION   LICENSE # _ _ _ _ _ _ _ _

                     The NARRATOR takes a pair of
                     sunglasses from their pocket and
                     hands them over.

OBAMA
I'm not running things anymore, and that means none of this
crap... is my responsibility.
           (to MICHELLE)
Michelle.

                     MICHELLE stands and joins him.

OBAMA
We're off to Tahiti to go jet-skiing. Obamas out.

                     Hand in hand, they both exit. A
                     beat follows.

CLINTON
Well, that was some weird shit.

                     Beat.

TRUMP
Can we move on to Mike Pence now?

                     PENCE hands TRUMP the book, who
                     then holds it for him to place
                     his hand upon.

NARRATOR
Of course.
           (to PENCE)
Michael Richard Pence, do you solemnly swear that you will
accept your fate of being forever remembered by history as
responsible for all of the terrible things that Donald
Trump goes on to do, to not fulfill a single one of your
responsibilities to ensure that the President follows the
law, and to waste thousands of dollars by storming out
sports events that you never wanted to go to in the first
place?

PENCE
I do.

                                         (CONTINUED)

CONTINUED:

                    NARRATOR
Then I do declare you to be the Vice-President.

                         All (except CLINTON and the
                         NARRATOR) begin to applaud.

                         Noticing BILL clapping, CLINTON
                         moves his hands down.

                    BILL
Sorry, Hillary. I just find it emotional.

                    CLINTON
I need to find a bar.

                    NARRATOR
I need to join you.

                         CLINTON and the NARRATOR exit as
                         TRUMP takes to the podium.

                    TRUMP
Well, Narrator, thank you very much. President Obama, I do
not know where he has gone. I guess he has to run to the
airport before his visa expires. Also, I would also like to
thank all of those great patriotic Americans who voted for
me.
                         (beat)
Today is a very special day because today we are taking
such great and fantastic power away from Washington, a man
who I hear is overrated, and giving it to Russia.

Throughout this brutal election campaign, ordinary American
voters have told me that they want great things like
schools, they want lots of schools, and also safe
neighborhoods. I have also been told that small business
owners want a strong economy and skilled people to work for
them. But in life, you do not always get what you want. If
they wanted those things, then they should have voted for
Crooked Hillary Clinton.

What I am going to do is make America great again. And to
do this, trust me, such fantastic things will be happening.
                         (MORE)

                                             (CONTINUED)

CONTINUED:
                          TRUMP (CONT'D)
Everything is going to be so great that you will not even
know that it is great. That is how great it is going to be.

There will be lots of jobs. We are going to create so many
jobs for people like lawyers. So many lawyers, and also
comedians. There is going to be so many lawyers and so many
comedians, that it is going to be like an N-B-C production
office in the year two thousand and ten.
Most importantly of all, I am going to give this country
what it really needs. We are going to have, prepare for
your minds to be blown, a space force. We are going to have
rockets, fast rockets that go whoosh. Also, we will have
some that go wheeee.

For the true patriots of this country, we are also going to
have such a great display of fireworks above our cities on
our Independence Day, June fifth, courtesy of little rocket
man and North Korea.

I know a lot of people are worried right now about the
safety and the security of your family, but to you, I ask a
question, in the event of a nuclear war, would it not be
cool to become a super hero?
                         (beat)
And now, I am going to hand over to Mike Pence.

                                   TRUMP stands back as PENCE takes
                                   to the podium.

                          PENCE
Well, what are we all standing around for? This is supposed
to be a party. Comrades, let's dance.

ACT II, SCENE SEVEN | THE INAUGURATION PARTY

                                   A BALLROOM where in an instant
                                   the dress of those on stage has
                                   changed to attire of distinctly
                                   Russian origin. Equally as
                                   Russian is the music now filling
                                   the stage.

                                                      (CONTINUED)

                              While the ENSEMBLE and others
                              remain on stage, PENCE and TRUMP
                              have disappeared.

                    CONWAY
Comrades, please welcome the President and Vice-President.

                              Synchronized, PENCE and TRUMP
                              return and begin to dance
                              Barynya center stage. Circled
                              around them, their guests clap
                              and cheer as they watch.

                              After a short time, PENCE and
                              TRUMP take a bow together and
                              then move to the side to allow
                              CONWAY and SPICER to take the
                              floor together.

                              Again, those around them clap
                              and cheer for a short while
                              until PENCE and TRUMP join them,
                              and all four dance together.
                              As the music begins to slow, the
                              dancing stops, and all on stage
                              stand arm in arm to sing.

                    ENSEMBLE (EXCEPT TRUMP)
                         (drunkenly)
/DONALD TRUMP IS OUR PRESIDENT, DONALD TRUMP IS OUR MAN. WE
ALL LOVE DONALD TRUMP, HE'S OUR MAN, DONALD TRUMP IS OUR
MAN. HEY!/

                              Silence, and then the music
                              builds once more for ERIC,
                              IVANKA, and JUNIOR to now take
                              center stage.

                              While IVANKA and JUNIOR dance
                              synchronized, however, ERIC
                              stands watching them both
                              confused until eventually he
                              drops the floor and begins to
                              spin himself around.

                                             (CONTINUED)

> As the three of them move to the
> side, next to take the floor is
> a topless PUTIN, who enters by
> cartwheeling from the wings
> before performing a solo.
>
> Finally, as PUTIN finishes, the
> entire stage begins to dance
> together until abruptly, the
> music stops, and the stage
> clears to leave BILL on his own.

                        BILL
I am going to be in so much trouble if Hillary finds out
that I stayed for the party.

ACT II, SCENE EIGHT | THE FIRST PRESS BRIEFING

> The WHITE HOUSE PRESS BRIEFING
> ROOM where the ENSEMBLE (as
> PRESS) sit facing a podium,
> behind which, the NARRATOR
> stands.

                        NARRATOR
With the inauguration over and the party at an end --

> SPICER enters and begins to push
> the NARRATOR away.

                        SPICER
Hey, hey, no. Not your place. Listen here, Narrator person,
I don't know who you are or what you're doing here, but
this is not your show, do you understand? Now get off this
stage before I strangle you with the piece of gum I'm
chewing right now.

> After pushing the NARRATOR
> offstage, he takes his place at
> the podium.

                                                   (CONTINUED)

                         SPICER
Okay, now I want all of you son's of bitches to listen up,
so I don't have to repeat myself. First up, it's item
number one, I have a hangover after the inauguration party
last night. It's what big boys and big girls get after they
drink alcohol. You'll all learn about that one day.

                         PRESS #1
Like the morning after impeachment.

                         SPICER
Right, I heard that. You, what's your name?

                         PRESS #1
Ayma.

                         SPICER
That should be Ayma, sir. Do you understand that? Let's try
it again, what's your name?

                         PRESS #1
Ayma, sir.

                         SPICER
Good, and what's your second name?

                         PRESS #1
Moron.

                         SPICER
Ayma Moron.

                    The ENSEMBLE laugh.

                         SPICER
Oh, right, I get it. It's a joke. It's joke around with
Spicy day, is it? Well, not on my watch. See me in my
office at the end of the day. I'm also taking ten points
away from C-N-N house for your pathetic attempt to be the
joker in the group.

                         PRESS #2
C-N-N house? Sean, this isn't some sort of school for
magic.

                                                    (CONTINUED)

                              SPICER
Well, you all could have fooled me, that's for sure. I read
all of your reports on the inauguration this morning, and
nearly all of you just conjured up the size of the crowd.
Staying with this, we come to item number two. I'm not
mentioning any names, okay, but I am looking at you when I
say this New York Times. You can't just lie about the
figures to make the President look bad. You were all there,
and you all saw the billions --

                              PRESS #3
Billions, Sean?

                              SPICER
Okay, millions then. Happy now? You all saw the millions of
people who came out to watch the President.

                              PRESS #4
Sean, most of them were protesters.

                              SPICER
Okay, but tell me this, would they have been there if it
wasn't for the President.

                              PRESS #4
They were protesting the President.

                              SPICER
But would they have been protesting the President if it
wasn't his inauguration? Would they have been protesting
Hillary Clinton?

                              PRESS #4
No, they would have been there to celebrate instead.

                              SPICER
Okay, that... that is sort of my point. Here's what's going
to happen, all of you are going to go and write me a new
draft of your inauguration reports using the correct crowd
size figures as homework, even you The Washington Post. I
want all of them on my desk first thing tomorrow, or I will
write home to your parents.

                         PRESS #5 raises their hand.

                                             (CONTINUED)

                              SPICER
Yes, you from Fox News.

                              PRESS #5
Master Hannity sent an apple for me to give you, sir.

                              SPICER
Well, you can tell Sean Hannity that I don't like apples. I
don't go within three feet of any fruit. But it's a nice
gesture, and so I'll tell you what, at recess, you can have
the first choice of toy to play with.

                              PRESS #2
Sean --

                              SPICER
What?

                              PRESS #2
Are you some sort of joke?

                              SPICER
Stop asking questions. The next person who asks me a
question can stand outside until we're done. Okay, we move
on now to item number three. For the stupid among you,
which is all of you, that is one less than four, but one
more than two. It says here that the President will later
today walk from the White House Residence across to the
Oval Office. I don't know what that is so don't ask.
Perhaps it's an office in some sort of Oval shape? I don't
know. Perhaps you can all Google it. To sign some executive
orders with Paul Ryan and Mitch McConnell.

                              PRESS #6
Sean, what will these executive orders be about?

                              SPICER
What did I just tell you all about asking questions? I'm
marking your name down.
                              (beat)
Okay, so it says here that there will be multiple, that
means more than one, executive orders signed that will be
great in nature. So there are some great things going to be
happening, report that, that is your news.
                              (MORE)
                                                        (CONTINUED)

CONTINUED:

                         SPICER (CONT'D)
Oh, and it also says that the President will be ordering
people to stop laughing at Mitch McConnell.
                    (beat)
Now during this walk to this circular shaped office, the
President will be joined by his third lady, and I am told
that she will be wearing a long white robe topped with a
wizard-like hat... no, wait, that's going to be the
President. It says Melania will be wearing a bag over her
head because she's embarrassed to be seen with her husband.

                         PRESS #1
Can we report that?

                         SPICER
No. You're all going to report this instead. The First
Lady, Melania Trump, loves... Why aren't you all writing
this down? Get writing before I write it on your faces
using C-N-N's blood for ink.

                    They all begin writing.

                         SPICER
Okay, the First Lady, Melania Trump, loves the President,
that's Donald Trump, very much. The two of them regularly,
and there's a note here that says regularly is at least
three times a week, make love together in the evenings.
Except for the President who makes love five times a week.

                              There's a flash as someone takes
                              a photo.

                         SPICER
Okay, which of you little assholes is taking photos? Was it
you, Washington Post?

                         PRESS #3
My editor asked me to get a photo because you're not
allowing cameras in here.

                         SPICER
Oh, and I suppose that you think you're just going to print
some photo of me in your newspaper with a caption about the
news? Something like this here.
                    (checking his notes)
                         (MORE)
                                              (CONTINUED)

CONTINUED:

                          SPICER (CONT'D)
Giant Weiner, Sean Spicer, confirms that the President is
not lacking down there.
                          (beat)
I don't want to see another camera. No more photos. Believe
it or not, some of us in this administration don't actually
photograph too well. I'm not mentioning names, but you all
know I'm on about Steve Bannon. And then there's Stephen
Miller, he doesn't photograph at all.

                          PRESS #3
Past administrations have always allowed these briefings to
be broadcast so they can be open to the people.

                          SPICER
This is not a past administration, is it? This is Spicer's
time, and what I say goes. It works like this. The
President decides what the news is, and then he tells me,
Sean Spicer. I then tell all of you what the news is, and
then you go and dumb it down for your readers and your
viewers so that they know what the news is.

                          PRESS #3
What is the news today?

                          SPICER
I haven't had the chance to discuss it with the President
yet.

                          PRESS #1
Sean, did you just call all of our readers and viewers dumb
right now? They are all voters.

                          SPICER
Of course, I'm calling them dumb. Three million more of
them voted illegally for Hillary Clinton rather than our
President, and for some reason, they all decided to vote in
California. I'm not sure what's going on there, but I would
say that's pretty dumb C-N-N.

                          PRESS #4
Can we quote you on that, Sean?

                                                  (CONTINUED)

                         SPICER
                    (mocking at first)
"Can we quote you on that, Sean?" How about I quote you on
your dying words as I strangle you with your iPhone
charger? And don't try to pretend you don't all have
iPhones, okay? I know that you liberal fake news people all
use Apple stuff. Siri told me.

                         PRESS #1
Sean, I really think that the administration has a duty to
show people what they're doing. It's only right that you
allow cameras in here.

                         SPICER
Well in here it's not what you think that matters. I decide
what happens, the President decides what I decide what
happens, and Comrade Vladimir Putin decides what the
President decides what I decide what happens. It is simple.

                         PRESS #1
                      (standing)
I'm sorry, but I think we all have a duty to the people
here. Who's with me?

                         PRESS #4
                      (standing)
She's right.

                         PRESS #3
                      (standing)
I don't think we should do any more reporting until the
cameras are turned back on.

                         PRESS #2
                      (standing)
I think it's time to boycott Sean Spicer.

                              They all stand, except for PRESS
                              #5.

                         SPICER
Oh really? So you're all going to be principled? You're all
going to rally together to stand up to this administration
and make a point?

                                              (CONTINUED)

                         Beat, and they all sit.

                         PRESS #4
Actually, I'm going to leave it to someone else.

                         PRESS #1
I'm sure there are protesters working on this stuff.

                         SPICER
That's what I thought. Okay, we come to item number four
now. The President will, that means he is going to, in a
few days time be hosting a woman from Germany who goes by
the name of... I think it's angled moo-cow.

                         PRESS #2
Sean, do you mean Angela Merkel, the Chancellor of Germany?

                         SPICER
I mean what I said. Don't make me repeat myself.

                         He checks his notes.

                         SPICER
Actually, now that I look at it, it might be Angle --

                         PRESS #2
Angela Merkel?

                         SPICER
Yes, that. Alright, none of you remember that I got that
name wrong, okay. You, C-N-N, are you remembering? I can
see you remembering right now.
                         (beat)
Okay, I think we're done here now. There are some minor
things about banning an entire religion and abolishing all
forms of healthcare, but the details aren't important.

                         He goes to leave as a mumble
                         breaks out.

                         PRESS #3
Banning a religion?

                                                      (CONTINUED)

                         PRESS #2
Abolishing healthcare? We need more information than that.

                         SPICER
Okay, I want fingers on lips.

                         PRESS #1
What?

                         SPICER
You heard me, fingers on lips.

                              Confused, they do as they're
                              told.

                         SPICER
Are you not all journalists in here?

                              They nod.

                         SPICER
Good, then look up the news and work it out for yourselves.
I'm going for a lie-down.

ACT II, SCENE NINE | MERKEL VISITS THE WHITE HOUSE

                              Remaining in the WHITE HOUSE
                              PRESS BRIEFING ROOM where the
                              ENSEMBLE (as PRESS) remain on
                              stage, now in front of two
                              podiums that stand between a
                              United States flag and a German
                              flag.

                         NARRATOR
                         (entering)
And so as Spicer said in the days ahead, Merkel flew to
meet with the orange guy who when first told he had won
simply said WHO!?. The first world leader to make the trip,
why? Every other had suddenly developed an injury, a four-
year dip. No one wanted to be the first to meet with their
new counterpart who was now the worst.
                         (MORE)

                                             (CONTINUED)

CONTINUED:

                          NARRATOR (CONT'D)
But at the end of the first of her trips, multiple days
filled with multiple blips, a duty she knows she has does
Angela, to straight out the President and to keep her hands
triangular.

                              PRESS #2
Does anyone else feel like we've been here for days?

                              NARRATOR
Ladies, gentlemen, and Fox News of the White House Press
Pool, I present to you the Chancellor of Germany, Angela
Merkel, and President Donald J. Trump.

                              ANGELA MERKEL and TRUMP enter
                              and take their places behind the
                              podiums.

                              TRUMP
Today, I am honored to welcome European President Angel
Murky to the White House.

                              MERKEL begins to drink from a
                              glass of water.

                              TRUMP
I have enjoyed speaking to her today, and I am sure that
she has greatly enjoyed speaking to me too, okay folks.

                              MERKEL spits out her water.

                              MERKEL
I apologize.

                              TRUMP
                          (ignoring MERKEL)
We have a great relationship, and let me tell you, there
has never been a time when our country has had more in
common with Germany.
                          (beat)
I would like now to hand over to Missus Merkel.
                          (to MERKEL)
Chancellor, thank you.

                                                  (CONTINUED)

PERFORMANCE LICENSE EDITION   LICENSE # _ _ _ _ _ _ _ _

                         MERKEL
Narrator, can you translate?

                              The NARRATOR nods.

                         MERKEL
Thank you.

                              She takes a deep breath.

                         MERKEL
Danke schön, so genannt Herr Präsident.

                         NARRATOR
Thank you very much, so-called Mister President.

                              TRUMP pulls out his phone and
                              begins to play a game on it.

                         MERKEL
Das ist alo der weg, den sie gewählt haben, Amerika?

                         NARRATOR
So this is the path you chose America?

                         MERKEL
Sie haben sich entschieden, den Fanta Fascist zu wählen.

                         NARRATOR
You have decided to elect the Fanta Fascist.

                         MERKEL
Ein wörtlicher großer käse.

                         NARRATOR
A literal big cheese.

                         MERKEL
Ein butterbefeuerter, sonnengebräunter xenophobie mit
händed in der größe von kinderhandschuhen.

                         NARRATOR
A butter-friend, sun-tanned xenophone with hands the size
of children's mittens.

                                                        (CONTINUED)

MERKEL

Der räuberische rassist des vierten reiches.

NARRATOR

The Rapacious Racist of the Fourth Reich.

MERKEL

Was zum verdammten wort hast du gedacht, Amerika?

NARRATOR

What the naughty word were you thinking, America?

MERKEL

Es ist als ob sie zweitausendsechzehn modell brandneue B-M-W genhandelt haben.

NARRATOR

It's as though you traded in brand new two thousand and sixteen model B-M-W.

MERKEL

In glattem schwarz.

NARRATOR

In smooth black.

MERKEL

Für neunzehnachtunddreißig Volkswagen Käfer in der sonne orange.

NARRATOR

For nineteen thirty-eight Volkswagen Beetle in sunshine orange.

MERKEL

Ernsthaft, der mann ist so dumm, der einzige grund warum er keinen atomkrieg begonnen hat ist dass er den startcode nicht buchstabieren kann.

NARRATOR

Seriously, the man is so stupid, the only reason he hasn't started a nuclear war is that he can't spell the launch codes.

(CONTINUED)

                         MERKEL
Sie sind nur eins, zwei, drei, vier, ich erkläre einen
atomkrieg.

                         NARRATOR
They're only one, two, three, four, I declare a nuclear
war.

                         MERKEL
Barack hat es mir gesagt.

                         NARRATOR
Barack told me.

                         MERKEL
                      (with lust)
Oh Barack, vie sehr vermisse ich ihn. Sicher, ich wusste
dass er nicht mehr Präsident sein konnte, aber ich dachte
Hillary würde in der lage sein mit ihm kaffee zu kochen um
über alte zeiten zu reden.

                         NARRATOR
Oh Barack, how I miss him so much. Sure, I knew he couldn't
be president anymore, but I thought that Hillary could set
up coffee with him so we could talk about old times.

                         MERKEL
Obwohl er vielleicht mehr zeit hat, mich zu besuchen. Ich
sagte ihm, Barack, wenn du jemals in Berlin bist, komm und
sag hallo und ich werde dich herumführen. Ich kenne die
besten plätze, wo wir uns hinsetzen und zu mittag essen
können, während die sonne untergeht, während wir uns über
wechselkursmechanismen und außenpolitik im Nahen Osten
unterhalten.

                         NARRATOR
Although he may...
                      (beat, then to MERKEL)
Sorry, could I have that slower?

                         MERKEL
Obwohl er vielleicht mehr zeit hat, mich zu besuchen.

                                        (CONTINUED)

CONTINUED:

                          NARRATOR
Although he may have more time to visit me.

                           MERKEL
Ich sagte ihm, Barack, wenn du jemals in Berlin bist, komm
und sag hallo und ich werde dich herumführen.

                          NARRATOR
I told him, Barack, if you're ever in Berlin, come and say
hello and I'll show you around.

                           MERKEL
Ich kenne die besten plätze, wo wir uns hinsetzen und zu
mittag essen können, während die sonne untergeht, während
wir uns über wechselkursmechanismen und außenpolitik im
Nahen Osten unterhalten.

                          NARRATOR
I know the best places where we can sit down and have lunch
while the sun goes down as we talk about foreign exchange
mechanisms and our policies in the Middle East.

                           MERKEL
Wir hätten so viel Spaß zusammen haben können. Nicht wie
Honky Honky Spaß, nein, ich meine, ha ha, Lachen Sie laut L-
O-L Spaß. ROFL.

                          NARRATOR
We could have had so much fun together. Not like Honky
Honky fun, no, I mean, ha ha, laugh loud L-O-L fun. ROFL.

                           MERKEL
Aber jetzt muss ich mit Trumpelstiltskin über handelsregeln
reden.

                          NARRATOR
But now I've to discuss trade rules with Trumpelstiltskin.

                           MERKEL
Ich habe neulich mit Justin Trudeau telefoniert. Theresa
May denkt nicht viel von ihm, aber ich denke, dass er ein
schöner mann ist. Seine arme sind so stark und er hat ein
gesicht, das mich heiß und verschwitzt macht.

                                                    (CONTINUED)

                    NARRATOR
I spoke to Justin Trudeau the other day. Theresa May does
not think much of him, bit I think he is a handsome man.
His arms are so strong and he has a face that makes me all
hot and sweaty.

                    MERKEL
Wie auch immer, er sagte, dass er darüber nachdachte,
Donald auf dem G-7—Gipfel im nächsten Jahr den falschen
platz zu nennen, damit wir ihn nicht ertagen mussten.

                    NARRATOR
Anyway, he said that he's considering giving Donald the
wrong location of the G-7 summit next year so we don't have
to endure him.

                    MERKEL
Es wäre immer so ein lustiger witz.

                    NARRATOR
It would be such a fun joke.

                    MERKEL
Ich schätze, ich sollte jetzt der mächtigen mango
zurückgeben, damit er euch alle noch mehr belügen kann.

                    NARRATOR
Well, I guess I should hand back over to the mighty mango
so he can lie to you some more.

                    MERKEL
P-S das pipi ist echt. Ich habe es gesehen.

                    NARRATOR
P-S the pee-pee tape is real. I've seen it.

                    MERKEL
Mister President, over to you.

                              TRUMP remains focussed on his
                              phone.

                    NARRATOR
Mister Trump, sir.

                                        (CONTINUED)

CONTINUED:

                          TRUMP
                       (looking up)
Oh, is the woman done now? I was playing golf on my phone.
I discovered that if I change the screen settings, I can
make the little man in the game look as orange as me.

                          MERKEL
Er hat auch die gleichen Hände wie du, du komplett
verdammter trottel.

                          NARRATOR
He also has the same size hands as you, you --

                          MERKEL
Actually, don't translate the rest of that. I need a drink
now.

                     She exits.

                          TRUMP
Does that mean I can go too? I want to watch the end of Fox
and Friends while my McMuffin is still warm.

                              The NARRATOR nods and TRUMP and
                              the ENSEMBLE exit.

ACT II, SCENE TEN | COOPER & CONWAY

                              The CNN STUDIO, where COOPER is
                              halfway through interviewing
                              (and arguing with) CONWAY on his
                              show.

                          NARRATOR
It's a fact that in any ordinary circumstances, the meeting
of two world leaders would be the day's news, but it also
remains that Donald J. Trump's opinion of what truly
matters are very different views. And so rather than to
praise the trade the United States from Germany hopes to
graze, he sends on Kellyanne Conway live to defend his
crowd size and popularly dive.

                     The NARRATOR exits.

                                            (CONTINUED)

CONTINUED:

                          COOPER
I'm just not sure that you actually understand, Kellyanne.
The role of the media and the press is to report the facts,
not to make the President look good.

                          CONWAY
I'm not sure that you're getting it, Anderson. The
President is good, and that's why what he says are the
facts. Why are you seeing to discredit the President?

                          COOPER
I'm not seeking to discredit the President. The President
is discrediting himself, and you're helping him to do that.

                          CONWAY
Well, I don't agree with that. You and the other members of
the liberal mainstream media have been lying about the size
of the inauguration crowd size for days now.

                          COOPER
Why are we back to the crowd size?

                          CONWAY
Do you know how many times Hillary Clinton visited places
like Bowling Green during the election? That small town is
the location of one of this country's worst-ever massacres,
and she didn't go to pay her respects once.

                          COOPER
Kellyanne, what are you on about? There's never been a
massacre in a place called Bowling Green.

                          CONWAY
Okay, it is very disrespectful for you to pretend that
nothing happened, Anderson. But I really don't expect
anything else from C-N-N because none of you care about
lives being lost in Republican states.

                          COOPER
When you're failing to defend yourself, you can't just
change the subject to a made-up massacre and then accuse an
entire network of being disrespectful because no one else
has heard of it.

                                                    (CONTINUED)

                          CONWAY
Actually yes I can do that, Anderson.

                          COOPER
You were on about crowd sizes, I believe?

                          CONWAY
You see, Anderson? It isn't me that's bringing up the
subject of crowd sizes, it's you.

                          COOPER
No, you brought it up and then tried to distract from it by
making something else up.

                          CONWAY
Why do you and C-N-N keep refusing to accept how many
people turned out to celebrate President Trump's
inauguration?

                          COOPER
We prefer to consider the facts, and all of the live
footage from the day shows that turnout was significantly
lower than any previous inauguration.

                          CONWAY
That's not true, and you know it, Anderson. Our Press
Secretary, Sean Spicer, has spent a lot of time trying to
explain the facts to your reporter at the White House, so
how can you still continue to get it wrong?

                          COOPER
Sean Spicer hid in the bushes outside our reporter's house
all night so that he could threaten them with a twig when
they left the next morning.

                          CONWAY
Sure, but after that, he pointed out that millions of
people turned out to see the President.

                          COOPER
Then he was lying.

                          CONWAY
No, he wasn't lying.

                                              (CONTINUED)

PERFORMANCE LICENSE EDITION   LICENSE # _ _ _ _ _ _ _ _

                         COOPER
Then what was he doing? Every single factual source proves
that what he was claiming is false.

                         CONWAY
He was giving alternative facts.

                         COOPER
I'm sorry?

                         CONWAY
Sean Spicer was giving alternative facts.

                    COOPER begins to laugh.

                         COOPER
I didn't have any trouble hearing you, Kellyanne.

                         CONWAY
There's no need to laugh, Anderson. You're supposed to be a
professional.

                         COOPER
I don't even know what to say.

                    He laughs harder.

                         CONWAY
That's okay. I know that you understand the truth now.

                         COOPER
It's not that, it's just stupid. It's so stupid.

                         CONWAY
I can wait until you're done. I'm more mature than this,
and I'm going to be the bigger person.

                    COOPER laughs harder still.

                         COOPER
You're on here representing the President of the United
States. What's going on?

                                              (CONTINUED)

>   Laughing even harder, he falls
>   off his chair onto the floor.

                         COOPER
How can any of this be happening?

>   The NARRATOR enters and rushes
>   to COOPER'S side.

                         NARRATOR
Anderson, speak to me, are you okay? Speak to me.

                         COOPER
Everything is just so stupid.

                         NARRATOR
                    (shouting out)
We need help here.

>   The NARRATOR exits before
>   rushing back with a first aid
>   kit, but as they approach COOPER
>   again, they are rugby tackled by
>   PAUL RYAN, who enters at speed.

                         RYAN
                    (to the NARRATOR)
Let me tell you what the problem is here. You want to help
Anderson Cooper, but Anderson Cooper hasn't paid for his
healthcare. Now not only has he collapsed, but he's going
to get worse if you do nothing. We can fix this problem
with a three-pronged approach. Number one, someone is going
to pay for his healthcare. Number two, you are going to
treat him. Number three, I am going to pass a law that bans
all mirrors, so that I never have to look at myself again.

>   RYAN release the NARRATOR as
>   they hand him a bundle of bills
>   from their pocket.

                         RYAN
I don't want to get into the specifics of what just
happened.

                                                  (CONTINUED)

                            He exits as the NARRATOR helps
                            COOPER back onto his chair.

                       COOPER
I think that it's time for us to take a commercial break
right now. Thank you, Kellyanne Conway, for joining me.

                            The NARRATOR exits as CONWAY
                            pulls out her phone and begins
                            to dial a number.

                       CONWAY
You know, Anderson, I really think that we're going to have
to rethink our relationship.

                       COOPER
What relationship? I don't want to rethink any relationship
with you. We don't have one, and I want to keep it that
way.

                       CONWAY
I'll talk to you after I've called my husband.

                            She puts the phone to her ear.

                       CONWAY
                     (on phone)
Hey George. Yes, I've just finished my interview with
Anderson Cooper, and I should be home soon. We can have
that special meal we've been planning tonight.
                     (beat)
You know Anderson, he's the one that looks like the love
child of Mike Pence's hair and Andy from Toy Story.

                            A PRODUCTION ASSISTANT enters
                            and hands COOPER a memo before
                            exiting.

                       COOPER
You might want to hold your plans, Kellyanne.

                       CONWAY
What?

                                        (CONTINUED)

                           COOPER
And we're live in three, two, one... Hello, and welcome
back to Anderson Cooper three-sixty with me, Anderson
Cooper. Still with me, senior aide to the President,
Kellyanne Conway, who I hope can give us her take on some
breaking news just in. F-B-I director James Comey has, in
the past few minutes, announced that he will be launching a
formal investigation into possible collusion between the
Trump campaign and the Russian Government. Kellyanne...

                           CONWAY
                        (on phone)
George, I'm going to have to call you back.

ACT II, SCENE ELEVEN | THE WHITE HOUSE DAY CARE CENTER

                              A WHITE HOUSE OFFICE where ERIC,
                              KUSHNER, and TRUMP stand holding
                              hands in a circle along with a
                              DAY CARE ASSISTANT.

                           NARRATOR
                        (entering)
With the candlelit dinner at home now to be eaten by George
Conway alone, Kellyanne sets off to the Whitehouse with
haste, the last words from Cooper still leaving a
particularly bad taste. Her boss is now the subject of
multiple questions, and she can't help but worry that to
answer them exactly what will be his suggestions.

But while with ideas of her own in mind she travels, ahead
Donald Trump is ensuring already that any plan just
unravels. For rather than calling his advisors to talk, he
calls in James Comey to tell him to walk. The F-B-I
Director on the spot fired. A move which only by idiots can
ever be admired.

But rather than let just the one man go, where to stop
firing, the President does not know. From an agency head,
and a chief of staff too, each one distracting from the
news that does brew.
                         (MORE)

                                              (CONTINUED)

CONTINUED:
                    NARRATOR (CONT'D)
But how many more departures can he get away with? All why
trying to keep on the truth, his solid gold lid.

             The NARRATOR exits.

                 DAY CARE ASSISTANT
Okay, so are we all ready to take it from the top again?
One, two, three...

                TRUMP/ ERIC/ DAY CARE ASSISTANT
/YOU PUT THE RACIST IN, THE RACIST OUT, YOU PUT A RACIST
BACK IN AND DENY WHAT IT'S ABOUT. WHEN THE PRESS ASK
QUESTIONS YOU IGNORE THEM ALL, THAT'S WHAT IT'S ALL ABOUT./

                 DAY CARE ASSISTANT
Very good, Donald. I think you're the best here. Do you
want a verse of your own?

                    TRUMP
/I BROUGHT JAMES COMEY IN, TO MY OFFICE, AND I FIRED HIM, I
FIRED HIM, I TOLD HIM TO GET OUT. I FIRED HIM, AND THEN THE
LOSER RAN, HE SQUEALED LIKE A LITTLE MOUSE./

                 CONWAY enters.

                 DAY CARE ASSISTANT
And who is this joining us? It looks as though we have a
new face. Come in and introduce yourself to the group.

                    CONWAY
Oh, no, I'm not here to join in. I was told the President
was here, and I need to speak to him.

                 DAY CARE ASSISTANT
Well, don't take too long. We're going to start doing some
painting soon.

             TRUMP approaches CONWAY.

                    TRUMP
What is it you want, Kellyanne Conway?

                                        (CONTINUED)

                         CONWAY
Just some dignity.
                    (beat)
Mister President, what is this place?

                         TRUMP
This is the White House day care center, Kellyanne Conway.

                         CONWAY
How come I've never heard of it before?

                         TRUMP
Why would you have? It is a secret group for top secret
agents. You have to be a big boy to be invited. We even
have codenames. I am Dusty Don, Sean Spicer usually comes,
and his codename is Bushmaster, Jared Kushner is the Silent
Stalker, and Eric Trump is --

                         CONWAY
Is he Eric, sir?

                         TRUMP
Do not be stupid. His codename is Evan.

                         CONWAY
Mister President, I need to speak to you about James Comey.

                         TRUMP
Do not worry about James Comey, Kellyanne Conway. He is
just a pastry chef at the F-B-I.

                         CONWAY
But Mister President, he's just announced that you and your
campaign is now under investigation for working with the
Russian Government.

                         TRUMP
I have already solved it. I fired him.

                              CONWAY lets out an involuntary
                              scream.

                         CONWAY
You fired him, sir?

                                             (CONTINUED)

                        TRUMP
I fired him.

                        CONWAY
Are you not worried that it's going to look like you're
obstructing justice?

                        TRUMP
What is that?

                        CONWAY
Oh, that's where someone's actions actively stop or delay
an investigation or justice being found.

                        TRUMP
I know what obstruction is, Kellyanne Conway. I mean, what
is justice?

                        CONWAY
I may not be the best person to tell you about that.

                        TRUMP
Either way, you are worrying without reason, Kellyanne
Conway.

                        CONWAY
What have you done, Sir?

                        TRUMP
I have fired loads of other people to distract from me
firing James Comey. Someone from the Office of Government
Ethics said it was inappropriate, and so I fired them too.

                        CONWAY
Mister President, this isn't going to look very good.

                        TRUMP
It will be okay. I have you to go and lie out there for me.

                    DAY CARE ASSISTANT
Donald, do you want to come and join us for Twinkle,
Twinkle, Little Star?

                                              (CONTINUED)

                         TRUMP
I have to go, Kellyanne Conway.

                              TRUMP turns away as CONWAY
                              reaches into her pocket for a
                              bottle of medication that she
                              begins to drink from.

                         TRUMP
                    (turning back)
One more thing, Kellyanne Conway. I have also just banned
all Muslims from entering the country.

                         CONWAY
                    (to herself, looking at the
                     bottle)
I'm going to need something stronger.

ACT II, SCENE TWELVE | THE SECOND PRESS BRIEFING

                              The WHITE HOUSE PRESS BRIEFING
                              ROOM and the ENSEMBLE (as PRESS,
                              excluding PRESS #4) sit waiting
                              in front of a podium.

                         NARRATOR
                    (entering)
Despite the best efforts to distract the President has made
to blur the facts, the press and the public believe still
wary for all of the President's answers feel too airy. For
them, there's something about James Comey's departures that
just doesn't add up, as though there's something being
hidden but ready to come up. And so it is that Sean Spicer
is sent to ensure that the reports of the press are all
equally as bent.

                              SPICER enters and notices the
                              NARRATOR.

                         SPICER
Hey, no. I've told you before. Get out!

                                             (CONTINUED)

CONTINUED:

                              The NARRATOR rushes to exit
                              before SPICER can reach them.

                         SPICER
                    (taking the podium)
Okay. You can shut up. You can shut up. You can shut up.
You can shut up. You especially can shut up, C-N-N, and New
York Times, you can shut up too.

Straight to it, item number one. You all seem to be having
some concerns about the recent staff changes around this
place, but let me tell you, you do not have any concerns,
is that clear? The President can fire who he wants when he
wants, okay.

                         PRESS #1
Sean, he just fired the F-B-I director while he was leading
an investigation into Russia's involvement with the
election and any help that the country offered to the Trump
campaign.

                         SPICER
Maybe you didn't understand it correctly, okay, or maybe
you're just really stupid, I don't know, but the President
did not fire James Comey because he was investigating him.
He fired James Comey because he was very mean to Hillary
Clinton about her emails.

                         PRESS #2
But the President was very mean to Hillary Clinton about
her emails. During the election, he got the crowds at all
of his rallies to shout that she should be locked up.

                         SPICER
Oh, so you finally say that he had crowds at his rallies
now and not a small gathering? Perhaps you can tell your
editor that, New York Times? But no, he didn't do that,
okay. You're making that up or just imagining it or
something.

                         PRESS #2
Sean, it's on tape.

                                                (CONTINUED)

                         SPICER
Well, then it's an imaginary tape.

                         PRESS #6
The President also said himself in an interview with Sean
Hannity on Fox News the other day that he fired Comey
specifically because of the investigation and because he
refused to pledge his loyalty to him, something that is now
leading calls for a special prosecutor to be appointed not
only to take over the Russia investigation but also to look
at possible obstruction by the President.

                    They all begin taking notes.

                         PRESS #3
That's a good tip. I didn't have that.

                         SPICER
Seriously, you want to do this, M-S-N-B-C?

                         PRESS #6
I don't understand.

                         SPICER
Okay, you all call yourselves journalists. So how come as
so-called professionals, you're all believing everything
you see on the news?

                         PRESS #6
Sean --

                         SPICER
Just because the President said something on a television
show, it does not make it the truth. Are we clear on that?

                         PRESS #2
But what about the special prosecutor?

                         SPICER
Okay, no more questions. If there are any more questions,
then you'll all be in my office, and last time that
happened to one of you, you didn't leave the same.

                                              (CONTINUED)

                          PRESS #1
                         (shaking)
I... I saw things I can't unsee.

                          SPICER
There will be no special pro... damn it.

                          PRESS #6
Prosecutor?

                          SPICER
Yes. There won't be one of those. Period.
                         (beat)
Now, moving on to item number two. The Justice Department
will later today be announcing that they are appointing a
special pro... not again.

                          PRESS #6
Special Prosecutor?

                          SPICER
Yes, that. And I am told to tell you that this will be for
a period, okay.

                          PRESS #2
Sean --

                          SPICER
I said no questions, New York Times. We're going to move on
from item number two to item number three. The President
has appointed a new director of communications who is
starting today. It says here his name is... oh Jesus.

                          PRESS #6
Do you need help?

                          SPICER
No, I do not need help M-S-N-B-C. I can pronounce the name.
It's just, it's --

                          ANTHONY SCARAMUCCI enters.

                                              (CONTINUED)
PERFORMANCE LICENSE EDITION   LICENSE # _ _ _ _ _ _ _ _

                            SCARAMUCCI
Me, Anthony Scaramucci! Hey, thanks for the introduction
there, Spicy, you little son of a bitch. How about we catch
up some time over my favorite dish, amuse-bouche? Or
perhaps we can catch a game, amuse-Mooch! Hey?

                              SPICER
Okay, that's it. I'm not doing this anymore. I sold the
last remaining bit of my soul and reputation for this job,
and I'm not prepared to now work with the abandoned twin of
some cartoon villain. Spicy is out.

                              SPICER exits as SCARAMUCCI takes
                              the podium.

                            SCARAMUCCI
Hey, what's that asshole's problem? I'm the Mooch! Everyone
loves the Mooch. Except for my wife, I've just heard she
wants a divorce. Mooch is sad. Poor Mooch.
                    (beat)
Hey, okay on to item number four. Steve Bannon sucks his
own cock.

                             PRESS #2
Can we quote you on that?

                            SCARAMUCCI
Yeah, why not? I'm the Mooch, and we all want it to be
true, don't we? Okay, item number five. The President has
fired Director of Communications, Anthony Scaramucci.
                    (waving)
Well, I'm off to go wrestle Reince Priebus. Hey, Mooch out!

                              SCARAMUCCI exits as SARAH
                              HUCKABEE SANDERS enters and
                              takes the podium.

                         HUCKABEE SANDERS
Hello there guys. I'm Sarah Huckabee Sanders, and I will be
taking over for Sean Spicer now that he has leaft the
building. Leaft, do you get it? Because he likes bushes.
Okay, item number six. Steve Bannon is also out. Now that's
out of the way, I want to tell you all a story about the
President.
                            (MORE)
                                                    (CONTINUED)

                    HUCKABEE SANDERS (CONT'D)
Once upon a time, there was a little boy called Donald,
that's the President, only guys? Only back then he wasn't
running the country.

                              The ENSEMBLE begins to stand and
                              exit.

                    HUCKABEE SANDERS
Hey, where are you all going? I've not finished my story.
                    (following them)
He was a little boy, of only two hundred and thirty-nine
pounds, and he had a daddy, we all have a daddy, right? We
can relate?...

ACT II, SCENE THIRTEEN | TRUMP FINDS OUT ABOUT MUELLER

                              The OVAL OFFICE, where a large
                              office cupboard now stands next
                              to the desk.

                              The room is empty except for
                              ERIC, who sits alone on the
                              floor, attempting to play a
                              xylophone.

                    NARRATOR
                    (entering)
And so as the news spreads of Mueller's arrival, the
feeling among many is that the ending is final. With a
distinguished career as a veteran and attorney, Robert
Mueller is the man appointed special counsel to end Donald
Trump's journey. But the orange mango who is scared to ever
dance the foreign tango still remains in bliss, for he
watches Fox News' reports on burger emojis that make the
truth easy to miss. But how long can he remain outside the
know? As long as it takes Kellyanne Conway to ruin his
presidential flow.

                              The NARRATOR exits.

                                             (CONTINUED)

                        TRUMP
                      (entering)
Okay, Eric Trump, take it from the top. This is going to be
so great.

                    ERIC begins to play.

                        TRUMP
/OH DO NOT GO BREAKING MY NON-DISCLOSURE AGREEMENT./

                        ERIC
/I COULDN'T READ IT IF I TRIED./

                        TRUMP
/OH HONEY DO NOT TELL OUR STORY./

                        ERIC
/I FORGOT MY LINE./

                        TRUMP
/OH DO NOT GO BREAKING MY NON-DISCLOSURE AGREEMENT./

                        ERIC
/ESPECIALLY IF ON DAD YOU PEE./

                        TRUMP
/OH HONEY WHEN YOU KNOCK ON MY DOOR./

                        ERIC
/I FORGOT MY LINE./

          TRUMP   ERIC
/NOBODY KNOWS IT./   /(I DON'T KNOW ANYTHING.)/

                    CONWAY enters as ERIC stops
                    playing.

                        CONWAY
Mister President, sir, and oh, Eric too. I hope that I'm
not interrupting anything important?

                        TRUMP
No, Kellyanne Conway, it is okay. What did you want?

                                        (CONTINUED)

CONTINUED:

                              CONWAY
It's about the Russia investigation, sir. There's been a
new development.

                              TRUMP
What do you mean, the Russia investigation? There should
not be any Russia investigation. I fried James Comey.

                              CONWAY
Yes, you did, that's the problem. There are quite a few
people, including many in the Justice Department, who think
that you only fired him because he was investigating you.

                              TRUMP
That is fake news. I also fired him because he refused to
pledge loyalty to me, the great Pres...

                              CONWAY
President, sir?

                              TRUMP
Thank you, Kellyanne Conway. Even I find it hard to say
sometimes.

                              CONWAY
You finally have something in common with the world, sir.

                              TRUMP
As I was saying, I also fired him because he refused to
pledge loyalty to me, the great President Donald J. Trump.
Steve Bannon did it.

                              CONWAY
Well yes, but Steve Bannon has also recently left to start
a new job as the interactive trench foot exhibit in a war
museum. Anyway, it sounds crazy, the Justice Department is
using your admission to Sean Hannity that you fired James
Comey over the investigation as evidence that you fired
James Comey over the investigation. They've appointed a
special counsel.

                              TRUMP
Where was Jeff Sessions? Why did he not stop this?

                                                (CONTINUED)

                         CONWAY
Jeff Sessions couldn't recall why he didn't stop it, but I
looked into it and found that he was busy selling a new
range of cookies at the store.

                         TRUMP moves over to his desk.

                         TRUMP
I have a great plan to solve this. I will just fire whoever
the special counsel is.

                                   He sits, and the sound of a
                                   whoopee cushion deflating fills
                                   the stage before he stands and
                                   holds it up.

                         ERIC
Dad made a naughty sound.

                         TRUMP
Kellyanne Conway, why is there a whoopee cushion on my
seat?

                         CONWAY
I don't know why, Mister President. Anyway, I'm not sure
that you can just fire the special counsel. It might not
look very good, and they've appointed someone who is quite
influential.

                         TRUMP
Who have they appointed, Kellyanne Conway?

                         CONWAY
                    (mumbling)
Robert Mueller.

                         TRUMP
Who?

                         CONWAY
Robert Mueller, sir.

                         TRUMP
Oh no.

                                                      (CONTINUED)

>   Beat, and then TRUMP slowly sits
>   back down on the whoopee
>   cushion.

                         CONWAY
I share your concerns, sir.

                         TRUMP
This is not so great.

>   CONWAY pulls out her phone and
>   begins to look at it.

                         CONWAY
But you might be okay, Mister President. Looking on
Twitter, it doesn't look as though he has any evidence that
you've done anything illegal and **OH GOD!**

                         TRUMP
What is it, Kellyanne Conway?

                         CONWAY
It looks as though he's just found evidence that you've
done things that are illegal.

                         TRUMP
What evidence?

                         CONWAY
Don Junior has just tweeted the messages he received from
Julian Assange last year, and also the guest list for the
meeting with the Russians at Trump Tower.

>   JUNIOR enters.

                         JUNIOR
Hey dad, I was wondering if you could possibly help me out
by signing an executive order to ban some of the hotels
that I don't own.

                         TRUMP
Donald Trump Junior, why did you just tweet about getting
help from Julian Assange and also the Russia meeting?

                                              (CONTINUED)

                         JUNIOR
Oh, well about that... well, I don't know.

                    Beat.

                         ERIC
Hey dad, didn't you tweet about the Russia meeting too?

                              TRUMP pulls out his own phone as
                              ERIC begins to lick his the
                              mallet of his xylophone as
                              though it's a lolly.

                         JUNIOR
                    (to ERIC)
Hey buddy, that thing isn't for eating. It's for playing.
You're supposed to tap it like this.
                    (demonstrating)
Okay, you got it? Now you try.

                         ERIC plays a note.

                         ERIC
It makes a sound.

                         JUNIOR
It does make a sound, yes.

                              As JUNIOR turns away, ERIC
                              begins to tap his own head with
                              the mallet and make a sound each
                              time.

                         JUNIOR
                    (to TRUMP)
Dad, what are you doing?

                              TRUMP looks up from his phone.

                         TRUMP
I am blocking Robert Mueller on Twitter so that he cannot
see what I said about the Russia meeting.

                                             (CONTINUED)
PERFORMANCE LICENSE EDITION   LICENSE # _ _ _ _ _ _ _ _

                              JUNIOR
Why don't you just delete the tweets?

                              TRUMP
Because blocking people makes me feel excited in a way that
Melania has not made me feel for six years.

                              JUNIOR
You know, I don't think I should have eaten lunch before
coming to see you.

                              TRUMP
It is also fun and just so great to block people, like this
person, because she said that the Pope does not like me,
and this person because they said I upset a cute dog.
Retweeting is also so great, and so I am going to do it now
to this person who says they love what I am doing. Clearly,
they like me so much because they have a cross and a flag
in their bio and have rated me out of ten in their name.
MAGA girl two four nine six eight nine two seven. And now I
also block this person for saying I should delete my
account... oh, I already have Crooked Hillary Clinton
blocked.

                         HUCKABEE SANDERS enters.

                         HUCKABEE SANDERS
Mister President, hello, and hello to everyone else. I've
got a story to tell you all. I was in my office just a few
moments ago when two men arrived with a large package for
you, Mister President, and they wanted to know where to
deliver it.

                              TRUMP
Was it Vladimir Putin. Because I already have enough of
those teddy bears with eyes that move and a microphone for
a nose.

                         HUCKABEE SANDERS
No, sir. Robert Mueller --

                                               (CONTINUED)
PERFORMANCE LICENSE EDITION   LICENSE # _ _ _ _ _ _ _ _

CONTINUED:

                          TRUMP
                        (standing)
Quick, Eric Trump, Donald Trump Junior, close the curtains
and barricade all of the doors. Kellyanne Conway, you start
digging us an escape tunnel.

                    HUCKABEE SANDERS
I think you misunderstood me, sir. The package isn't Robert
Mueller, it's just from Robert Mueller. He sent it.

                          CONWAY
Mueller sent it? But what is it?

                    HUCKABEE SANDERS
I don't know, Kellyanne.

                          TRUMP
Have it brought in here.

                              HUCKABEE SANDERS exits and then
                              returns a moment later with two
                              DELIVERY MEN carrying a large
                              and flat wrapped package.

                          TRUMP
                    (pointing at his desk)
Place it on here.

                              After doing as instructed, the
                              DELIVERY MEN exit as TRUMP
                              unwraps the package, and all
                              (except ERIC) gather around.

                          JUNIOR
So you know, that looks like a portrait.

                              TRUMP holds it up to show a
                              portrait of Robert Mueller.

                          CONWAY
Okay, so does anyone think that it's suspicious that Robert
Mueller is sending a portrait of himself?

                                                    (CONTINUED)

                          TRUMP
Clearly, he is just sending it to show that there are no
hard feelings between us. He is a smart man, Kellyanne
Conway, and smart men often sent portraits of themselves to
show that they are smart.

                          CONWAY
I'm still suspicious of it, sir.

                          TRUMP
                     (ignoring CONWAY)
I think that it would look so great on this wall here.

                              He takes the portrait and puts
                              it up on the wall behind his
                              desk.

                          TRUMP
And now he can sit over me as my guardian angel of not
being under investigation.

                              As they all turn away from the
                              portrait, it 'opens' as if a
                              door and the real ROBERT MUELLER
                              appears and begins to listen to
                              the conversation.

                          CONWAY
But, Mister President, you are under investigation.

                          MUELLER nods.

                          TRUMP
Wrong. Robert Mueller would not have sent me a present if I
was under investigation.
                     (to JUNIOR)
Donald Trump Junior, can you go and get Mike Pence?

                          JUNIOR
Sure. I'll go get him for you right now.

                          JUNIOR exits.

                                                   (CONTINUED)

                         CONWAY
Mister Trump, I really think you should be talking to a
lawyer.

                         TRUMP
Okay, if you insist, Kellyanne Conway --

                         TRUMP turns to the cupboard next
                         to his desk as PENCE enters
                         wearing ear muffs.

                         PENCE
Mister President, sir. You asked to see me.

                         TRUMP
Mike Pence, why are you wearing ear muffs?

                         PENCE remains silent, and so
                         TRUMP walks over and lifts off
                         his ear muffs.

                         TRUMP
Mike Pence, I said, why are you wearing ear muffs?

                         PENCE
Because my lawyer advised me to wear them whenever I am
around you. He said that if I can't hear what you're
saying, then it's much easier to plead innocent.

                         PENCE puts the ear muffs back
                         on.

                         TRUMP
Mike Pence, we need your help.

                         Beat.

                         PENCE
I would love to stay and catch up with all of you, but if
none of you mind, I have my inauguration to start planning.

                         PENCE exits.

                                            (CONTINUED)
PERFORMANCE LICENSE EDITION   LICENSE # _ _ _ _ _ _ _ _

                         TRUMP
Do you think he will invite all of us?

                         CONWAY
Mister Trump, you've got more important things to worry
about.

                         TRUMP
Quite right, Kellyanne Conway.

                              TRUMP turns back to the
                              cupboard.

                         CONWAY
What are you doing, sir?

                         TRUMP
I am calling Michael Cohen. Michael Cohen.

                              The cupboard shakes for a moment
                              then goes still before COHEN
                              walks out of it.

                         COHEN
You called, boss?

                              CONWAY and HUCKABEE SANDERS
                              watch in shock while ERIC points
                              with wonder.

                         ERIC
Magic trick.

                         CONWAY
What were you doing in a cupboard?

                         COHEN
Oh, it's where I live now, Kellyanne. I had to sell my
house to help get the boss out of some trouble.
                         (to TRUMP)
Nasty business with Robert Mueller. I've just heard more
news too, he's got Paul Manafort, the guy's in jail right
now.

                                             (CONTINUED)

                         TRUMP
Who is Paul Manafort?

                         CONWAY
He used to get the coffee around here before I started.

                         TRUMP
Kellyanne Conway, go and send his family some flowers for
their loss, and also work on convincing one of his children
to start a fire in his filing cabinet.

                         CONWAY
I'll get straight to it, Mister President.

                    CONWAY exits.

                         TRUMP
So, Michael Cohen, what is your plan to get me out of this
investigation?

                         COHEN
I'm still working on coming up with something. Perhaps you
should consider hiring another lawyer to help?

                         TRUMP
I am already ahead of you, Michael Cohen.
                    (to HUCKABEE SANDERS)
Sarah Huckabee Sanders, can you go and find me Rudy
Giuliani?

                    HUCKABEE SANDERS
I can certainly do that for you, Mister President. It
sounds like it could be the start of a great adventure.

                    HUCKABEE SANDERS exits.

                         COHEN
About another matter, though, boss. I got a call earlier
from a guy. He claims to be a lawyer representing a Stormy
Daniels. You know, that porn star that you fu --

                         TRUMP
Michael Cohen, I am going to have to stop you there. There
is a child in the room.

                                             (CONTINUED)

                         COHEN
That porn start whose... missus Eric you stuck your mister
Eric in.

                         ERIC
Hey, that's an Eric kiss.

                              MUELLER coughs, and they look at
                              him.

                         MUELLER
Excuse me.

                         TRUMP
You are excused, Mister Robert Mueller.

                              They look away from Mueller.

                         COHEN
Anyway, boss, this guy said they're getting ready to sue
you because you never signed a non-disclosure agreement
with her.

                         TRUMP
That is fake news. I always sign non-disclosure agreements.
The only one that I have not signed is the one you gave me
before my speech last year, which I have right here...

                              He pulls the agreement from one
                              of the desk draws and begins to
                              look through it.

                         TRUMP
And this one is between Donald J. Trump and... what does
this say here, Michael Cohen?

                              COHEN moves closer.

                         COHEN
Stormy Daniels. It says Stormy Daniels and you forgot to
sign it. You told me that you never forgot to sign
anything.

                                                     (CONTINUED)

                         TRUMP
I do not remember saying that.

                         COHEN
Well, this could be a big problem, boss. This guy is a bald
guy, and no Breitbart reading kind neither. He may turn out
to be nearly as crooked as you some day, but he's got real
certificates. Not just those you get printed from some word
processor when you graduate Trump U.

                         TRUMP
Okay, we need a plan.

                    RUDY GIULIANI enters.

                         GIULIANI
Well, if you need a plan, then I am your man.

                         TRUMP
Rudy Giuliani.

                         GIULIANI
That's my name, and let me tell you... /YOU'VE GOT TROUBLE,
RIGHT HERE IN THIS OFFICE, I'M TALKING TROUBLE WITH A
CAPITAL T WHICH ALSO STANDS FOR TREASON./
                    (beat)
/BUT DON'T YOU WORRY, FOR SIR I HAVE A PLAN, WE'RE GOING TO
SAY TO EVERYONE ASKING THAT YOU'RE GUILTY./

                         TRUMP
I do not understand.

                         GIULIANI
/WE'RE GOING TO SAY THAT YOU'RE GUILTY./

                         COHEN
That he's guilty?

                         GIULIANI
/THAT HE'S GUILTY. WE SAY IT SO MUCH WE CONFUSE THEM ALL
INTO THINKING YOU'RE NOT./

                         COHEN
Into thinking that he's not guilty?

                                        (CONTINUED)

                        GIULIANI
/THAT'S RIGHT./

                        TRUMP
Why are you singing

                        GIULIANI
It's supposed to be a musical.

                        COHEN
No. It's supposed to be an alternative musical.

                    Beat.

                        COHEN
Boss, we still need to come up with a plan that might
actually work.

                        GIULIANI
I've just said, we're going to say he's guilty.

                        COHEN
But will it work, though?

                        TRUMP
Rudy Giuliani, will it work?

                        GIULIANI
Well, we've been saying it about Hillary Clinton for years,
and she's still not in jail.

                        TRUMP
Okay, Rudy Giuliani, I want you to go on all of the fake
news tonight and tell them that I am guilty. Michael Cohen,
I want you to take a shower because you smell like a not so
great bag of fried chicken, and then I want you to sort out
this Stormy Daniels problem.

                        GIULIANI
That's it, Donald, you've got it.

                        COHEN
Sure thing, boss.

                                        (CONTINUED)
PERFORMANCE LICENSE EDITION   LICENSE # _ _ _ _ _ _ _ _ _

                                   As COHEN and GIULIANI exit,
                                   TRUMP turns back to ERIC.

                         TRUMP
Okay, Eric Trump, whenever you are ready.

                                   ERIC begins to play.

                         TRUMP
/AND I THINK IT IS GOING TO BE A SHORT, SHORT TIME,
'TILL MUELLER INVESTIGATES ME AND FINDS,
I AM NOT THE MAN MY VOTERS THINK IS INNOCENT,
OH, NO, NO, NO. KIM JONG UN IS A ROCKET MAN.
SHORT, AND FAT, BURNING UP HIS COUNTRY ALL ALONE.../

                                   TRUMP exits as MUELLER looks
                                   down at ERIC and begins to
                                   smile.

ACT II, SCENE FOURTEEN | MUELLER INTERROGATES ERIC

                                   OUTSIDE THE WHITE HOUSE where a
                                   toy car is parked.

                         NARRATOR
                       (entering)
It would be true to say that across the administration, the
level of intelligence is not so high, but for one member,
it's lower and all who see him only sigh. But maybe his
family believe his heart is in the right place, even if he
struggles daily to tie up his own shoelace. Or perhaps it
is that he has to stay for he knows too much, a possibility
that some want to know if the case truly is as such. Eric
Trump has been the kid who has sat through every meeting
and seen exactly who his father has been greeting. But is
he loyal to his family name? Or can Robert Mueller use him
to his investigation's gain?

                                   ERIC enters and climbs into the
                                   car before he begins pushing
                                   himself around the stage, making
                                   engine noises.

                                              (CONTINUED)

PERFORMANCE LICENSE EDITION   LICENSE # _ _ _ _ _ _ _ _

> After a moment, the NARRATOR is
> joined by two FBI AGENTS, and
> together, they sneak up behind
> ERIC and push the car offstage.

                    ERIC (OFF)
Hey, where are you taking me? I'm the dumb one.

> Lights out, and for a moment,
> nothing, until a single
> spotlight goes up on ERIC on sat
> sitting opposite a desk.

                    ERIC
What's going on? I can see the light. Am I dead? I feel
like this looks like how dad describes a date.

                    FBI AGENT #1 (OFF)
Are you Eric Frederick Trump?

                    ERIC
No. I'm just Eric.

                    FBI AGENT #2 (OFF)
Are you the son of President Donald J. Trump?

                    ERIC
He prefers if we call him Lord Führer at home.

> The stage lights up to reveal an
> interrogation room.
>
> ERIC looks around as footsteps
> grow in volume until the two FBI
> AGENTS enter along with ROBERT
> MUELLER.

                    MUELLER
Mister Trump...

> He goes to shake ERIC'S hand,
> but rather than reciprocate,
> ERIC grabs and licks his.

                                        (CONTINUED)

CONTINUED:

                         MUELLER
Mister Trump, I am Robert Mueller.

                    He sits opposite ERIC.

                         ERIC
Son of a bitch.

                         MUELLER
I'm sorry?

                         ERIC
That's what dad calls you.

                         MUELLER
Well, that's who I wish to speak to you about today, Mister
Trump.

                         ERIC
I'm not allowed to talk to strangers.

                         MUELLER
Don't think of me as a stranger. Think of me as a distant
but kind uncle of yours.

                         ERIC
Can I have some candy?

                         MUELLER
I'm not sure I understand you, Mister Trump.

                         ERIC
I want candy. Uncles give candy.

                         MUELLER
Okay, I'm not that sort of uncle. I just want to ask you a
few questions and get a few answers.

                         ERIC
Can I have candy after?

                         MUELLER
                    (to FBI AGENTS)
Does either of you have some sweets we can give this kid?

                                            (CONTINUED)

>   One of them reaches into their
>   pocket and pulls out a bag of
>   M&Ms to hand to ERIC.

                              FBI AGENT #1
I've only got these, sir.

                              ERIC
Uncle Mueller, I'm not allowed candy.

                              MUELLER
Well, I'm letting you have them as a special treat. Think
of me as a naughty uncle that lets you do things you
normally wouldn't be allowed to do.

                              ERIC
Like when dad asks Ivanka to call him an uncle, so it
sounds less creepy?

                              MUELLER
Mister Trump, I'm going to need you to swear an oath right
now that you're going to tell us the truth.

                              ERIC
I can't do that, Uncle Mueller. Junior says it's bad to
swear.

                              MUELLER
Look, Mister Trump, I just want to ask you about your
father and what he did during the election last year, and I
need you to promise that you'll tell the truth.

                              ERIC
Can we go eat pizza and watch a movie after?

                              MUELLER
Mister Trump, if you help us out here, then I promise that
I will personally arrange for you to meet the star of your
favorite movie.

                              ERIC
Cool. I've always wanted to meet a talking snowman.

                                                      (CONTINUED)

                        MUELLER
So do we have an arrangement?

                        ERIC
Okay, but I can't tell you about any of the stuff that dad
said I'm not allowed to talk about.

                        MUELLER
What did he say that you're not allowed to talk about?

                        ERIC
The help he got from the Russia meeting, Vladimir Putin
voting multiple times in Wisconsin, fake news online
attacking Hillary Clinton, and WikiLeaks hacking the D-N-C
for him.

                        MUELLER
Is there anything else he said you can't talk about?

                        ERIC

Future mom.

                        MUELLER
Who is future mom?

                        ERIC
She's the porn star that dad has Eric kisses with. But he
doesn't want anyone to know about her because his Uncle
Cohen paid her one hundred and thirty thousand dollars to
stay quiet.

                        MUELLER
One hundred and thirty thousand dollars? Why doesn't he
just use the internet like everyone else?

                        ERIC
Sometimes they only get paid one hundred and twenty
thousand.

                        Beat.

                                              (CONTINUED)

                              MUELLER
                          (to FBI AGENTS)
This kid is so stupid, I don't know whether to punch him or
kiss him for making our job easier.

                               ERIC
Don't kiss me. The doctor said it might be contagious.

                              MUELLER
Now, Mister Trump, you love your father, right?

                               ERIC
What is love?

                              MUELLER
Oh, love... well, love is what the majority of Americans
will be feeling towards me when I wrap up this
investigation.

                               ERIC
Will anyone ever feel love towards me?

                              MUELLER
I'm sure we can get you a pet if you want to try to
experience it yourself.

                               ERIC
No. I don't want a Reince Priebus.

                              MUELLER
I don't follow you, Mister Trump.

                               ERIC
That's what Uncle Scaramucci always called him. I miss
Uncle Scaramucci, but dad said he had to go away to a
better place.

                              MUELLER
I don't want to interrupt your story, Mister Trump, but I'd
quite like to wrap up this interview soon. So, I'm going to
ask you again, do you love your father?

                               ERIC
I think so.

                                                    (CONTINUED)

                              MUELLER
Very good, that makes this easier. Now, there's a very good
chance that he's soon going to be locked up for a very long
time, do you understand me?

                              ERIC
Is that like when he asks Ivanka to bring the chains?

                              MUELLER
Back to your father being in jail, Mister Trump. I'm sure
that if you loved him, you wouldn't want him to be alone
for the rest of his life, would you?

                              ERIC
No, but he could just get a mirror. That's what I do when I
want a friend to play with. I'm not talking to that friend
anymore, though. He said I look funny.

                              MUELLER
Well, what we want to arrange for your father is something
similar to that, only with real people. His friends and his
family, for example. So can you help us out with that, so
he isn't alone?

                              ERIC
Sure.

                              MUELLER
So who do you think we should lock up with him for the
company? Anyone who has similar interests to him like
treason and sexual assault?

                              ERIC
Well, there's Jared Kushner and Donald Trump Junior.

                              MUELLER begins to note the names
                              down.

                              ERIC
Michael Cohen, Kellyanne Conway, Sean Spicer, Vladimir
Putin, Ivanka Trump, Eric Trump, Michael Flynn, Stephen
Miller, Steve Bannon, Rudy Giuliani, Jeff Sessions,
European mom, and a some guy named George.

                                                    (CONTINUED)

Beat.

                    MUELLER
                (to FBI AGENTS)
Look at this kid.
                (to ERIC)
Well, Mister Trump, that's all that I need to ask you.
You've been a big help to me and your country.

                    ERIC
Do I get to meet a talking snowman now?

                    MUELLER
Meet a talking snowman?... Well, I'll tell you what, if you
come back here next week, you can meet one, okay? But just
remember to bring your father and your brother too, you
wouldn't want them to miss out now, would you?

                    ERIC
What about Jared Kushner?

                    MUELLER
Now you're getting it. Well, run along then and tell them
all the exciting news.

                    ERIC
Thank you, Uncle Mueller. I love you.

                    MUELLER
And right now, I love you too, kid.

                         ERIC begins walking offstage.

                    MUELLER
The exit is the other way, Mister Trump.

                    ERIC
I knew that.

                         He changes direction and exits.

                         MUELLER stands and puts his arms
                         around the FBI AGENTS.

                                        (CONTINUED)
PERFORMANCE LICENSE EDITION   LICENSE # _ _ _ _ _ _ _ _

                          MUELLER
You know, I think we can go out and celebrate tonight. I
think we've got those treasonous assholes.

ACT II, SCENE FIFTEEN | MICHAEL COHEN FLIPS

                              The OVAL OFFICE, where JUNIOR
                              sits tied to a chair while TRUMP
                              is taunting him by holding
                              hairspray just out of reach.

                          NARRATOR
                         (entering)
With now in hand the knowledge that from Eric Trump he did
demand, Robert Mueller sets forth to have his team raid
offices from the south, east, west, and to the north.
Lawyers, secretaries, and a tea boy too, Flynn, Manafort,
and Michael Cohen, to name just a few. The net is now
closing fast around the President, and many around him know
exactly by this what is meant. Every other day a new name
jumps ship, and with a lifeboat ready sits Mueller if they
promise to talk from their lip. But with a team of lawyers
working to work the lies which they mill, Donald Trump sits
confident of being found innocent somehow even still. Sure
his son Junior shared on Twitter evidence and more, but
that is why now he sits tied to a chair on the Oval Office
floor. For his father to solve it is still sure of his
plan, but then still little does he know he's about to lose
his favorite lawyer man.

                          The NARRATOR exits.

                          TRUMP
You are not getting your hairspray back until you have sent
that tweet, Donald Trump Junior.

                          JUNIOR
But dad, if I don't spray my hair at least once an hour,
then I end up looking like you.

                                             (CONTINUED)

                          TRUMP
Then pull out your phone and get tweeting, otherwise I will
leave you tied up and make you babysit your brother
tonight, and just a little F-Y-I, we have not changed his
diaper.

                          JUNIOR
Okay, fine.

                    He pulls out his phone.

                          JUNIOR
                    (to himself, reading)
"I welcome this opportunity to share this statement to set
out the circumstances around the reported Russia meeting at
Trump Tower last year."
                    (to TRUMP)
What do you want me to say?

                          TRUMP
It has been reported by the lying fake news media that I
met with Russia. I did meet with Russia, but nothing
happened, and I did not do anything illegal. If I did do
anything illegal, then it was the fault of Crooked Hillary
Clinton. P-S, my father was not at the meeting.

                    COHEN enters.

                          COHEN
You know, boss, you're wasting your time. There's no point
in trying to fight it.

                          TRUMP
What are you talking about, Michael Cohen?

                          COHEN
I'm talking about how it's not going to make a difference.
Everyone already knows about that Russia meeting and
everything that happened at it. You tweeted about it, Don
Junior tweeted about it, and Comrade Putin even set a photo
from it as the header of the Kremlin's profile.

                                                      (CONTINUED)

CONTINUED:

                         TRUMP
I am not worried, Michael Cohen. We are just going to deny
the Russia meeting, and then they have no more evidence.

                         COHEN
I wouldn't be sure of that, boss. Last I heard, Robert
Mueller sat down with one of your children the other day
and asked some questions.

                         TRUMP
None of them would be stupid enough to have told the truth.

                         COHEN
It was Eric Trump.

                    Beat.

                         TRUMP
We are so screwed.

                         COHEN
Exactly, boss. Robert Mueller now has all the evidence he
needs.

                         TRUMP
I still do not need to worry. I still have you as my
lawyer, and as long as you are here, there will always be
someone to pay the bribes to get me out of any situation.

                         COHEN
Well actually, about that, boss. I've come to hand in my
resignation to you. I've been speaking to the Mueller team,
and they've offered me an out. I want to flip.

                         TRUMP
You do not get an out, Michael Cohen. No one in this
administration gets a way out. There are no redemptions
from this.

                    GIULIANI enters.

                         TRUMP
Rudy Giuliani, have you heard this? Michael Cohen says he
is going to flip.

                                            (CONTINUED)

>   GIULIANI grabs COHEN by the
>   head.

                            GIULIANI
I'm sure he's just having a joke with us.

                            COHEN
Hey, get off me. I'm not joking around here.

>   COHEN breaks free.

                            COHEN
They came and raided my office this morning and found
evidence of everything. There's nothing more I can do for
you now, and I don't think there's anything you can do
either, boss.

                            TRUMP
What are you saying, Michael Cohen?

                            COHEN
I'm saying that right now, I'm pretty sure there's a Stormy
coming right for you.

>   Beat.

                            TRUMP
Please, Michael Cohen. There must still be something that
you can do for me?

                            COHEN
Mister Trump, I'm not even a real lawyer. I couldn't even
get a place at Trump U. I had to get my degree from Trump U
Junior.

                            TRUMP
I can offer you money. I can offer you lots of great green
American dirty bribe money.

                            COHEN
Boss, you still haven't paid me back for paying off all
those lawsuits for you. Besides, Robert Mueller has offered
me something you never could.
                            (MORE)

                                              (CONTINUED)

CONTINUED:

                         COHEN (CONT'D)
A nice comfortable cell where I get three meals a day, new
clothes, and never have to speak to another member of the
public ever again.

                         TRUMP
Please, Michael Cohen. Stay and help me.

                         COHEN
No, Mister Trump. This is the end. It's over. You've never
respected me, and the other lawyers bully me --

                         GIULIANI
That's not true.

                         COHEN
Yes, it is. You always steal my lunch money, and you even
wrote to the President of the Bar Association to tell her I
have posters of her on my bedroom walls.

                         GIULIANI
It was a good joke.

                         COHEN
I don't even have a bedroom. I have to live in a bush now
because the boss evicted me from my cupboard.

                         TRUMP
It was prime real estate, Michael Cohen. You know that.

                         COHEN
Have you got any idea what it's like to have Sean Spicer as
a roommate?

                         TRUMP
What about if I give you your cupboard back?

                         COHEN
It's too late. Robert Mueller is going to bring you and
everyone around you down. And you know what, I'm going to
help them as much as I can. You're a bad man, Mister Trump,
and everyone is going to find out what you've done to their
country. You're not the boss of me anymore... boss.

                                              (CONTINUED)

PERFORMANCE LICENSE EDITION   LICENSE # _ _ _ _ _ _ _ _

>   Beat, and then COHEN exits as
>   CONWAY and ERIC enter.

                              CONWAY
Mister President, do you need a moment? That looked as
though it was emotional.

                              TRUMP
Kellyanne Conway, we just lost a very fine, and a very
great, member of our catering team.

                              CONWAY
Well anyway, sir, I think that we're going to need to come
up with a new idea.

                              GIULIANI
What's wrong with my idea? It's working. We've told
everyone that the President is guilty and he's not been
arrested yet.

                              CONWAY
Yet.

                              GIULIANI
They can't arrest a sitting president. They wouldn't try.

                              CONWAY
No, but they can wait until he's not a sitting president.
And they can also arrest all of us now.

                              GIULIANI
Then we will them that we're all guilty. That everyone is
guilty. What are they going to do about it? Arrest all of
us?

                              CONWAY
They are trying to. Just last week, they indicted twelve
household cleaners, eleven gardeners gardening, ten lawyers
lying, nine drivers driving, eight butlers buttling, seven
librarians reading, six stewards seating, five-clothes-
valets, four table waiters, three bell boys, two tea
blenders and the former campaign barista.

>   ERIC begins to clap.

                                            (CONTINUED)

                         CONWAY
                        (to ERIC)
Thank you.

                        (to TRUMP)
So you see, sir, I really think we need to try doing
something different.

                         TRUMP
Have we tried calling it all a witch hunt in the hope that
it makes it just go away? Or we use thoughts and prayers?

                         CONWAY
We only use thoughts and prayers for problems we could
actually fix if we wanted to, sir.

                         TRUMP
What about paper towels? Have we tried paper towels?

                         CONWAY
Paper towels don't really do anything, sir... ever.

                         TRUMP
What about Jeff Sessions? Why can't he just close down the
investigation?

                         CONWAY
Oh, about Jeff Sessions. I saw him earlier, and he said he
was planning on coming to see you, but he's going to have
to reschedule because he's got to spend the day trying to
recall which rainbow he left his pot of gold at the end of.

Also, Mister President, if you don't mind me asking, why is
Donald Trump Junior tied to a chair?

                         JUNIOR
Can someone untie me now?

                         TRUMP
I cannot let you out, Donald Trump Junior. I used a lock
and gave the key to Eric Trump to keep it safe.

                    They all look to ERIC.

                                                  (CONTINUED)

                           ERIC
That was a key? I thought it was candy.

                    KUSHNER enters.

                          CONWAY
So what are we going to do about Robert Mueller, sir?

                          TRUMP
Jared Kushner, do you have any ideas?

                    KUSHNER holds up a cue card.

                          CONWAY
                        (reading)
"No. I have no idea about anything and don't know why I'm
still here."
                        (beat)
Jared Kushner has no idea about anything and doesn't know
why he's still here, sir.

                           ERIC
Why don't we just run away?

                         GIULIANI
The kid has a point. Running away could work.

                          TRUMP
Kellyanne Conway, what language do they speak in South
America?

                          CONWAY
They speak Spanish in many places, sir. Why do you ask?

                          TRUMP
Puedo hablar Español.

                          CONWAY
Mister President?

                          TRUMP
I said I can speak Spanish. My father taught it to me when
I was a little boy and told me that if I ever get into
trouble, then I should run away to South America.

                                           (CONTINUED)

                    CONWAY
But what about your children, sir?

                    JUNIOR
Yo tambien puedo hablar Español.

                    TRUMP
Donald Trump Junior and Ivanka Trump are both fluent. Even
Eric Trump knows some words.

                    ERIC
Guten tag.

                    CONWAY
Mister President, are you suggesting that we just leave all
of this behind? That we just run away from the mess we've
created so that someone else has to clean it up?

                    TRUMP
Yes, I am.

                    CONWAY
I'm in. What do we do?

                    TRUMP
Rudy Giuliani, I need you to stay behind and make sure that
no one knows we have gone anywhere.

                    GIULIANI
I can do that, and when they come after me, I'll just tell
them that I'm guilty. What's the worst they can do?

                    CONWAY
Prosecute you for treason.

                    GIULIANI
They only prosecute you if they like you, Kellyanne.

                    TRUMP
Donald Trump Junior, you are going to stay tied to that
chair until we can get the key back.

                                            (CONTINUED)

                          JUNIOR
Why can't we just tell Eric where babies come from so he
brings it back up straight away?

                          ERIC
I already know where babies come from. The baby fairy puts
them under your pillow at night.

                          TRUMP
                    (to JUNIOR)
Because no one wants to clean up that mess.
                    (to CONWAY)
Kellyanne Conway, I need you to go and get Ivanka Trump,
and also some glasses and some fake mustaches, and then
meet us at the airport in one hour.

                          CONWAY
Mister President, just one thing, sir. I really like this
plan, okay, but don't we need to leave someone behind to
take the blame for us.

                          TRUMP
Kellyanne Conway, I have already thought about this, and I
know of such a great goat.

                              Slowly, they all turn to stare
                              at KUSHNER, who, after staring
                              back for a moment, turns around
                              his cue card to reveal, "Why are
                              you all looking at me?"

ACT II, SCENE SIXTEEN | THE ESCAPE TO SOUTH AMERICA

                              An AIRPORT TERMINAL where
                              CONWAY, ERIC, IVANKA, and TRUMP,
                              along with JUNIOR (still tied to
                              a chair), all of them are
                              wearing glasses and a fake
                              mustache, are talking to a CHECK-
                              IN agent.

                                              (CONTINUED)

                            NARRATOR
                          (entering)
And so with Cohen having flipped, next comes the inevitable
sinking of the ship. The days of freedom are now limited
for those at the top, and they know they have no choice but
to flee from the chop. Donald J. Trump with two of his sons
and Ivanka too, along with Kellyanne Conway, who completes
their few. Mike Pence has already fled the nest, and not
one of them cares who is arrested from the rest.

                                        The NARRATOR exits as HANNITY
                                        enters but stands to watch from
                                        the side.

                            TRUMP
Hello check-in person, we are here for the flight to South
America even though I hear it is overrated. There is five
of us.
                          (looking around)
Make that four of us, we should probably check Donald Trump
Junior in as baggage because we still cannot untie him.

                            ERIC
I haven't been for poo-poo yet.

                        CHECK-IN AGENT
And do any of you have a preference of where you'd like to
sit on the plane?

                            TRUMP
As far along the right-wing as possible.

                        CHECK-IN AGENT
And other than this chair, do you have any baggage to
check?

                            CONWAY
I might need to pay some excess charges here. I've picked
up a lot since I started working for Mister Trump.

                                        The CHECK-IN AGENT hands over
                                        their boarding passes.

                                                    (CONTINUED)

                    CHECK-IN AGENT
Here are your boarding passes, and if you'd like to make
your way through security, boarding will begin in just over
an hour.

                    TRUMP
Eric Trump, make sure you have your clear school bag ready
for security to check.

                              The CHECK-IN AGENT moves to push
                              JUNIOR offstage.

                    IVANKA
Daddy, why isn't Jared Kushner coming?

                    TRUMP
Jared Kushner was a great guy, but... Kellyanne Conway, can
you take this one?

                    CONWAY
Sure thing, Mister Trump.
                         (putting her arm around
                         IVANKA)
Ivanka, let me tell you a story about how there are plenty
more fish in the South American Sea.

                         CONWAY and IVANKA exit.

                    ERIC
Hey, where's European mom?

                    TRUMP
She said she's having dinner with a lawyer tonight.

                              Beat, and then HANNITY
                              approaches them.

                    HANNITY
Donald J. Trump.

                         TRUMP turns to him.

                    TRUMP
Sean Hannity.

                                             (CONTINUED)
PERFORMANCE LICENSE EDITION   LICENSE # _ _ _ _ _ _ _ _

                              ERIC
Dad, are we going away for a long time? Because Uncle
Mueller promised that he would introduce us all to a
talking snowman.

                              TRUMP
Eric Trump, if you are good and leave us alone, I will buy
you a talking snowman toy from the shop.

                              ERIC
I can be a good boy. If I try hard, I can even be a real
boy.

                         ERIC exits.

                              HANNITY
President Trump, sir.

                              TRUMP
Sean Hannity.

                              HANNITY
Does it have to end this way? I thought that we were all
going to grow old together in prison. You, me, and everyone
else. I thought Betsy DeVos would count her days in prison
in elephants.

                              TRUMP
You could come with us, Sean Hannity. It would be great.

                              HANNITY
But if I leave, who will look after Tucker Carlson? He
needs me as a role model otherwise, he might grow up to be
a respected journalist.

                              TRUMP
You do such fantastic work with that man, Sean Hannity.

                              HANNITY
Will I ever see you again?

                                              (CONTINUED)

                          TRUMP
Of course, you will see me again. You will see my face
every day on all of the wanted posters. They are going to
be <u>huge</u>.

                          HANNITY watches as TRUMP exits.

                          HANNITY
You were a good friend, Mister President.

                          A moment, and then HANNITY takes
                          a deep breath as PUTIN enters
                          and places his arm around his
                          shoulders.

                          PUTIN
Don't not worry about Donald. Tell me, how you like to be
world leader in year two thousand and twenty?

                          Together, they exit.

ACT II, SCENE SEVENTEEN | KUSHNER IN THE OVAL OFFICE

                          The OVAL OFFICE, where KUSHNER
                          sits alone behind the desk
                          looking around confused and
                          scared.

                          NARRATOR
                          (entering)
And so we reach at last the end of our first part, and
still yet to show Trump is any sign of a heart. And so
while to South America he now takes flight, there is
another who sits in the Oval Office on this night. For it
is that Jared Kushner, in all the commotion, has received
an unexpected promotion. From the bottom to the top, being
president is now his job. But little is Jared aware of just
how badly he is about to fare.

                          The NARRATOR exits.

                                              (CONTINUED)

                              For a moment, KUSHNER continues
                              to look around, and then
                              suddenly, there's loud banging
                              and lights fill the stage as the
                              ENSEMBLE (as FBI AGENTS) storm
                              on stage and surround him.

                         FBI AGENT #1
We're looking for the President.

                              Beat, and then KUSHNER begins to
                              raise his hands.

                         KUSHNER
I want my mommy.

                              Lights out.

                    END OF PART ONE

PART TWO

ACT III : "THE SECOND YEAR"

ACT III, PRE-SHOW | PRE-SHOW

>   As the audience returns to the
>   auditorium for phase two, they
>   are greeted by a stage which is
>   lit by a sidle center spotlight.
>
>   In the middle of the spotlight,
>   a gravestone stands atop a small
>   mound of earth with the words
>   "R.I.P. America," etched into
>   the stone.
>
>   Once the audience is seated, the
>   lights in the auditorium go
>   down, and the voice of HILLARY
>   CLINTON fills the room.

                    CLINTON (PRE-RECORDED)
Hello again, America. It is Hillary Rodham Clinton here
once more. Still here. Oh, I am still here. Of course, I am
still here. I am not going anywhere. I never have, and I
never will. You do not get rid of Hillary Rodham Clinton
that easily.

I am here to welcome all of you, whether you be a man, a
woman, a small man, or even a small woman - unless you did
not vote for me, that is. If that is the case, then I think
that I speak for all of us when I say that you can go off
and have some sexual intercourse with yourself. To the rest
of you, welcome to this here performance of part two of
TRUMPED: An Alternative Musical. Still one-hundred percent
James Corden free.

This second part of the show is the sequel to the first
part of the show. The only sequel. Please, let this be the
only sequel. Please, god. We are all really going to need
to face some facts here, America. There may be some very
difficult choices ahead.
                         (MORE)
                                              (CONTINUED)

CONTINUED:
                              CLINTON (PRE-RECORDED) (CONT'D)
And I am not talking about whether it is time to put
Florida out of its misery. I am talking about the wall.
If some of us are stupid enough actually to vote for that
man a second time, then we really are going to need it. We
are going to need it so that we all have something to bash
our heads against daily in frustration.

Before this performance gets underway, I would just like to
remind you once again that you need to switch off all of
your mobile phones and other electronic devices. If Mike
Pence sees any of them, then he might attempt to set up
witch trials again, and the last time he did that, I lost
my first primary.

Also, Russia. Russia might be using them to listen in, and
the producers of this show would rather they did not know
what was is in. They have not yet trained to run away fast
enough.

So sit back and relax... Well, not back and probably not
relax. Trump is still the President after all, and none of
us have been able to do either for some time. Instead, sit
forward and tense, or in the fetal position crying in the
nearest corner with a gentle, comforting rocking motion.

Finally, thank you for your co-operation and remember to
vote for me the next time I run for office. I will even
offer you Bernie's policy of healthcare for all, because
let us face it, by the time that I am finally president, we
are all going to be of an age where it would come in really
useful.

Please enjoy the show.

                         The spotlight fades, and the
                         stage falls into darkness.

ACT III, SCENE ONE | FOX & FRIENDS

                         For a short moment, the stage
                         remains dark.

                                              (CONTINUED)

                         FOX NEWS PRODUCER (OFF)
Please get into position. We're ready to go live.

                              Lights up on the FOX & FRIENDS
                              STUDIO in New York City.

                              Sat on a couch ready to present
                              their show live to the nation,
                              STEVE DOOCY, AINSLEY EARHARDT,
                              and BRIAN KILMEADE. EARHARDT is
                              busy tidying KILMEADE's suit as
                              the FOX NEWS PRODUCER enters.

                              Opening title music begins to
                              play.

                         FOX NEWS PRODUCER
And we are live in five... four... three... two... and
go...

                              The FOX NEWS PRODUCER exits.

                         DOOCY
Good morning, patriots.

                         EARHARDT
You know, Steve? I heard that it's a good morning too.
Hello there, America.

                         DOOCY
It's not just a good morning, though, is it, Ainsley?

                         EARHARDT
That's right, Steve. It's also a very good start to the
week, isn't it?

                         DOOCY
That's right, Ainsley. Happy Monday, loyal subjects.

                         EARHARDT
How was your weekend, Brian?

                         KILMEADE
It was exciting.

                                                  (CONTINUED)
PERFORMANCE LICENSE EDITION   LICENSE # _ _ _ _ _ _ _ _

                          EARHARDT
That's great --

                          KILMEADE
I got to fly in a helicopter when it came to rescue me from
a lake after I fell in the water while fishing. I couldn't
swim back to my boat because I was scared by what I thought
was a shark in the water. But it wasn't a shark, it was
just my reflection.

                          EARHARDT
Great.

                          KILMEADE
I think it was a hammerhead, actually.

                          DOOCY
Well, do you know what is not so great today, Ainsley?

                          EARHARDT
I don't, Steve. Why don't you tell me and all of those who
are watching us at home?

                          DOOCY
I'll do just that, Ainsley. It's not great that nobody
knows where the President is right now. He hasn't been seen
for weeks.

                          EARHARDT
That's right, Steve. If you're watching us today, Mister
Trump, let us know that you're okay. Send us a sign.

                          KILMEADE
I think our viewers are very rude. We are always telling
them things, but they never tell us anything back.

                          EARHARDT
What do you think has happened to the President, Brian?

                          KILMEADE
Perhaps he's not very well?

                          DOOCY and EARHARDT both laugh.

                                              (CONTINUED)

                              DOOCY
Ha. Ha. Ha. That's very funny, Brian.

                              EARHARDT
But what an absurd suggestion. Our President could never be
ill. He's far too healthy for that.

                              DOOCY
That's right, Ainsley. Remember, Brian, his last medical
showed us that he's a healthy two hundred and thirty-nine
pounds.

                              KILMEADE
Does anyone know what that is in Dollars?

                              EARHARDT
Perhaps he's been kidnapped?

                              KILMEADE
By Hillary Clinton?

                              EARHARDT
You know, that could be true, Brian.

                              DOOCY
It wouldn't surprise me.

                              EARHARDT
Not at all, Steve.

                              DOOCY
Well, that really is some breaking news happening on Fox
and Friends this morning. Our President has been kidnapped
by none other than Hillary Clinton. You heard it here
first.

                              EARHARDT
Perhaps she is hiding him in the same place that she has
been hiding all of those emails from the American people,
Steve?

                         CLINTON enters.

                                                    (CONTINUED)

CONTINUED:

                         CLINTON
Seriously? I mean, seriously? Why are you people all still
so obsessed with me? The election was over a year ago.

                         DOOCY
Was it really over a year ago, though? Or is the concept of
time just a liberal conspiracy against real Americans.

                         CLINTON
You know what? Just delete your program.

                         KILMEADE begins to cheer.

                         EARHARDT
She isn't being nice to us, Brian. The nasty woman said a
bad thing.

                         KILMEADE
Oh.

                         KILMEADE stops cheering and
                         instead begins to cry.

                         KILMEADE
That was the meanest thing anyone has ever said to me.

                         EARHARDT
It's okay, Brian. Isn't it, Steve?

                         DOOCY
That's right, Ainsley.
                         (to CLINTON)
Look at what you've done now. You've made Brian cry.

                         KILMEADE
I want my mom.

ACT III, SCENE TWO | PUTIN IN THE OVAL OFFICE

                         The NARRATOR enters at the front
                         of an otherwise dark stage.

                                           (CONTINUED)

                          NARRATOR
And so we return when some weeks have passed since Donald
J. Trump handed over his mast to another which prompted
within the White House a notable change of cast.

It was Jared Kushner who took the fall, and off to jail he
was ordered when on Trump he refused to talk or even
scrawl. But still seeks Mueller for answers and truth,
though with the dynasty out of the way, it is much harder
to sleuth.

Meanwhile, across America, opinions are mixed, with some to
say the President's departure was one to save the nation
from certain doom. In contrast, others feel he did little
to help when he boarded that flight to South America while
upon his foot, paper from an airport bathroom.

Though one fact cannot be disputed --

                              The NARRATOR is interrupted by
                              the entrance of a cloaked figure
                              of "death."

                              As the figure approaches, it
                              removes its hood to reveal that
                              they are actually CLINTON
                              dressed in a black Grim Reaper
                              pantsuit.

                          NARRATOR
Hillary, what are you doing here?

                          CLINTON
Me? Oh, well, I'm just here to remind all of these fine
American people in the audience that I do still exist.

                              CLINTON begins to wave at the
                              audience.

                          NARRATOR
But weren't you here doing that just a moment ago

                                                     (CONTINUED)

CONTINUED:

                         CLINTON
Well, yes, I was. But in these current times, things happen
quickly, and people forget easily.

                              CLINTON points at an audience
                              member in the front row.

                         CLINTON
                    (to audience member)
It's you. Hello! How good to see you again... for the very
first time. How are you?

                         NARRATOR
Why are you dressed like that?

                         CLINTON
Like this? It is a costume. I have decided that it would be
appropriate for me to embrace my pure form and become the
ghost of elections past.

                         NARRATOR
But you don't look like a ghost. You're closer to a grim
reaper.

                         CLINTON
I know that. But I was talking to Bill, and he reckons that
the whole point of dressing up is to look different from
how you usually do.

                         NARRATOR
I still don't understand why you're dressing up.

                         CLINTON
I want to be able to take my rightful place in the Oval
Office, and so I am here to watch over the slow and painful
death of Donald Trump's political career.

                         NARRATOR
In the same way he did to you?

                         CLINTON
No. In fact, he did not do that. Something cannot die if it
is already dead. And you can trust me on that.
                         (MORE)

                                                (CONTINUED)

CONTINUED:

                         CLINTON (CONT'D)
I searched it up on the internet. Or as the cool people
say, I went and **Binged** it.

                         NARRATOR

Google?

                         CLINTON
No. Google is what Bill and I save for our special
quadrennial date nights. Or as most people call them, the
midterms. We get together, turn up on people's campaign
trails, and leave them completely screwed.

                              VLADIMIR PUTIN enters from the
                              darkness at the back of the
                              stage.

                         PUTIN
Do either of you have intention of getting on with show?
Some of us have important annex of nations to be doing
later.

                         CLINTON
You know, Vladimir. I often wonder why you did not choose
to help me instead of Donald. I was the better candidate.

                         PUTIN
We did offer. You deleted email we sent without reading it.

                         Beat.

                         CLINTON
Okay. Let us get on with the show.

                         PUTIN

Good.

                              PUTIN retreats back into the
                              darkness.

                         CLINTON
So has Donald Trump's political career died yet, Narrator?

                         NARRATOR
You'll need to come back at the end of the next act.

                                              (CONTINUED)
PERFORMANCE LICENSE EDITION   LICENSE # _ _ _ _ _ _ _ _

                         CLINTON
Then I will watch on from the wings waiting for my moment.
But can I stick around for just this bit? Only if you do
not mind?

                         NARRATOR
Well, I --

                         CLINTON
Great! I am sure that we will be the greatest of friends.
We already get along like... well, I do not really know. I
have never got on with anything before.
                    (beat)
Do continue.

                         NARRATOR
Thank you.
                    (to audience)
Though one fact cannot be disputed. While Donald may have
run off with his family to the America in the south, those
who now take his place in the Oval Office do so with no
couth.

                         CLINTON
That is right. There are some very bad people in there.
                    (leaning in)
And spoiler alert. It is Vladimir Putin and Sean Hannity. I
have read the script.

                         NARRATOR
Hillary, we're not supposed to tell them that much.

                         CLINTON
I am sorry. My mistake. I have never been that good at
knowing when I should leave.

                         NARRATOR
Now would be good.

                         CLINTON and the NARRATOR exit.

                                                    (CONTINUED)

                         Lights go up on THE OVAL OFFICE,
                         where PUTIN sits with his feet
                         on the desk while in front, SEAN
                         HANNITY stands rehearsing.

                    HANNITY
                 (mid-rehearsal)
... And now, we come to our final story of the night, and
it's about those unpatriotic Democrats again. This time,
get this, they are going after our veterans. That's right,
those Democrats are calling for tougher sanctions on Russia
and the Russian people after everything they did fighting
alongside our boys in W-W-Two. Well, we here on Hannity
salute the sacrifices made by those brave Russian soldiers,
and we call upon the Democrats to start showing them the
respect they deserve.

                    PUTIN
Good. It be very good. I think it get message we want
across most well.

                    HANNITY
Thank you, Comrade Putin, sir.

                         Footsteps grow in volume from
                         offstage.

                    PUTIN
Quick. I think someone be coming. I should not be here.

                         As HANNITY rushes to make
                         himself look casual, PUTIN
                         presses a small button on top of
                         the desk. The entire desk, and
                         PUTIN with it, swivels around to
                         be replaced by an empty replica.

                         ROBERT MUELLER enters carrying a
                         file.

                    HANNITY
Mister Mueller. I wasn't expecting to see you here.

                                              (CONTINUED)

                          MUELLER
I could say the same thing about yourself, Mister Hannity.
The Oval Office is, I do not believe, the Fox News studio.

                          HANNITY
Oh, well I was just --

                          MUELLER
Mister Hannity, do you know the current whereabouts of the
President?

                          Beat.

                          PUTIN (OFF)
                       (shouting out)
No, you do not.

                          HANNITY
                       (to MUELLER)
No, I do not.

                          MUELLER
I'm sorry?

                          HANNITY
No one knows where the President is right now.

                                   MUELLER slams his file down on
                                   the desk. The desk swivels back
                                   around to reveal PUTIN, looking
                                   shocked. MUELLER doesn't notice.

                          MUELLER
Mister Hannity, may I remind you that multiple eyewitnesses
claim that you were the last person to see the President
before his disappearance last month.

                                   In a panic, PUTIN presses the
                                   button and disappears again.

                          HANNITY
I have already testified under oath. I don't know anything.

                                                        (CONTINUED)
PERFORMANCE LICENSE EDITION   LICENSE # _ _ _ _ _ _ _ _

CONTINUED:

                         MUELLER
I already know that you don't know anything, Mister
Hannity. But do you know where President Trump is?

                         HANNITY
No.

                    MUELLER picks his file up.

                         MUELLER
I hope that you're telling me the truth right now, Mister
Hannity. For your own sake.

                    He goes to leave but turns back
                    at the last moment.

                         MUELLER
Remember, Mister Hannity. I will be watching you. I am
always watching you.

                    MUELLER exits.

                         PUTIN (OFF)
                       (shouting out)
Is he gone?

                         HANNITY
He's gone.

                    The desk swivels back, and PUTIN
                    reappears.

                         PUTIN
Eyewitnesses? I thought we had all sent to gulag.

                         HANNITY
That's a very funny joke, Comrade Putin, sir.

                         PUTIN
I not joke. I never joke. But, you know, I actually be
getting tired of need to hide each time he come looking for
evidence. If I be honest, I actually be starting to miss
Donald.

                                              (CONTINUED)

                         HANNITY
So am I, Comrade Putin, sir.

                         PUTIN
And Donald was such good value. Whenever I needed laugh, I
just pick up phone and tell him foolish thing to do, and he
go and do it.

                         HANNITY
Very true, Comrade Putin, sir.

                              PUTIN stands and goes to put his
                              arm around HANNITY's shoulder.

                         PUTIN
Come now, Sean. You have not agree with all Putin says. It
almost me like something does bother you for past weeks.
Tell Putin what it be.

                         HANNITY
Well, this may sound dumb, but I'm worried that I might be
going to prison soon.

                         PUTIN
No. Of course, you not sound dumb. There be real chance you
be going to American gulag soon.

                         HANNITY
And if I only have a few months of freedom left, then I
don't want to spend them running for president. I want to
be around so that I can see Tucker Carlson grow into a real
boy.

                         PUTIN
I see. Well, perhaps it not be bad idea to bring back
Donald then. I be thinking of it for few days now. After
all, Fox and Friends have noticed he gone, and they notice
nothing.

                         HANNITY
It's a very good idea, Comrade Putin, sir.

                         PUTIN
Good. I be glad you agree. I leave you to get him them.

                                                      (CONTINUED)

> PUTIN goes to leave.

                    HANNITY
Me? But I don't know where he is.

                    PUTIN
Oh, Donald be in South America. He sent postcard.

                    HANNITY
South America?

                    PUTIN
Just follow trail of toilet paper that look like it once be
stuck to shoe bottom.

ACT III, SCENE THREE | THE TRUMP RANCH

> The kitchen of a TRADITIONAL
> SOUTH AMERICAN RANCH. A small
> ramp leads to a raised area with
> a table and refrigerator. Behind
> them, the front door. At the
> side of the scene, an open fire
> where IVANKA TRUMP teaches ERIC
> TRUMP math.
>
> As South American folk music
> plays in the background, the
> NARRATOR enters.

                    NARRATOR
And so with the mission set out by Putin now a personal
goal for Sean Hannity, to South America he travels to bring
back to America the President to further the excruciation
of humanity.

But for the Trump family who Sean seeks to find, life has
changed, and just last week, a thirty-year lease on their
own ranch signed. And so the return of Donald is far from
set in stone, no matter the consequences for Hannity if the
President does not retake America's throne.

                                                        (CONTINUED)

> The NARRATOR exits as the music
> fades out.

                    IVANKA
Now tell me, what is four plus five?

                    ERIC
Nine?

                    IVANKA
No. It's six. Remember, we are in the Southern Hemisphere,
so everything is upside down.

> DONALD TRUMP enters through the
> front door.

                    TRUMP
You know, Eric Trump and Ivanka Trump, moving to South
America, was the very greatest decision that I, Donald J.
Trump, has ever made. This really is the life for us. Eric
Trump is finally learning to count to ten...

                    ERIC
One. Three. Two.

                    TRUMP
And I have just joined the local golf club. They said that
I had just enough money on me to cover the joining fee. It
was lucky I took that extra one million two hundred and
twenty-nine thousand four hundred and eleven with me.

                    ERIC
Nine. Eight.

                    TRUMP
Now, where is my greatest son, Donald Trump Junior?

                    IVANKA
He is working in his room, daddy.

                    TRUMP
I should shout for him to come here.
                    (shouting out)
Donald Trump Junior, come here.

                                        (CONTINUED)

>   DONALD TRUMP JUNIOR enters. He
>   is still tied to a chair from
>   the end of the previous act.

                         JUNIOR
Hey dad, I heard you shouting me.

                         TRUMP
Come here, Donald Trump Junior.

                         JUNIOR
Up there?

                         TRUMP
Yes. Up here, Donald Trump Junior. To the top of this ramp.

                         JUNIOR
Okay, you know, dad, it's really not easy for me to do that
right now. If you just untied me then --

                         TRUMP
I have already told you. I lost the key.

>   Slowly, JUNIOR uses his feet to
>   push the chair to the bottom of
>   the ramp and then slowly up it.

                         TRUMP
                    (as JUNIOR approaches)
I need you to go and get my guitar for me, Donald Trump
Junior.

                         JUNIOR
Your guitar?

                         TRUMP
It is in my bedroom.

>   JUNIOR looks back down the ramp.

                         JUNIOR
You know what? Fine. I'll go get it.

                                              (CONTINUED)

CONTINUED:

>   JUNIOR makes his way back down
>   the ramp and exits as TRUMP
>   takes a seat at the table.

                         TRUMP
So, Eric Trump, what have you learned today?

                         ERIC
Four. Ten. Five. Seven. Six.

                         TRUMP
That is my social security number. How did you get that?
                    (beat)
Hey, Eric Trump, how rich am I?

                         ERIC
Jeff Bezos plus one Dollar.

                         TRUMP
What a great child.

>   JUNIOR returns, now with a
>   guitar. Everyone watches as he
>   makes his way back up the ramp.
>
>   At the top of the ramp, he hands
>   the guitar to TRUMP and joins
>   him at the table.

                         TRUMP
And now, I am going to play you all a great song. This is
going to be the greatest song performed by the greatest
person in the greatest way.

>   TRUMP coughs and strums the
>   guitar once.

                         TRUMP
/DO NOT CRY FOR ME, AMERICA./ Yeah!

>   TRUMP nods and looks pleased
>   with himself.

                                                    (CONTINUED)

                         TRUMP
You are all supposed to clap. How about this one?

                                   TRUMP coughs and strums the
                                   guitar once more.

                         TRUMP
/IF I REALLY WERE A RICH MAN./ Yeah!

                                   There is a sudden knock on the
                                   door behind him.

                         TRUMP
That was not a clap.
                    (standing)
Quick. It might be Robert Mueller with questions. Ivanka
Trump, you need to hide. Eric Trump, you can stay here, we
can afford to lose you.

                                   IVANKA rushes into the wings.

                         JUNIOR
And what about me, dad?

                                   TRUMP grabs the back of JUNIOR's
                                   chair and pushes him down the
                                   ramp with enough force that he
                                   continues offstage.

                         TRUMP
                    (to himself)
What about me? What about me? I know.

                                   TRUMP stands by the door, puts
                                   his hands over his face, and
                                   then turns away from it.

                                   Another knock.

                         TRUMP
                    (shouting out)
Beep. Donald J. Trump is not available at the moment.
Please leave a message for Donald J. Trump after the
beep... Bing, bing, bong, bong.

                                               (CONTINUED)
PERFORMANCE LICENSE EDITION   LICENSE # _ _ _ _ _ _ _

                    Another knock.

                    TRUMP
Okay. Plan number B.
                    (shouting out)
We are not here. No one is here.

                    Another knock.

                    TRUMP
This will be okay. It will be okay.

                              Cautiously, TRUMP turns back to
                              the door and pulls back the
                              curtain to see who is there.

                    IVANKA
                    (returning)
Who is it, daddy?

                    TRUMP
Sean Hannity.

                              ERIC screams as TRUMP lets the
                              curtain fall back down.

                    ERIC
Sorry. I thought you said a vampire.

                    Another knock.

                    TRUMP
Quick. Hide. It might be Robert Mueller --

                    IVANKA
It's Sean Hannity, daddy.

                    TRUMP
How do you know?

                    IVANKA
You just said it was.

                                             (CONTINUED)

CONTINUED:

>   TRUMP opens the door, and
>   HANNITY enters, looking as
>   though he's faced a long
>   journey.

                         HANNITY
I am so glad that I've found you, sir. I've been looking
for the right place for days.

>   TRUMP stares at HANNITY without
>   showing any emotion.

                         TRUMP
Sean Hannity.

                         HANNITY
Mister President, sir. You have no idea how good it is to
see you again.

                         TRUMP
Sean Hannity, it is always good to see me.

>   JUNIOR returns.

                         JUNIOR
Is it safe?

                         HANNITY
And Junior, you're here too.
                    (to IVANKA)
And get this, Ivanka too. I'm so glad to find the three of
you here.
                    (to ERIC)
And Eric.

                         IVANKA
Hello, Sean. You are honored to meet my father again.

>   TRUMP gestures for HANNITY to
>   take his attention away from
>   IVANKA.

                         TRUMP
I am here, Sean Hannity. I am not over there.

                                        (CONTINUED)

                         HANNITY
I'm sorry, Mister President. I didn't mean to give you any
undivided attention.

                                   JUNIOR begins to make his way
                                   back up the ramp as TRUMP sits
                                   at the table and gestures for
                                   HANNITY to do the same.

                         TRUMP
So what can I do for you, Sean Hannity?
                    (to JUNIOR)
Donald Trump Junior, fetch me a diet cola.

                         JUNIOR
Where are they?

                         TRUMP
They are in the refrigerator.

                                   JUNIOR begins to move closer to
                                   the refrigerator as...

                         TRUMP
Not that refrigerator. I have my own private Presidential
refrigerator in my bedroom. It is so cold. It is the most
coldest refrigerator ever. Even standing close to it makes
you deny global warming and causes all of your nipples to
go as hard as entry to Trump University.

                         JUNIOR
Do I have to go?

                         TRUMP
Yes. I have to talk to Sean Hannity.

                                   JUNIOR makes his way back down
                                   the ramp and exits once more.

                         TRUMP
So what can I do for you, Sean Hannity?

                         HANNITY
Well, Mister President, sir, I've come to take you home.

                                                  (CONTINUED)

                              TRUMP
But I am home. This is my home, Sean Hannity.

                             HANNITY
I meant your real home, sir. The United States of America.
You're our President, sir. And we need you back.

                              TRUMP
I am sorry, Sean Hannity, but I am not coming back. This is
my home now. It is so great. We have got our life set out.
I have even ordered a no foreign immigrants sign for the
front door. I wanted to own Jeff Bezos, so instead of
Amazon, I ordered it from el Amazonas.

                             HANNITY
But, Mister President, we need you. I need you. I can get
away with so much more while you're around. And America
needs you to come and save us all from the Democrats and
the liberals. Who knows where the next big threat might
come from? It could be from electronic cigarettes. We are
going to need your leadership to protect us from things
that could kill literally six of us. We need to leave here,
break Jared out of prison, get back to the Oval Office, and
get back to work.

                             IVANKA
                           (with lust)
Jared?

                              TRUMP
He did not say Jared Kushner. He said... Jobs. Many jobs. I
have created so many jobs. Good jobs. A lot of distracting
jobs. Jobs. Yeah!

                         ERIC applauds.

                              TRUMP
Thank you, Eric Trump.

                                   JUNIOR returns with a can of
                                   diet cola and begins making his
                                   way back up the ramp.

                                                      (CONTINUED)

                        HANNITY
And you could create so many more jobs, Mister President.
Get this. You could truly make America great again.

                        TRUMP
Are you saying that I have not already made America great
again, Sean Hannity? I am the greatest President ever. I
had Siri read to me from Twitter that since people have
thought I left the country, I have the highest approval
ratings ever.

                        HANNITY
I meant that you could make America great again, again. You
could be the greatest ever Donald J. Trump.

                                As JUNIOR makes his way to the
                                top of the ramp, he drops the
                                can, and it rolls back down.

                        TRUMP
I am sorry, Sean Hannity.
                    (to JUNIOR)
Go and get that can, Donald Trump Junior.
                    (to HANNITY)
But I do not want to come back.

                        JUNIOR
Make Eric get it.

                        TRUMP
Eric Trump, get that can from the floor.

                                ERIC stands and walks over to
                                the can.

                        TRUMP
                    (to HANNITY)
I like my life here, Sean Hannity. No one wants to ask me
questions and there are no Russians to blackmail me.

                        HANNITY
Some would say that it's your constitutional duty to
return, Mister President.

                                                    (CONTINUED)
PERFORMANCE LICENSE EDITION   LICENSE # _ _ _ _ _ _ _ _

                         ERIC opens the can, and it
                         sprays in his face.

                    TRUMP
Eric Trump, go and get another diet cola.
                    (to HANNITY)
I do not know a mister constitution, Sean Hannity.

                    ERIC
Make Junior go and get it.

                    TRUMP
Donald Trump Junior, go and get another diet cola.
                    (to HANNITY)
The only way I would ever return is if we run out of diet
cola or anything like that.

                    JUNIOR
I can't get another. That was the last one.
                    (beat)
We don't have any regular cola either, or anything like
that.

                    Beat.

                    TRUMP
Sean Hannity, I have reconsidered. So long as I get to fly
in first-class and they serve fried chicken on the plane, I
will come home.

                    HANNITY
I'm sorry to let you down, Mister President. But we can't
fly back. Robert Mueller and his team still want to
question you, and they might be waiting at the airport.

                    TRUMP
What are you suggesting?

                    HANNITY
We'll have to make our way back to Washington unnoticed. We
have to journey north to Mexico and then cross the border
on foot.

                                               (CONTINUED)

                          JUNIOR
You mean, we have to walk?

                          HANNITY
It's the only option we've got.

                          TRUMP
Can we stop for fried chicken on the way?

                          ERIC
Can I get a toy with mine?

                          TRUMP
And Eric Trump will have a toy with his.

                          HANNITY
I'm sure that we'll be able to find food, Mister President.

                          TRUMP
                        (standing)
Okay, Ivanka Trump, I want you to stay close to me so that
we do not lose you. Donald Trump Junior, I want you to keep
an eye on Eric Trump and try to lose him.

                                   ERIC runs to hug JUNIOR at the
                                   top of the ramp.

                          ERIC
Yay! Road trip buddy.

                                   As ERIC releases JUNIOR, he
                                   knocks him back down the ramp
                                   and offstage.

                          JUNIOR
                        (returning)
You know, dad? I think this would be a lot easier if I
weren't still tied to this chair.

                                   TRUMP reaches into his pocket
                                   and pulls out a small key which
                                   he uses to untie JUNIOR.

                                                  (CONTINUED)

CONTINUED:

                          JUNIOR
I thought you said that you'd lost the key?

                          TRUMP
I did say that I had lost the key.

                          JUNIOR
Then why have you just pulled it out of your pocket?

                          TRUMP
I found it again.

                    Beat.

                          IVANKA
Daddy, what are you going to do about Kellyanne? She isn't
home yet.

                          TRUMP
I will leave her a note.

                              TRUMP goes to the table to
                              scribble on a piece of paper.

                          HANNITY
Is there anything I can do, Mister Trump?

                              TRUMP looks at HANNITY.

                          TRUMP
Sean Hannity, I have a special job for you.

ACT III, SCENE FOUR | THE BORDER CROSSING

                              A BORDER CROSSING point between
                              Mexico and the United States
                              where DMITRY SUREFIRE and PETROV
                              SUREFIRE stand either side of a
                              door marked "door to the United
                              States."

                                                    (CONTINUED)

NARRATOR
(entering)
With Hannity succeeding in talking around his friend to
make him feel about a return convinced, the President and
his party set off home to ensure once more that the nation
is winced.

But before setting foot on his kingdom's land, there are
issues to arise for Donald from earlier policies that were
not well planned. For he, his family, and Sean Hannity, it
does not matter what their personal vanity, their hopes of
returning without issue to American ground are all soon to
be drowned.

The NARRATOR exits.

DMITRY
Do you think new job we have is promotion, Petrov?

PETROV
I do, Dmitry.

DMITRY
I applied for Space Force, but they rejected me.

PETROV
Space Force? Why apply for Space Force?

DMITRY
I want to go into space, Petrov.

PETROV
We need not join Space Force to visit space, Dmitry. We be
Russian. Russia own space. We go to space whenever we want.

DMITRY
Can we go now? It be better than standing here.

PETROV looks at him, worried.

PETROV
Speak cautious, Dmitry. Boss may be listening to us. And
besides, I think Comrade Putin know what he be doing when
he place us here. We have essential job, no?

(CONTINUED)

                         DMITRY
What job?

                         PETROV
We have to guard America against the bad people.

                         DMITRY
What do you mean the bad people?

                         PETROV
I mean all the bad people, Dmitry. The criminals. The
conmen. The rapists.

                         HANNITY enters carrying TRUMP on
                         his shoulders.

                         HANNITY
I think we've made it, Mister President.

                         TRUMP
I think I can smell the freedom, Sean Hannity.

                         DMITRY
Oh, the bad people. I know what you mean, Petrov.

                         TRUMP climbs down as IVANKA
                         enters, followed by JUNIOR, who
                         holds the end of a children's
                         walking harness worn by ERIC.

                         TRUMP
                    (to the group)
I will handle this.

                         As TRUMP approaches the door,
                         DMITRY and PETROV step in to
                         block him.

                         TRUMP walks back casually, and
                         they step aside. A moment later,
                         TRUMP turns back to them, and
                         they step in once more.

                                              (CONTINUED)

                         TRUMP
                    (to the group)
Someone else handle this.

                                        IVANKA now steps forward. As
                                        with her father, DMITRY and
                                        PETROV stand in to block her.

                         IVANKA
Hello. You are both honored to meet my father today. Can we
all please come in?

                         PETROV

There be no entry.

                         DMITRY

We not let anyone in.

                              JUNIOR steps forward.

                         JUNIOR
But we are American citizens. And not just citizens. We are
natural-born citizens. Me, my father, my sister, Sean
Hannity, all of us natural born. And Eric...
                    (beat)
He's an American.

                         ERIC

I wee freedom showers.

                         PETROV
But do you have papers in correct order?

                         DMITRY
Anyone could claim they are American. But can you prove it?

                         HANNITY
                    (to TRUMP)
Why don't we just go around the side of the door, Mister
President? They can't guard everywhere.

                         TRUMP
We cannot go around it, Sean Hannity. There is a wall. A
great big wall. I built it.

                                             (CONTINUED)

>   HANNITY leans to look at either
>   side of the door.

                         HANNITY
Mister President, sir. There is no wall. I can see that
there isn't. No wall has been built here.

                         TRUMP
Are you calling me a liar, Sean Hannity?

                         HANNITY
No, Mister President. I was just pointing out that --

                         TRUMP
Sean Hannity, stop right there, or I will have to report
this to Comrade Putin.

>   DMITRY and PETROV look worried.

                         JUNIOR
                    (to DMITRY and PETROV)
You know, we know Comrade Putin personally. He wouldn't be
happy if he knew you weren't letting us in.

                         PETROV
We are under instructions not to let anyone through.

                         HANNITY
                    (stepping forward)
You want papers? Take these papers.

>   HANNITY takes a pile of bills
>   from his pocket and hands them
>   to DMITRY and PETROV.

                         HANNITY
Can we come through now?

>   DMITRY and PETROV step aside to
>   let them through the door.

                         TRUMP
Did you see my negotiating? Did you all see how great I
was? That was some great negotiating.

                                             (CONTINUED)

                            HANNITY
You did very well, Mister President.

                                      DMITRY and PETROV begin to count
                                      the bills.

                            DMITRY
This is real money, Petrov.

                            PETROV
Real United States Dollar, Dmitry.

                            HANNITY
                        (hanging back)
Hey, those aren't just United States Dollars. Those are
freedom bucks.

ACT III, SCENE FIVE | BREAKING KUSHNER OUT

                                      From the depths of a dark stage,
                                      a single voice shouts out.

                        COHEN (IN DARKNESS)
                        (shouting out)
Hello. I want to see the manager. The boss. This is not
what I signed up for.

                                      A spotlight shines upon a PRISON
                                      CELL where MICHAEL COHEN sits on
                                      a bed.

                            COHEN
                        (shouting out)
I was told that if I flipped on boss Trump, then I'd get a
light sentence. This is no light sentence. I didn't sign up
to be sharing no cell with this guy.

                                      A second spotlight shines upon
                                      JARED KUSHNER, who sits in the
                                      corner of the cell rocking.

                                                          (CONTINUED)

                          KUSHNER
                   (muttering to himself)
I don't know... I want my mommy... where the President
is... I'm innocent... I don't know anything... It wasn't
Mister Trump or me... Ivanka... I want my mommy...

                          NARRATOR
                       (entering)
The border crossed eventually and back onto the soil of
their home nation, but still, there's work to be done as
another waits to be broken out on permanent probation.

              KUSHNER sobs loudly.

                           COHEN
                     (shouting out)
Oh, great. And now he's crying again. Can't a felon get no
peace around these parts?

                          NARRATOR
For in a cell sits crying advisor Jared Kushner, and for
company, former lawyer Michael Cohen. The earlier here for
refusing to talk the truth about Trump, which all know he
is all-knowing.

                              The NARRATOR exits as other
                              voices begin to come from the
                              opposite wing.

                       HANNITY (OFF)
I think we just have to take a left here, Mister President.
And then this should be the corridor to the cells.

                        TRUMP (OFF)
Okay, Sean Hannity. So, here is my great plan.
                         (beat)
Donald Trump Junior, tell us what my great plan is.

                       JUNIOR (OFF)
Okay, so here is what is going to happen. Dad, Sean, you're
both going to try the door to the cell and use strength to
break it down. I'm going to go up into the ceiling and then
lower myself down into the cell from above.

                                              (CONTINUED)

CONTINUED:

                              ERIC (OFF)
I'm going to push this button.

                         Flashing lights and alarms fill
                         the stage.

                              JUNIOR (OFF)
Turn it off.

                         The lights and alarms stop.

                              TRUMP (OFF)
Donald Trump Junior, take Eric Trump with you.

                              JUNIOR (OFF)
Fine. But keep Ivanka with you.

                              TRUMP (OFF)
Okay.

                         Offstage there is the sound of
                         movement followed by silence.

                              HANNITY (OFF)
Hold on, Mister President. I think I've found the light
switch.

                              TRUMP (OFF)
How do you know, Sean Hannity?

                         The stage lights up.

                              HANNITY
Because it turned the lights on.

                              COHEN
                         (shouting out)
Hey, what's going on? I don't remember asking for no light.

                         HANNITY, IVANKA and TRUMP enter.

                         Noticing KUSHNER, IVANKA runs up
                         to the bars of the cell as he
                         looks up at her.

                                              (CONTINUED)

CONTINUED:

                    IVANKA
                 (lovingly)
Jared.

                         KUSHNER stands and approaches
                         IVANKA. For a moment, they gaze
                         into each other's eyes.

                    IVANKA
You are honored to be broken out of jail by my father
today.

                    TRUMP
                 (to HANNITY)
Do we really need Jared Kushner?

                         KUSHNER reaches into his pocket
                         and pulls out paper and a pen,
                         which he uses to begin writing.

                    HANNITY
I think so, Mister President. We've come this far.

                         KUSHNER hands the paper to
                         IVANKA.

                    IVANKA
                 (reading)
"I love you, Ivanka. But your father tricked me and told me
to wait for him in the Oval Office."
                 (to KUSHNER)
Oh, that is just my father's sense of humor.
                 (reading)
"The F-B-I came looking for him so they could ask him some
questions. Instead, they arrested me because I wouldn't
talk."

                         COHEN stands and approaches.

                    COHEN
You know, speaking of questions, I've got a few. What are
you all doing here? I don't want to be involved with you
guys no more.
                    (MORE)

                                              (CONTINUED)

                          COHEN (CONT'D)
Also, does anyone know what time they're bringing the snack
cart around? I'd love some potato chips right about now.

                          TRUMP
                       (to HANNITY)
Sean Hannity, who is this man?

                          HANNITY
It's Michael Cohen, Mister President. He was your lawyer.

                    TRUMP turns to COHEN.

                          TRUMP
I do not know you. I have never met you.

                          COHEN
I know you, though, boss. You're a bad man.

                          HANNITY
                       (to TRUMP)
We should be getting on with breaking Jared out before a
guard comes along.

                              TRUMP attempts to open the cell
                              door, but it doesn't open.

                          TRUMP
It is not opening, Sean Hannity. It must be rigged.

                              TRUMP tries once more, this time
                              with more force. Failing again,
                              he watches HANNITY walk over and
                              open it easily on his first try.

                          TRUMP
Close the door, Sean Hannity.

                              HANNITY closes the door.

                              TRUMP grabs the handle and leans
                              against the door. It opens, and
                              he falls forward into the cell.

                                              (CONTINUED)

CONTINUED:

                         TRUMP
That was easy.

                         COHEN
It's supposed to be easy. It's so the guards can get in if
they need to.

                                   From the top of the stage,
                                   JUNIOR begins to be lowered into
                                   the cell on a rope.

                         JUNIOR
Any luck on that side?

                         TRUMP
I have got it open, Donald Trump Junior.

                                   JUNIOR reaches the ground and
                                   unties himself from the rope.

                         JUNIOR
                      (shouting up)
Hey, buddy, father's got it open. You can come down now.

                         ERIC (OFF)
Okay.

                         JUNIOR
                      (to TRUMP)
So, how did you do it, dad?

                         TRUMP
I used great skill and great strength.

                                   At the top of the stage, ERIC's
                                   head appears, followed by his
                                   body, as he is lowered upside
                                   down with his rope tied to just
                                   one ankle.

                         ERIC
Hey, Junior, all of my blood is rushing to my head. I'm
going to look like dad soon.

                                                     (CONTINUED)

CONTINUED:

                    TRUMP
You do not have any blood, Eric Trump.

                    ERIC
Hey, Junior, was I supposed to tie the other end of the
rope to something first?

                         Beat, and then ERIC falls the
                         final few feet before the other
                         end of the rope follows.

                    TRUMP
Why is it so cold in here?

                    COHEN
There's an open window at the end of the corridor.

                    TRUMP
I know how to fix this.

                         TRUMP goes to close the door.

                    COHEN/ HANNITY/ IVANKA/ JUNIOR
NO!

                         KUSHNER holds up a piece of
                         paper with "NO!" written on it
                         as the door closes.

                    TRUMP
Why is it still cold?

                    COHEN
Because the cell is made out of metal bars with gaps in
between them.

                    TRUMP
We should just go somewhere warmer then.

                         TRUMP attempts to open the door
                         again but fails.

                    TRUMP
Why won't it open, Sean Hannity?

                                        (CONTINUED)
PERFORMANCE LICENSE EDITION   LICENSE # _ _ _ _ _ _ _ _

                        HANNITY
I think it only opens from the outside, Mister President.
                    (to JUNIOR)
Can we get out the way you came in?

                                JUNIOR pulls on the rope he was
                                lowered in on. It falls to the
                                ground.

                        JUNIOR
Eric, did you forget to tie the end of both ropes?

                                Beat, and then they all turn to
                                look at ERIC who is stuck with
                                his head in the bars.

                        ERIC
My head hurts.

ACT III, SCENE SIX | BACK IN THE OVAL OFFICE

                                A dark stage except for a single
                                centered spotlight into which
                                the NARRATOR enters.

                        NARRATOR
And so five become six as Kushner takes his place back in
the occult. But before plans can continue, they must return
to the White House for there is another with whom they all
must consult.

Further too, more old friends die hard, and they're ready
to return to fight the fight against each every nationwide
liberal at heart. While upon their mater's fleeing they
worried first for their own well-being, with the
President's return now so imminent --

                                MIKE PENCE enters wearing a
                                leather jacket and carrying a
                                carton of milk.

                                                    (CONTINUED)

                         PENCE
Mister President, I'm back, sir. I have the milk you asked
for.

                                   PENCE notices the NARRATOR is
                                   alone.

                         PENCE
Oh, is the President not here?

                         NARRATOR
He's not got back yet.

                         PENCE
I'll come back soon then.

                         NARRATOR
Where have you been?

                         PENCE
I went to fetch some milk

                         NARRATOR
For a month?

                         PENCE
It's good milk.

                                   PENCE turns to exit, revealing
                                   as he does that the back of his
                                   jacket is embossed with an "I
                                   LOVE VEGAS" slogan.

                                   As PENCE exits, the NARRATOR
                                   turns their attention back to
                                   the audience.

                         NARRATOR
While upon their master's fleeing, they worried first for
their own well-being, with the President's return now so
imminent, so are loyalties and a following ever equally non-
discriminant.

                                             (CONTINUED)

                              THE NARRATOR exits as lights go
                              up on the OVAL OFFICE, where
                              PUTIN sits alone with his feet
                              up on the desk.

                              To one side stands a large crate
                              covered in mailing stickers.

                              ERIC, HANNITY, IVANKA, JUNIOR,
                              KUSHNER, and TRUMP enter.

                    TRUMP
Who would ever have thought that a get out of jail free
card would have actually worked?

                    JUNIOR
You know, it's lucky that those guards had lost the one
from their set.

                              PUTIN stands and approaches.

                    PUTIN
                  (drawn out)
Donald...

                              TRUMP flinches as PUTIN hugs
                              him.

                    PUTIN
It be good to have you back. Now dance for Putin.

                    TRUMP
I do not want to dance.

                    PUTIN
I said dance.

                              TRUMP begins to dance on the
                              spot.

                    PUTIN
It be just like old time. You can stop now.

                              TRUMP stops dancing.

                                              (CONTINUED)
PERFORMANCE LICENSE EDITION   LICENSE # _ _ _ _ _ _ _ _

                              PUTIN
                          (to HANNITY)
You did work good.

                              HANNITY
Thank you, Comrade Putin, sir.

                              PUTIN
                          (to TRUMP)
So, Donald. With you back, I think it be time that we
increase moves to take control of all America, no?

                         PUTIN returns to the desk.

                              TRUMP
I thought I made the decisions around here?

                                   As he sits, PUTIN shakes his
                                   head.

                              PUTIN
No.
                          (to HANNITY)
Sean, go back to Fox News and wait for instruction.

                              HANNITY
Yes, sir.

                              HANNITY bows and exits.

                              IVANKA
                          (to PUTIN)
Daddy, can Jared and I have some free time to catch up?

                              TRUMP
Of --

                              PUTIN
                          (to IVANKA)
Yes, you may.

                                   TRUMP looks at PUTIN and then to
                                   IVANKA.

                                                      (CONTINUED)

                         TRUMP
I though that --

                    IVANKA and KUSHNER exit.

                         PUTIN
Now, Donald. Before we get down to business.
                    (gesturing at the crate)
This package came for you earlier.

                    TRUMP approaches the crate.

                         TRUMP
What is it?

                         PUTIN
It be big box. But I hear voices from inside earlier.

                         TRUMP
                    (to crate)
Hello.

                    A beat, and then a muffled voice
                    comes from within the crate.

                    CONWAY (IN CRATE)
Mister Trump, is that you?

                         TRUMP
                    (to crate)
Hello.

                    PUTIN grabs a crowbar from under
                    the desk and uses it on the
                    crate. The front falls open to
                    reveal KELLYANNE CONWAY stuck
                    upside down.

                         PUTIN
I not be expecting that.

                         CONWAY
Is it safe to come out now?

                                        (CONTINUED)
PERFORMANCE LICENSE EDITION   LICENSE # _ _ _ _ _ _ _ _

                          PUTIN
It be safe.

                    CONWAY falls out of the crate.

                          CONWAY
                       (standing up)
I got your note, Mister Trump.

                          TRUMP
Hello, Kellyanne Conway.

                          CONWAY
Mister President. I am ready to serve at your pleasure once
more.

                    CONWAY goes to bow but loses her
                    balance and falls over.

                          PUTIN
Perhaps she need moment.

                          JUNIOR
You know, I was expecting something more impressive.

                          PUTIN
What do you want Putin to do? Put her back in box and rig
door with firework for second opening? Order parade? No.
Kellyanne got left behind so got shipped because ride share
app not go that far. What you expect? She came out of box
because box be what she in. It be simple.

                          TRUMP
But --

                          PUTIN
Donald. Shut up.

                    Approaching footsteps come from
                    offstage.

                          PUTIN
We all need hide. Now.

                                              (CONTINUED)

                              All panicking, CONWAY returns to
                              the crate as JUNIOR goes to hide
                              behind a curtain, and ERIC moves
                              to the wall and sticks a nearby
                              lampshade on his head.

                    TRUMP
What do I do?

                    PUTIN
Come here.

                              TRUMP joins PUTIN at the desk,
                              the later pushing the button for
                              them to swivel around.

                              MUELLER enters and looks around.

                    MUELLER
                  (to himself)
It seems different in here. I'm sure I just heard voices
too. And there is something funny in the air.
                  (sniffing)
The smell of cheap cologne, fried chicken, South East
Florida, and the third cubicle along in the bathroom of a
Tuscaloosa fast food place at closing on the day of a kid's
birthday party.

                              MUELLER walks over to a window
                              and opens the curtain next to
                              the one where JUNIOR is hidden.

                    MUELLER
Why's it so dark in here?

                              MUELLER looks over and points at
                              the lampshade on ERIC's head.

                    MUELLER
Someone should get that light looked at. I've never seen
one looking so dim.

                              MUELLER takes a final look
                              around.

                                        (CONTINUED)

                         MUELLER
Well, it doesn't look like there's any Trumps in here. I'll
try the fast-food restaurants.

                         MUELLER exits.

                         They wait for a moment before
                         coming out from their hiding
                         places. ERIC walks forward with
                         the lampshade stuck on his head.

                         ERIC
Can I get some help here?

                         JUNIOR
I'm coming, buddy.

                         JUNIOR goes to help ERIC.

                         TRUMP
                         (to PUTIN)
How long has the desk done that?

                         PUTIN
Ever since you leave. I had feature put in so I can easily
hide when people come with question.

                         TRUMP
Can I have a go?

                         PUTIN
If you must.

                         TRUMP pushes the button on the
                         desk, and he and PUTIN swivel.

                         TRUMP (OFF)
I want to get one of these.

                         They swivel back.

                         PUTIN
This be yours.

                                                    (CONTINUED)

                    TRUMP
I want to press it again.

                    PUTIN
Donald.

                              TRUMP presses the button again,
                              and they swivel back out of
                              sight. A moment later, they
                              return. TRUMP presses it again,
                              and again, and again.

                    PUTIN
DONALD!

                              The next time the desk comes
                              back around, PUTIN and TRUMP are
                              replaced by CLINTON.

                    CLINTON
Ah. Ha. Ha. Ha. I told you. I told you that it would
happen, and none of you believed me. But here I am. My
rightful home. Hillary Rodham Clinton in the Oval Office.
This is how it should be. I have dreamt of this moment. I
am the Presid --

                              The desk swivels back to PUTIN
                              and TRUMP.

                    CLINTON (OFF)
No. This is my moment.

                              The desk swivels back to CLINTON
                              and then back and forth between
                              her and PUTIN and TRUMP before
                              stopping on CLINTON.

                    CLINTON
No one can take this moment away from me.

                              The desk swivels back...

                                                  (CONTINUED)

CONTINUED:

                         CLINTON
                      (disappearing)
          Oh. It turns out they can.

                              ... this time to TRUMP and PENCE
                              who still holding the milk.

                              Beat.

                         PENCE
          I got that milk you asked me to fetch, Mister President.

                              PENCE and TRUMP stand and move
                              to one side.

                              The desk swivels once more, and
                              PUTIN returns.

                         PUTIN
          You know, I think that desk really need putting on slower
          setting.

                         TRUMP
                       (to PENCE)
          It is good to see you again, Mike Pence.

                         PENCE
          I have missed you, Mister President, sir.

                         PUTIN
          Okay, yes. There be time to catch up later. We have work
          now.

                         PENCE
          I do apologize. Do continue.

                              PUTIN moves back to the desk.

                         PUTIN
          Good. So, I be thinking. We need effort to secure way of
          ensuring our regime continue for long-term.

                         PENCE
          What did you have in mind, Comrade?

                                             (CONTINUED)

                          PUTIN
Supreme Court. It be time we get a new pick for Donald
before he be impeached.

                          PENCE
But there isn't a vacancy?

                          PUTIN
Oh. Not worry about small matter like that. Putin has plan
for that. Putin always have plan.
                    (to TRUMP)
Donald, I have other work I must do now. But before I
leave, dance one more time for Putin.

                          TRUMP

I do not want to dance.

                          PUTIN

I said dance.

                              TRUMP performs a short dance on
                              the spot.

                          PUTIN

Such good value.

                              PUTIN presses the button on the
                              desk, and he disappears to be
                              replaced by the NARRATOR.

                          NARRATOR
                    (walking forward)
And so back together are Trump and friends ready to stamp
down more authority, all with the aid of Putin's new plan
for further control now being an administration priority.

But playing most on the mind of Donald and the rest, a
problem to which half can now attest. For an insecure
border is what they believe sits on the country's southern
end, but luckily for the President, it is a matter to which
Mike Pence and Kellyanne Conway have plans to attend.

                          The NARRATOR exits.

                                                   (CONTINUED)

                         PENCE
Mister President, sir, you may remember, before your
departure, you were discussing ways to secure the border.

                         TRUMP
I want to build a great big wall, Mike Pence.

                         PENCE
Well, sir, Kellyanne Conway and I would like to show you
some prototypes that we were working on before you left.

                         TRUMP
Did Mexico pay for them?

                         PENCE
No. They said they wouldn't.

                         TRUMP
Then who did pay for them?

                         CONWAY
No one paid for them, Mister President. We paid ourselves.

                         TRUMP
I cannot have that, Kellyanne Conway. If Mexico refuses to
pay for them, then someone else should.
                    (to JUNIOR)
Donald Trump Junior, did you pay any tax last year?

                         JUNIOR
No. Not me.

                         TRUMP
Eric Trump, did you pay any tax last year?

                         ERIC
I run away before they can tell me what the fare is.

                         TRUMP
Mike Pence, did you pay any tax last year?

                         PENCE
I am officially a church for tax purposes, sir.

                                              (CONTINUED)

                         TRUMP
Kellyanne Conway, did you pay any tax last year?

                         CONWAY
Yes, I did.

                         TRUMP
I need to borrow money.

                         CONWAY
How much do you need?

                         TRUMP
I'll check.
                    (to PENCE)
Mike Pence, how much did you and Kellyanne Conway spend to
build the wall?

                         PENCE
Ten thousand dollars, sir.

                         TRUMP
                    (to CONWAY)
Kellyanne Conway, I need to borrow twenty thousand dollars.

                         CONWAY
Sure thing, Mister President.

                              CONWAY pulls a checkbook out of
                              her pocket, writes a check and
                              hands it to TRUMP.

                         CONWAY
Just make sure I get it back.

                              TRUMP rips the check in two and
                              pockets one half.

                         TRUMP
                    (to PENCE)
Mike Pence, I have found someone to give you ten thousand
dollars to cover the wall.

                                             (CONTINUED)
PERFORMANCE LICENSE EDITION   LICENSE # _ _ _ _ _ _ _ _

                          PENCE
That is very kind of you, Mister President.

                              TRUMP hands PENCE the other half
                              of the check.

                          PENCE
And here is your five thousand dollars, Kellyanne.

                              PENCE rips the half check in two
                              and hands one piece to CONWAY.

                          CONWAY
You're very kind, Mike.

                          TRUMP
Now show me these walls.

                          PENCE
Kellyanne, could you fetch the first prototype, please?

                              CONWAY exits.

                          PENCE
So this is our first idea, Mister Trump.

                              CONWAY enters pulling along a
                              wooden fence, with a door in the
                              middle, mounted on wheels.

                          TRUMP
What is it, Mike Pence?

                          PENCE
It is a wooden fence, Mister President.

                          JUNIOR
It's got a door in the middle of it.

                          TRUMP
Why has it got a door in the middle of it?

                                                    (CONTINUED)

                         CONWAY
The door is there so that we can open it to kick all of the
bad people out of our country.

                         JUNIOR
But doesn't that mean that bad people can also come into
the country?

                         PENCE
I offer you my assurances, the door does not allow any --

                              The door opens, and the NARRATOR
                              walks through.

                         PENCE
Kellyanne, I think that we may have to reconsider the
wooden fence.

                              CONWAY exits with the fence.

                         NARRATOR
Ever predictable was the failure of Conway and Pence's
first wooden attempt, but no matter, for a second they have
with far fewer splinters, though with a chance of growing
unkempt.

                              The NARRATOR exits as CONWAY
                              enters pulling along a large
                              hedge on wheels.

                         PENCE
This is our second idea.

                         TRUMP
What is it?

                         PENCE
It is a hedge, Mister President.

                         CONWAY
We are proposing to build a border hedge. It's a more
environmentally friendly option.

                                                   (CONTINUED)

CONTINUED:

                         TRUMP
I do not like environmentally friendly, Kellyanne Conway.

                         JUNIOR
Could we get it made out of plastic in China?

                         CONWAY
Yes, we could. And look at the benefits of the design.
There is no door.

                                   The NARRATOR enters with a
                                   chainsaw which they use to cut
                                   through the hedge.

                         PENCE
I'm not so sure about the hedge, Kellyanne. Bring out our
third idea.

                                   CONWAY exits with the hedge.

                         NARRATOR
Green though it may be, their second idea fails to show
bloom, while even for their third that waits in the wings,
even there for improvements, there still exists room.

                                   The NARRATOR exits as CONWAY
                                   enters pulling along a brick
                                   wall on wheels.

                         PENCE
And this is our third idea, Mister President.

                         CONWAY
It's brick. Solid brick. No door and no way to cut through.

                                   The NARRATOR enters with a
                                   ladder which they use to climb
                                   to the top of the wall.

                         PENCE
We forgot about ladders, Mister President.

                                   The NARRATOR climbs back down.

                                                  (CONTINUED)

                          PENCE
Kellyanne, do you have our fourth prototype ready?

                          CONWAY
It's ready.

                              CONWAY exits with the brick
                              wall.

                          NARRATOR
And so even solid brick is not a solution that is bestowed
by Trump an honored tick. But one final idea they have
ready to show, and it's one that can be painful for those
who get close without the know.

                              CONWAY enters pulling along an
                              electric fence on wheels.

                          PENCE
Now this, Mister President. This is an electric fence.

                          CONWAY
                        (to the NARRATOR)
Go on. Try your metal chainsaw or your metal ladder now.

                              The NARRATOR approaches the
                              fence with caution.

                          NARRATOR
Eric, come here.

                              ERIC walks over to the NARRATOR,
                              who whispers in his ear.

                          ERIC
Okay.

                              ERIC closes his eyes, sticks out
                              his tongue, and then moves
                              slowly closer toward the fence.

                              The entire room goes dark with a
                              loud ban.

                                                    (CONTINUED)

CONTINUED:

                    ERIC (IN DARKNESS)
You said it tasted like candy.

                    NARRATOR
                  (to CONWAY)
No, it works.

                    TRUMP
Mike Pence, Kellyanne Conway, this is a very good idea. But
it needs one small change to make it a very great idea.

                    PENCE
What do you suggest, Mister President?

                    TRUMP
Electric is for liberals. They are not so smart. But I am
smart. I do not want electric. I want coal.

                    Beat.

                    PENCE
You want a coal fence?

                    TRUMP
Correct.

                    PENCE
Kellyanne?

                    CONWAY
                  (to TRUMP)
Sir, I'm not sure that what you're suggesting would
actually be possible.

                    TRUMP
Make it possible.

                         CONWAY and PENCE look at each
                         other for a brief moment.

                    PENCE
We will try our best, Mister President.

                                              (CONTINUED)

                         TRUMP
Good. Now I need to go on executive time. There are a lot
of important things I need to do.
                    (to JUNIOR)
Donald Trump Junior, take Eric Trump for a walk so that he
can go toilet.
                    (to CONWAY)
Kellyanne Conway, go and make me a coal fence.
                    (to PENCE)
Mike Pence.

                         PENCE
I'm at your service, sir.

                              CONWAY exits with the electric
                              fence as ERIC, JUNIOR, and the
                              NARRATOR follow.

                         TRUMP
I need you to go and mail a letter for me.

                              TRUMP picks up a small golden
                              envelope from the desk.

                         TRUMP
This is for my good friend, Kim Jong-Un.

                              TRUMP hands PENCE the envelope.

                         TRUMP
The envelope is not small. My hands are just <u>huge</u>.

                         PENCE
I will make sure that this gets where it needs to go,
Mister President.

                         TRUMP
Good job, Mike Pence.

                         PENCE
And what are you going to be doing, sir?

                                             (CONTINUED)

CONTINUED:

                         TRUMP
I have to prepare for the G-Seven, Mike Pence. But first, I
have a very important meeting.

                         PENCE
I will leave you to it then, sir.

                              PENCE bows and exits as TRUMP
                              sits at the desk and reaches for
                              the phone.

                         TRUMP
                       (on phone)
Can you fetch my lawyer's checkbook?

                              Beat, and then the room goes
                              dark once more with another loud
                              bang.

                         ERIC (OFF)
Ouch.

ACT III, SCENE SEVEN | JUSTICE KENNEDY

                              A spotlight shines upon a BUS
                              STOP in the middle of the stage
                              where JUSTICE KENNEDY stands
                              waiting alone.

                         NARRATOR
                       (entering)
And so as for all new tasks are set, it falls to Putin to
ensure a way for a preferable Supreme Court quota soon to
be met. And so he follows for multiple days until comes the
chance to convince another to do as he says.

                              The NARRATOR exits as a man
                              wearing a hood enters and stands
                              behind KENNEDY.

                         PUTIN (UNDER HOOD)
Pst. Psssst. Hey.

                                             (CONTINUED)

>   KENNEDY starts as he turns to
>   see the man lowering his hood to
>   reveal they are PUTIN.

                    KENNEDY
Oh. Vladimir. I didn't see you there.

                    PUTIN
I need have word with you.

                    KENNEDY
What do you mean have a word with me? I haven't done
anything wrong. I've done everything you've asked me to.

                    PUTIN
I need you resign seat on Supreme Court.

                    KENNEDY
Why would you want me to do that? I'm on your side

                    PUTIN
Because investigation continue and Donald likely to be
impeached soon. We have short time to secure court for
years that come.

                    KENNEDY
But I'm not that old. And I like my job.

>   PUTIN pulls several photos from
>   his pocket.

                    PUTIN
                (showing first photo)
See this? This --

                    KENNEDY
That's me.

                    PUTIN
                (showing second photo)
Good. Now, this. This be photo of man doing unspeakable
thing to warthog at local zoo.

                                        (CONTINUED)

                         KENNEDY
I don't get what you... Hold on, isn't that --

                         PUTIN
Yes, it be him. But we must not say, or he may sue.
                    (showing third photo)
This be activation key for well known photo editing
software package for P-C and other platform.

                    KENNEDY takes the photo.

                         PUTIN
We make multiple copy.

                         Beat.

                         KENNEDY
I'll resign my seat.

ACT III, SCENE EIGHT | THE G7 SUMMIT

                              The MANOIR RICHELIEU hotel in LA
                              MALBAIE, CANADA, where TRUMP
                              sits at a table at the back of
                              the stage while EMMANUEL MACRON
                              and ANGELA MERKEL stand to
                              confront him.

                         NARRATOR
                         (entering)
While for the President at home, the future looks to be
ever increasingly bleak, on the international stage, he
sees new opportunities and foreign policies ready for his
own unique Trump brand tweak.

                         MERKEL
                         (to TRUMP)
For the last time, Donald. Stop asking that man if you can
see the menu. He is the Prime Minister of Italy.

                                             (CONTINUED)

                          TRUMP
He was very rude to me, Angled Mackerel. I ordered a diet
cola from him over an hour ago, and he has still not
brought it to me.

                          NARRATOR
For leaving behind an investigation ongoing, it is to the
forty-fifth G-Seven summit in Quebec where he flies so he
can undertake some world leader elbowing.

                          MACRON
                        (to TRUMP)
He is not a waiter. And that woman who you asked security
to move along because she was sat on the floor crying, that
was Theresa May.

                          NARRATOR
For this is where gather the leader of the world's greatest
nations together all in one place, and their host for the
summit, a Prime Minister who many believe has the most
beautiful face.

                              JUSTIN TRUDEAU enters and shakes
                              hands with the NARRATOR.

                          TRUDEAU
Oh, hello. Welcome to Canada. Do you like my socks?
                        (showing off his socks)
You've got your very own pair in your hotel room. They come
with our compliments.

                              At the back of the stage, MERKEL
                              notices TRUDEAU.

                          MERKEL
                        (to MACRON)
Oh, Emmanuel, Justin is here.

                              MACRON turns around as TRUDEAU
                              approaches and shakes hands.

                          TRUDEAU
Welcome to Canada as our honored guests. It's good to see
you again, Chancellor Merkel. And you too President Macron.

                                              (CONTINUED)

                    TRUMP coughs loudly.

                    TRUDEAU
                  (to TRUMP)
Oh, I'm sorry. Would you like something for that cough
you've got there, Donald?

                    MACRON
                  (to TRUDEAU)
Thank you for the socks, Prime Minister. France thanks you
very much for your nation's kind generosity.

                    TRUDEAU
Oh, please. Call me Justin.

                    MERKEL
Can I call you Justin as well?

                    TRUMP coughs again.

                    TRUDEAU
                  (to TRUMP)
Are you certain I can't get you anything for that cough
there, Donald?

                    MACRON
                  (to TRUDEAU)
It really is a spectacular event that you are hosting for
us all here. I can only hope that we are able to live up to
the same next year.

                    TRUDEAU
Oh merci. Ce n'est vraiment rien du tout. Je suis sûr que
la France en fera plus qu'assez et j'ai hâte d'avoir
l'honneur d'être en votre présence lors de l'accueil de
l'année prochaine.

                    Beat.

                    MERKEL
                  (to herself)
Oh. He speaks French too.
                  (to TRUDEAU)
Can I have your autograph?

                                        (CONTINUED)

                         TRUDEAU
                        (laughing)
I don't do autographs. But how about we all get a photo
together?

                              TRUDEAU walks over to the
                              NARRATOR and hands them his
                              phone.

                         TRUDEAU
Do you mind?

                         NARRATOR
Not at all.

                              TRUDEAU leads MACRON and MERKEL
                              to the center of the stage.

                         TRUDEAU
Just here, I think.

                              As they get into position, TRUMP
                              stands, approaches from behind,
                              and pushes his way to the front.

                         TRUMP
America first.

                         NARRATOR
And three... two... one...

                              A flash fills the stage as
                              MACRON, MERKEL, and TRUDEAU all
                              pull faces behind TRUMP.

                              TRUMP turns around as they start
                              to laugh.

                         TRUMP
What is so funny?

                         MERKEL
Oh, nothing.

                                                    (CONTINUED)
PERFORMANCE LICENSE EDITION   LICENSE # _ _ _ _ _ _ _ _

CONTINUED:

                          MACRON
Let's take another.

                                        They get into position for a
                                        second photo.

                          NARRATOR
Three... two... one...

                                        Again, a flash as MACRON,
                                        MERKEL, and TRUDEAU all pull
                                        faces.

                          TRUDEAU
One more. For the memories

                          NARRATOR
Three... two... one...

                                        Another flash as MACRON, MERKEL,
                                        and TRUDEAU once more all pull
                                        faces.

                          NARRATOR
I'm not sure I quite got it that time. I'll try again.
Three... two... one...

                                        Another flash and MACRON,
                                        MERKEL, and TRUDEAU pull faces
                                        before MERKEL rushes forward
                                        with her own phone.

                          MERKEL
Can you take one on my phone too?

                                        The NARRATOR takes her phone as
                                        MERKEL rushes back into place.

                          MERKEL
Oh, I do love my job sometimes.

                          TRUDEAU
Now, lunch, I think?

                                                        (CONTINUED)
PERFORMANCE LICENSE EDITION   LICENSE # _ _ _ _ _ _ _ _

                         MACRON
It would be an honor to dine with you, Prime Minister.

                                   TRUDEAU gestures toward the
                                   wings.

                         TRUDEAU
After you then, Mister President. Chancellor Merkel.

                                   MACRON, MERKEL, and TRUDEAU go
                                   to leave.

                         TRUMP
Where are you all going? I demand that you stay.
                    (noticing the NARRATOR)
Just you and me, huh?

                         NARRATOR
I'm contractually obliged to be here.

ACT III, SCENE NINE | TRUMP MEETS THE QUEEN

                                   The NARRATOR remains on stage.

                         NARRATOR
And so was between Trudeau and Co the real discussions are
set to begin, a surprise is to await them for when they all
next awake from their hotel bed, for Donald J. Trump has
departed early to meet with a different world leader
instead.

Setting off on Air Force One to fly thousands of miles
across the sea, for that is where his next bilateral
meeting is set to be. With a dictator, a tyrant, that's the
term that some place, debatable, perhaps, but still it
rings true that their power comes solely through a family
trace.

This is why the President is so excited to greet a ruler
whom when many meet, they bow right down to her feet, and
with whom he seeks to get a photo to post with his tweet.
                         (MORE)

                                                  (CONTINUED)

CONTINUED:

NARRATOR (CONT'D)

And so it's lucky for him that efforts have failed to have
him from the country banned, for it means that still he
gets his chance to meet the Queen of England.

                         The NARRATOR exits as lights go
                         up on a ROOM WITHIN BUCKINGHAM
                         PALACE, where PRINCE CHARLES and
                         PRINCE PHILIP sit halfway
                         through a game of chess.

                    CHARLES

Check.

                         PHILIP leans into the board.

                    PHILIP

I am checking.

                         THE QUEEN enters looking angry.

                    THE QUEEN

Whose bloody idea was it for me to meet with that orange
turd from our former colony?
                    (to CHARLES)
Charlie, is this your idea of a joke?

                    CHARLES

The Prime Minister called and asked if we could host him
for a day. I had to say yes, mummy. I did not know what
else I could have said.

                    THE QUEEN

You could have said that we were going out? We could still
say that we are going out, could we not?

                    CHARLES

Not really, mummy. They are due to arrive at any moment.

                    THE QUEEN

Any moment? Oh, bugger the biscuit corgis! I have not had
any time to lock away the crown jewels.

                         PHILIP makes a move on the
                         chessboard.

                                        (CONTINUED)

                         PHILIP
                      (to CHARLES)
Check.

                         CHARLES
                     (to THE QUEEN)
It will all be okay, mummy. He is only here for one day.

                         CHARLES goes to make a move.

                         THE QUEEN
Charlie, if you dare that that queen, then I shall have you
sent to the Tower of London.

                         CHARLES
Oh. Well, I --

                         PHILIP
I think that is checkmate to me then, old boy. Bad luck
indeed.

                         THE QUEEN
                      (to CHARLES)
Bollock the scone swan! This is not going to be okay,
Charlie. You are not the one who will have to inform the
butler to clean up after him. I dare not think how long it
will take them to cover the scent.

                         CHARLES checks the board.

                         CHARLES
                      (to PHILIP)
Hold on, why do you have three kings?

                         PHILIP
I inherited them.

                         THE QUEEN
Chuff the afternoon finger sandwich! Will you stop playing
games? You are going to come with me right this moment and
help me greet him, Charlie.

                         CHARLES
Do I have to, mummy?

                                              (CONTINUED)

CONTINUED:

                         THE QUEEN
Who is Queen?

                         PHILIP
She has got you there.

                         THE QUEEN
I do not know why you are looking as though your fifty to
one came in at Ascott. You are coming too. You have much
more in common with him than I do.

                         PHILIP
Do I have to?

                         THE QUEEN
Who is Queen?

                         PHILIP
Bugger.

                         Lights fade on the scene as the
                         NARRATOR returns.

                         NARRATOR
Reluctant though all are to meet for the first time their
transatlantic head of state counterpart - a man whose name
in this country at least means simply a fart - they know
they have a diplomatic duty to fulfill, one that comes with
a rare opportunity for the most offensive in the room not
to be old Prince Phil.

                         The NARRATOR exits as the lights
                         go back up, this time on the
                         BUCKINGHAM PALACE VISITORS
                         ENTRANCE where a GUARD stands.

                         ERIC, dressed as a tourist,
                         enters and approaches the guard.

                         ERIC
Hey. You're wearing a hat. I want a hat.

                         ERIC reaches for the GUARD's
                         hat.

                                             (CONTINUED)

> GUARD

SIR, STAND BACK! DO NOT TOUCH THE QUEEN'S GUARD.

> ERIC
> (upset)

I don't want a hat anymore.

>> TRUMP enters with IVANKA and
>> JUNIOR, the latter two also
>> dressed as tourists.
>>
>> JUNIOR rushes to ERIC.

> JUNIOR

Hey, buddy. What's up?

> ERIC
> (pointing at the GUARD)

That man.

>> JUNIOR confronts the GUARD.

> JUNIOR

Hey, bud, what do you think you're doing to my little
brother?

> GUARD

DO NOT QUESTION THE QUEEN'S GUARD.

>> TRUMP steps forward.

> TRUMP
> (to JUNIOR)

Let me negotiate this, Donald Trump Junior.
> (to the GUARD)

Let us in.

> GUARD

YOU WISH TO ENTER THE PALACE?

> TRUMP

Yes.

(CONTINUED)

                          GUARD
                      (changed tone)
In which case, welcome to the official Buckingham Palace
tour. Please note that all visitors and their bags will be
required to undergo a security search. Do you have your
tickets, please?

                          TRUMP
I am here to see the Queen of not so Great Britain.

                          GUARD
You are not permitted to visit the Queen as part of the
tour, sir.

                          TRUMP
Why not?

                          GUARD
Because she is the Queen, sir.

                          TRUMP
I was told that if I came here, then I would get to meet
the Queen.

                          GUARD
Sir, this is a tour. You get to see where the Queen lives,
and you get a free pencil at the end, but you do not get to
meet the Queen herself.

                              THE QUEEN enters with CHARLES
                              and PHILIP.

                        THE QUEEN
Gob-smack the kerfuffled pork pie! That Fanta-colored
flatulent fascist fornicator has already arrived.

                          TRUMP
                      (to the GUARD)
I hereby demand --

                          GUARD
STEP BACK, SIR, OR I SHALL HAVE TO REMOVE YOU BY FORCE.

                              THE QUEEN approaches.

                                             (CONTINUED)

> THE QUEEN

No. No. It is okay. He is the President of the United
States.

> GUARD

I know who he is, your majesty. Why do you think I am
trying to remove him?

> THE QUEEN

Very good point. But we do actually have to talk to him.
Even if he does look like a bloated pufferfish in need of
an enema.

> GUARD

If that is your wish, your majesty.

> THE QUEEN

No, of course, it is not my wish. Why would I wish for
this? And do not question your queen again, or I shall have
you arrest yourself for treason. Now, go away.

> GUARD

Of course, your majesty.

                    The GUARD bows and exits.

> THE QUEEN

So, you are Donald Trump, are you?

> TRUMP

Listen, old lady, no autographs right now. I am waiting to
see some old bat in some hat.

> ERIC

And I want a pencil.

> THE QUEEN

I am the Queen.
                    (to CHARLES and PHILIP)
Charlie. Philip. Come over and greet our guests with me.

                              TRUMP pulls out a five-pound
                              note and holds it next to THE
                              QUEEN's head.

                                             (CONTINUED)

CONTINUED:

                         TRUMP
You do not look like the Queen.

                       THE QUEEN
No? What about if I turn this way?

                              THE QUEEN turns her head to
                              match the direction on the note.

                         TRUMP
According to this, you are only worth five English dollars.
Did you know that I am worth billions and billions of
dollars?

                       THE QUEEN
                    (ignoring TRUMP)
Shall I introduce you?
                    (gesturing at CHARLES)
This is my son, Charles, or Charlie as I call him. He is
the Prince of Wales.

                       CHARLES
So very lovely to meet you all.

                         TRUMP
Let me introduce you to my very great son... Eric Trump,
get out of the way.

                              TRUMP pulls JUNIOR in front of
                              ERIC.

                         TRUMP
This is Donald Trump Junior. He is just like me, only he is
junior.

                              JUNIOR reaches to shake hands
                              with them all, and then TRUMP.

                        JUNIOR
You know, it really is nice to meet all of you today.

                         TRUMP
It is very nice to meet you too, Donald Trump Junior. Let
me introduce you to the Queen.

                                              (CONTINUED)

                         THE QUEEN
Quite.
                    (gesturing at PHILIP)
And this is my husband and Charlie's father, the --

                          TRUMP
                     (to PHILIP)
You must be the king of the seas.

                    Beat.

                         THE QUEEN
No. He is the Duke of Edinburgh. Knacker the stewed trouser
press, are you always this dim?

                              PHILIP steps forward to shake
                              hands with TRUMP.

                          PHILIP
The wife was telling me that you are a keen racist. We must
talk about that. I am also a racist in my spare time, you
know?

                          TRUMP
That is fake news, Mister Edinburgh. I am not a racist.

                          PHILIP
That is fake news, Mister Edinburgh. I am not a racist.

                          TRUMP
I do not hate foreigners for no reason like a racist would.

                          PHILIP
Well then, why do you hate them?

                          TRUMP
I hate them because I can.

                    Beat.

                          PHILIP
You really are some offensive old fellow, are you not? You
must give me some tips on that before you depart.

                                        (CONTINUED)

CONTINUED:

                              TRUMP brings IVANKA forward.

                         TRUMP
This is my daughter, Ivanka Trump.

                         IVANKA
You are all honored to meet me today.

                       THE QUEEN
                   (gesturing at ERIC)
And who is this young gentleman here?

                         TRUMP
That is Eric Trump. We have to bring him because...
                     (to JUNIOR)
Donald Trump Junior, why did we have to bring him?

                        JUNIOR
The babysitter canceled.

                       THE QUEEN
                     (to ERIC)
And tell me, young sir. Are you enjoying your visit to the
palace today?

                         ERIC
I saw a dog.

                       THE QUEEN
Well, gander at the antique fish pâte!

                        PHILIP
                     (to all)
That does remind me. I was in my study just the other
morrow reading the latest Bill O'Reilly when one of those
damned corgis came in and proceeded to take a massive dump
on the hearthrug. That is right, a massive ordure right in
front of me. And I had the fire on too. It did not half
cause the maid some trouble. The smell reminded me of that
time I had to visit Hull.

                       THE QUEEN
Philip.

                                            (CONTINUED)

                         PHILIP
Yes?

                         THE QUEEN
Do shut up.

                         PHILIP
Oh. Okay then.

                         THE QUEEN
                      (to CHARLES)
Charlie, why do not you take these three younger guests for
a tour of the palace?

                         CHARLES
I have an engagement in --

                         THE QUEEN
Do not make me cut your allowance again.

                         CHARLES
Yes, fine then.
                  (to JUNIOR, ERIC and IVANKA)
Do come this way.

                         CHARLES begins to lead ERIC,
                         IVANKA, and JUNIOR offstage.

                         CHARLES
So you are the President's children, are you?

                         ERIC
What kind of whale are you?

                         CHARLES
Sorry, what? I, oh...

                         CHARLES, ERIC, IVANKA, and
                         JUNIOR exit.

                         THE QUEEN
So, Mister Trump, I hear that you like to visit Scotland? I
have a place up there, do not you know?

                                              (CONTINUED)
PERFORMANCE LICENSE EDITION   LICENSE # _ _ _ _ _ _ _ _

                    TRUMP
Listen, Queenie. No one loves Scotland more than me, and
there is no one that Scotland loves more than Donald J.
Trump.

                    THE QUEEN
You will not get any disagreement from me. Why, do butter
the village bus stop! Half of them up there wish for me to
be abolished.

                    TRUMP
I have a golf course up there. Some say the best golf
course. I play golf. I play great. Do you play golf?

                    THE QUEEN
No. Not me personally. I have a man to do that for me.

                    TRUMP
You have a great place here.

                    THE QUEEN
Thank you very much. I inherited many of the objects you
can see.
                    (pointing at a painting)
Like this one here. My father was given it by Winston
Churchill himself.

                    PHILIP
It was told that Churchill used to have it hanging in his
office during the war.

                    THE QUEEN
                    (suddenly stern)
Anoint the palace cabbage patch! Philip, do not mention the
war.

                    PHILIP
Why not? He was on the same side as us.

                    THE QUEEN
No, he was not.

                    PHILIP
Oh, right.

                                              (CONTINUED)

                    THE QUEEN
                    (to TRUMP)
Mister Trump, would you like to come and see the palace
gardens? I can show you around, and then we could get a
photographer to take some photographs for the newsprint?

                    TRUMP
Good idea, Queenie. And then after that, we should talk
business.

                              THE QUEEN begins to exit with
                              PHILIP following.

                    TRUMP
I have some great ideas to turn this place into a hotel.

                              TRUMP barges past THE QUEEN and
                              exits first. A moment later, he
                              returns.

                    TRUMP
Which way is it?

                    THE QUEEN
Right and then left.

                    TRUMP
Thank you.

                         TRUMP exits again.

                    THE QUEEN
Bloody hell and waltz with the gardener's budgerigar. He
really is as stupid as he looks on the television.

                              PHILIP and THE QUEEN exit as the
                              lights go down.

ACT III, SCENE TEN | PUTIN IN THE BATH

> As the NARRATOR enters a dark
> stage, from somewhere behind
> them comes the sound of bathroom
> singing.

NARRATOR

A meeting with royalty is one never to be forgotten, but
equally as necessary for the President is a need to fix at
home the issue of the public for on the truth they begin to
cotton. And so it is back in the air for a short few hours
across the sea, for a meeting that's to take place in a
third and neutral ground country.

But while the press gathers downstairs to ask questions in
their pre-scheduled conference, in his Helsinki hotel room
sits Trump's rendezvous bathing to remove his feelings so
tense.

> A light shines upon the scene
> behind the NARRATOR, where PUTIN
> sits in a bubble bath singing to
> himself. After a moment, he
> stops singing and looks around.

PUTIN

Can I not get just little privacy here?

> PUTIN shakes his head and then
> reaches for a bath brush to wash
> his back.

NARRATOR

But while Vladimir Putin sits to use his brush to scratch
his back, there is a clear sense that privacy is the
commodity which right now he does lack.

PUTIN

Of course. Anyone can see that. Here I wash, and hundreds
of people be watching.

> As the NARRATOR exits, there is
> a loud knock.

(CONTINUED)

CONTINUED:

                         PUTIN
                    (shouting out)
What be it now? I am bathing.

                         There is another knock.

                         PUTIN
Fine. Come on in. But be quick.

                         DMITRY and PETROV enter with the
                         latter carrying a soccer ball.

                         DMITRY
Comrade Putin, sir.

                         PUTIN
You know, most world leaders be able to wash without
disturbance. What do you want?

                         PETROV
Our apologies, Comrade, sir. We do not mean to disturb, but
we bring news.

                         PUTIN
What news?

                         PETROV holds the ball out.

                         PETROV
Ball.

                         Beat.

                         PUTIN
I be missing something.

                         DMITRY
We fit camera and microphone as instructed, Comrade.

                         PUTIN
You came whole way here and disturb bath just so you be
able to tell me you put camera in ball?

                                                   (CONTINUED)

CONTINUED:

                         PETROV
And microphone, Comrade.

                         PUTIN
Could news not wait until after I bathe?

                         DMITRY
We thought you enjoy news right away, Comrade.

                         PUTIN
You two really be largest idiots in whole of Russia. If you
be American, you be in Senate by now.

                         PETROV
Comrade, if I can ask, why you need ball?

                         DMITRY
Did you not have idea to give Comrade Trump rubber duck for
same purpose?

                         PUTIN
Donald keep rubber duck in bathroom, and it not be sight
anyone should ever see.

                         DMITRY
I see.

                         PUTIN
No. You really do not want. That man fake tans in way not
fit for human audience.

                         PETROV
Is there anything else you need, Comrade?

                         PUTIN
Yes. I need you leave Putin to bathe. I have hair of mine
to wash.

                         DMITRY
But, Comrade, you do not --

                         PUTIN
Leave.

                                                    (CONTINUED)

CONTINUED:

> DMITRY and PETROV exit as PUTIN
> begins to sing once more.
>
> The lights fade.

ACT III, SCENE ELEVEN | HELSINKI

> Lights up on two podiums set out
> in front of the flags of the
> United States and Russia. In
> front of the podiums sits the
> ENSEMBLE (as PRESS, excluding
> PRESS #2).

                    NARRATOR
                 (entering)
Ready to stand and share confident the United States aims,
all while unabashedly furthering his string of provably
false claims, Donald Trump is the first to arrive, ready to
with Putin publicly beg, steal, and foremost contrive.

> TRUMP enters at the edge of the
> stage and stands typing on his
> phone.

                    NARRATOR
While now fully relaxed and ready for any question that may
lie ahead, Vladimir Putin is just moments behind, though
having forgotten what still sits atop his head.

> The NARRATOR exits as PUTIN
> enters by TRUMP wearing a
> flowery shower cap.

                    PUTIN
Donald. I be glad to have talk before press.

                    TRUMP
Hold on. I am just sending a tweet.
                 (to himself, reading)
"And the Queen was very mean to me. Sad. Very bad for her
people." And send.

                                        (CONTINUED)

                    TRUMP puts his phone away.

                         TRUMP
What is it, Comrade Vladimir Putin, sir?

                         PUTIN
I be worried members of your press ask question they should
not ask. Awkward question.

                         TRUMP
I do not understand.

                         PUTIN
About Russia. They ask about Russia. They think Russia had
hand in election win of yours.

                         TRUMP
But you did?

                         PUTIN
Actually, we had two hand, Donald. But point be they should
not know. You need tell them that Russia did not have
involvement in election.

                         TRUMP
Can you not deal with them?

                         PUTIN
There be laws against Russian approach in Finland.

                         TRUMP
So what do I do?

                         PUTIN
I just say. Tell them Russia had no part.

                         TRUMP
I understand.

                         PUTIN
Tell them you be sure of this.

                         TRUMP
I understand.

                                              (CONTINUED)

CONTINUED:

                         PUTIN
Good. Now let us go out there.

                                    PUTIN sets off toward the
                                    podiums.

                         TRUMP
I do not understand.

                                    PUTIN stops and turns back.

                         TRUMP
Why are you wearing a hat?

                         PUTIN
I be wearing nothing on head.

                         TRUMP
I can see it.

                         PUTIN
I wear nothing on head, Donald.
                         (beat)
Now come. And just do what I do.

                                    PUTIN and TRUMP make their way
                                    to their podiums.

                         PUTIN
                      (to PRESS)
Stand.
                      (beat)
No, really. When I enter room, you stand. Now. Stand. All
of you.

                                    The PRESS stand.

                         PUTIN
Good. Now sit.

                                  The PRESS sit.

                         PUTIN
Members of press, welcome.

                                          (CONTINUED)

>   PUTIN puts his arm out as though
>   to greet them. TRUMP copies him.

                         PUTIN
Welcome to Helsinki.

                         TRUMP
Welcome to Helsinki.

                         PUTIN
I be glad to have opportunity to speak with Donald today to
discuss ties between nation. And we be glad now to answer
question you have.

                         TRUMP
I am glad to have the opportunity to speak with Donald
Trump today to discuss the ties between our nations. And we
are glad to have this chance to answer any questions you
have.

>   PUTIN coughs. TRUMP copies him.

                         PUTIN
Donald. What are you doing?

                         TRUMP
Donald Trump. What are you doing?

                         PUTIN
DONALD!

                         TRUMP
You told me to do what you do.

                         PUTIN
Not everything I do.

>   PUTIN scratches an itch. TRUMP
>   copies him.

                         PUTIN
Just... Do not be weird.
                    (to PRESS)
Okay. Who has question?

                                          (CONTINUED)

CONTINUED:

                              The PRESS remains silent as
                              TRUMP pulls his phone back out.

                    PUTIN
No question at all? Not one?

                              The PRESS remain silent.

                    PUTIN
There be major news in your country about belief that
Russia hacked election and not one of you have question?

                    PRESS #1
We don't need to ask them. We already know you'll deny it,
and we already know what the President has to say

                    PUTIN
How could it be you know what Donald is to say? He answer
no question.

                    PRESS #6
              (holding up their phone)
He tweeted.
              (reading from phone)
"Just spoken to Vlad. Good meeting. He tells me that I must
tell you all Russia had no involvement in the election.
Dot. Dot. Dot" --

                    TRUMP
              (to himself, reading)
"Dot. Dot. Dot. And now I have to have press conference
with loser press. Total losers. Very sad." And tweet.

                    PUTIN
DONALD!

                              TRUMP looks up.

                    TRUMP
I was tweeting.

                    PUTIN
              (to PRESS)
Okay. Is there any question?

                                        (CONTINUED)

                    PRESS #3
Yes. Hello. Washington Post here. What exactly are you
wearing on your head?

                    PUTIN
They be daffodils. I like way they look.
                    (to PRESS)
Next question.

                    PRESS #4
N-B-C here.

                    PUTIN
Go ahead.

                    PRESS #4
Yes. You've just mentioned how there is a belief in America
by many that Russia interfered in the two thousand and
sixteen elections, and recently there have also been
several alleged Russian spies that have been arrested --

                    PUTIN
Arrested? I know not of arrest.
                    (to TRUMP)
Donald. Do you know of arrest?

                    TRUMP
I do not know anything, Vladimir Putin, almighty. N-B-C is
just talking fake news.

                    PRESS #4
But, Mister President, you tweeted about them just an hour
ago.

                    TRUMP
                    (drawn out)
Fake news.

                    PUTIN
Continue with question.

                                                    (CONTINUED)

                              PRESS #4
Do you think that these beliefs of Russian interference and
these arrests are going to damage relations between the
United States and Russia?

                         PUTIN laughs.

                              PUTIN
Damage relation? No. There be no damage relation. Relation
between Putin's Russia and Putin's America be at all-time
high.

                              PUTIN gestures to someone in the
                              wings.

                              PUTIN
You actually remind me I have gift for Donald to show good
friends we are.

                              PETROV enters carrying the
                              soccer ball and hands it to
                              PUTIN.

                              PUTIN
This be ball from World Cup Russia set to win this year.

                              PUTIN hands the ball to TRUMP as
                              PETROV exits.

                              PUTIN
Donald. I wish you take ball as token of good thing.

                              TRUMP
Thank you, Vladimir Putin. I will treasure this.

          TRUMP   PUTIN
I have a special shelf in my   Just please do not keep in
bathroom.   bathroom.

                              PUTIN
No. God. Please. Anywhere but that.
                    (to PRESS)
Any more question?

                                                   (CONTINUED)

PRESS #5

Fox News here. I have a question for President Trump.

TRUMP

Go ahead, Fox News.

PRESS #5

I want to ask you about the Supreme Court.

PUTIN

Finally. Good question.

PRESS #5

President Trump, the resignation of Justice Kennedy from
the Supreme Court has left a vacancy for you to fill. Have
you got any ideas of who you might nominate yet?

TRUMP

That is a great question, and I have a great answer. I am
going to nominate someone who is great. I cannot tell you
who yet, but they will be great.

PRESS #5

Can you not give us any name?

TRUMP
(to PUTIN)
Vladimir Putin, who am I going to --

PUTIN

Donald! Be quiet.
(to PRESS)
Next question. No more question? Good. Leave.

PRESS #1

I have a question.

PUTIN

No. No more question. You go now. Go before Putin annex
Helsinki and have you arrested.

PRESS #1

But --

(CONTINUED)

PUTIN

GO!

The PRESS leaves in a hurry.

TRUMP
(to PUTIN)
Was it something I said?

PUTIN
Donald. You do not ask me suspicious question when there be witness.

TRUMP
But who am I going to nominate?

PUTIN
Putin not know. I thought, perhaps you choose. Can you think of anyone who be good?

TRUMP
Ivanka?

PUTIN
No. Not Ivanka. They need have experience. Why not you go back home and think about people?

TRUMP
Wait. I have an idea.

PUTIN
Who?

TRUMP
It has gone.

PUTIN
Look. Donald. Just choose someone who be not... bad.

Lights out.

ACT III, SCENE TWELVE | BRETT KAVANAUGH

>   The NARRATOR enters.

                         NARRATOR
While all across America suspicious as to Russia's election
involvement continue to rise, Donald Trump returns home to
implement a way to ensure his stability, a new seat on the
Supreme Court, his pick for the nation still a surprise.
For who to choose is the question that on his mind is a
plague, for he needs naught but a man to save him a trip to
The Netherland's The Hague. But eventually, a name comes to
him, and so he sets off to the bar, for he has a new job to
hire onto his team, Brett Kavanaugh.

>   The NARRATOR exits as the lights
>   go up on a BAR is D.C., Where a
>   JUDGE sits relaxed at the bar
>   talking to the BARTENDER.

                         JUDGE
And so the teacher asked my son what comes at the end of a
sentence and he answered an appeal.

>   The BARTENDER laughs.

                         BARTENDER
Can I get you another, judge?

>   The JUDGE finishes his drink.

                         JUDGE
Yeah. I've got time for one more.

>   TRUMP enters and looks around.

                         JUDGE
Did I ever tell you about the Christmas card I got from a
lawyer last year? He said he wishes, but cannot guarantee,
my family a happy Christmas.

>   The BARTENDER laughs again as
>   TRUMP approaches.

>   (CONTINUED)

                         TRUMP
I am looking for a judge.

                         BARTENDER
                    (gesturing at the JUDGE)
Well, here's a Judge right here.

                         TRUMP
                    (to the JUDGE)
Brett Kavanaugh, I am here to --

                         JUDGE
I'm not Brett Kavanaugh.

                         TRUMP
Do you know Brett Kavanaugh?

                              At the far end of the stage,
                              BRETT KAVANAUGH enters and
                              stands watching.

                         JUDGE
                    (gesturing at the BARTENDER)
He does.

                         BARTENDER
Yeah. I know Brett Kavanaugh, alright.

                         TRUMP
Do you know where I can find him?

                         BARTENDER
Do I know where you can find Brett Kavanaugh?
                    (beat)
Sure. I know where you can find Brett Kavanaugh.

                              A pause, and then the BARTENDER
                              points over to KAVANAUGH.

                         BARTENDER
He's over there.

                              As attention turns to KAVANAUGH,
                              he takes a long sniff.

                                             (CONTINUED)

                         KAVANAUGH
ARE WE READY TO DO SOME BOOFING?

                                   Loud music begins to play as
                                   KAVANAUGH puts his hands in the
                                   air. A moment later, the
                                   BARTENDER kicks something behind
                                   the bar, and silence falls.

                         BARTENDER
Shut that stuff up, Brett. There's a guy here to see you.

                                   KAVANAUGH approaches.

                         KAVANAUGH
                         (to TRUMP)
I didn't expect to ever see you here, Mister President. I
didn't think that you were cool. I thought you were a
lightweight.
                         (to the BARTENDER)
I'm meeting P-J and Squee here in ten, so I'll take three
beers.

                         BARTENDER
Three beers coming up.

                         KAVANAUGH
And they'll take one each as well.

                         BARTENDER
Five beers coming up.

                         KAVANAUGH
                         (to TRUMP)
I like beer, Mister President. Do you like beer?

                                   The BARTENDER places a beer on
                                   top of the bar. KAVANAUGH takes
                                   it and downs it in one.

                         KAVANAUGH
                         (while drinking)
DOWN! DOWN! DOWN! DOWN! DOWN! DOWN! DOWN! DOWN! DOWN!

                                             (CONTINUED)

                         KAVANAUGH slams the glass back
                         onto the bar.

                    KAVANAUGH
I love beer. You know how you love golden showers? Well, I
love them too. Mine are beer.

                         KAVANAUGH takes another long
                         sniff.

                    KAVANAUGH
Have you ever played devil's triangle, Mister President? I
can show you how to play if you want?

                    TRUMP
Brett Kavanaugh, are you drunk?

                         KAVANAUGH bends and looks back
                         through his own legs.

                    KAVANAUGH
No. I don't think so. I can still feel my feet.

                         KAVANAUGH stands back up.

                    KAVANAUGH
So what brings you here?

                    TRUMP
I came to ask if you would like to join the Supreme Court.

                    KAVANAUGH
The Supreme Court? Sounds cool. What would I have to do?

                    TRUMP
Dress up as a wizard and make sure I don't get arrested.

                    KAVANAUGH
I'm not sure. I have a pretty full schedule. When would you
need me?

                    TRUMP
For the rest of your life.

                                              (CONTINUED)

                          KAVANAUGH
Hold on. I'll check my calendar.

                                   KAVANAUGH pulls a large folded
                                   calendar from his pocket,
                                   flattens it, and then begins to
                                   examine it.

                          KAVANAUGH
I'll have to move a few lifting sessions around, but I can
make it work.

                                   The BARTENDER down a second beer
                                   and KAVANAUGH downs it.

                          KAVANAUGH
So when do I start?

                          TRUMP
You have to be confirmed by loser Congress first.

                          KAVANAUGH
That bunch of asses? Easy. Now can I get you a beer, Mister
President?
                          (to the BARTENDER)
Two more beers.
                          (to TRUMP)
And what do you want?

                          TRUMP
I am going to leave now. Even for me, you are too much.

                                   TRUMP goes to leave.

                          KAVANAUGH
                          (calling after TRUMP)
Hey, Mister President.

                                   TRUMP turns back as KAVANAUGH
                                   downs the third beer from the
                                   BARTENDER.

                          KAVANAUGH
Does it matter if I don't have a great past?

                                                        (CONTINUED)

> Beat.

                              TRUMP
Apparently not.

ACT III, SCENE THIRTEEN | THE KAVANAUGH HEARING

> On stage, a SENATE COMMITTEE
> ROOM set out for a hearing. Next
> to it, a SMALL LOCKER ROOM where
> KAVANAUGH sits on the floor
> doing sit-ups with a towel.

                            NARRATOR
                           (entering)
And so now chosen is the President's second Supreme Court
pick. Though his chosen one's confirmation is set to be
anything but slick. For questions soon arise about Brett
Kavanaugh's past, and before long, a collection of claims
has quickly amassed. And so in the Senate, a committee
hearing is held, an opportunity hope Republicans, to ensure
that all uncertainties are quelled.

> The NARRATOR exits as Senators
> JOHN CORNYN, TED CRUZ, JEFF
> FLAKE, LINDSEY GRAHAM, CHUCK
> GRASSLEY, and ORRIN HATCH enter.

                            GRASSLEY
Okay. Now let's take our seats and get this over with
before the Democrats get back from lunch.

> The group take their seats.

                            GRASSLEY
Earlier, we heard from a woman. That was interesting. She
said some things and I'm sure that some of us listened. But
now, we are going to come to the main event and talk to the
legend that is Judge Brett Kavanaugh.

                            HATCH
Are we not waiting for that woman we hired to do our jobs
for us?

                                              (CONTINUED)

                         CORNYN
The political prop we hired to look as though we care?

                         HATCH
That's the one.

                         GRASSLEY
I really don't think we need a woman this time around. I'm
sure that we can question this, I think we can all agree,
cool dude, on our own.

                              There is a murmur of agreement
                              from all except FLAKE, who
                              audibly gulps.

                         GRASSLEY
Okay. So if we're all ready --

                              The sudden appearance of DIANE
                              FEINSTEIN from under the desk
                              interrupts proceedings.

                         FEINSTEIN
Now hold on one moment.

                         GRASSLEY
Ranking Member Feinstein. What are you doing hiding under
the desk?

                         FEINSTEIN
I was eating my lunch down here because I had a feeling
that you bastards would try something clever.

                         GRASSLEY
I don't know what --

                         FEINSTEIN
And then I remembered that you're all Republicans so it
wouldn't be clever. It would just be evil.

                         GRASSLEY
Well, we're just about to begin.

                                                    (CONTINUED)

FEINSTEIN
Are we not waiting for the rest of my party.

GRASSLEY
We really don't have the time, I'm afraid. I have to go for
a round of golf later on, and Lindsey Graham here, he has
his first anger management session tonight.

GRAHAM
**IT'S BECAUSE I GET REAL ANGRY NOW. I'M ANGRY THAT THE WHITE
MAN IS UNDER ATTACK. I'M ANGRY THAT --**

                    GRASSLEY bangs a gavel.

GRAHAM
I yield my time.

GRASSLEY
Okay, so now I think it's time that we brought in he who is
the man, the one and the only, Brett Kavanaugh.

                    KAVANAUGH stands, wipes his face
                    with the towel, flexes, and then
                    approaches the SENATORS.

GRAHAM
**AND IN THE RED CORNER, INTRODUCING JUDGE BRETT KAVANAUGH. A
FORMER INTER-STATE BOOFING CHAMPION IN HIGH SCHOOL, HE WAS
THE FIRST MAN TO DISCOVER ALL FOUR CORNERS OF THE DEVIL'S
TRIANGLE, AND HE IS YOUR NEXT JUSTICE OF THE SUPREME COURT!**

                    KAVANAUGH takes his seat, and as
                    silence falls, he sniffs.

KAVANAUGH
**Before any of you ask me a question, I have a question for
all of you.**

GRASSLEY
Ask away, Mister Kavanaugh.

KAVANAUGH
Do any of you have a beer?

                                              (CONTINUED)
PERFORMANCE LICENSE EDITION   LICENSE # _ _ _ _ _ _ _ _

                                                GRASSLEY looks around at his
                                                fellow SENATORS as all, except
                                                FEINSTEIN, who looks disgusted,
                                                shake their heads.

                                        GRASSLEY

I'm afraid not.

                                      KAVANAUGH

Dang it. Not even a light? I'm feeling real parched right
about now.

                                      GRASSLEY

We can offer you a glass of water?

                                      KAVANAUGH

I'll take a pint of that.

                                      GRASSLEY

Okay. Well, while we wait for that, would you like to give
us your opening statement, Judge Kavanaugh?

                                      KAVANAUGH

I'll do that. I just... I need a moment.

                                                Overcome with emotion, KAVANAUGH
                                                sniffs and wipes his face before
                                                pulling a piece of paper from
                                                his pocket.

                                        KAVANAUGH

I'm sorry. It's just a hard time for me right now. And
these words, they are my words. They come from deep within
my heart. I sat down, on my own one night, and I came up
with these words which I offer to you now.
                          (beat, then reading from the
                           paper)
"You should begin by telling them that you're grateful for
the opportunity to clear your name, Brett. That will get
them onto your side right from the start."
                          (looking up)
I am grateful for the opportunity to clear my name --

                                              (CONTINUED)

                          FEINSTEIN
I'd like to say something.

                                    GRASSLEY bangs a gavel.

                          GRASSLEY
Continue, Brett Kavanaugh.

                          KAVANAUGH
                          (reading)
"After that, tell them that you're --"

                                    The NARRATOR enters with a
                                    bottle of water.

                          KAVANAUGH
WHAT? I asked for a pint of water. Not some dumb plastic
bottle. Do I look like some kid who can't use a big boy
glass?

                          NARRATOR
There weren't any glasses.

                                    KAVANAUGH takes the bottle and
                                    fails in his attempt to open it.

                          KAVANAUGH
CAN YOU... Can you open it for me?

                                    The NARRATOR takes the bottle,
                                    opens it with ease, and then
                                    hands it back to KAVANAUGH.

                          KAVANAUGH
Thank you.

                                    KAVANAUGH takes one mouthful
                                    from the bottle and then empties
                                    the rest over his face before
                                    throwing the bottle to one side
                                    and returning to his notes.

                                                        (CONTINUED)

                          KAVANAUGH
                          (reading)
"Don't forget to tell them that you're incest..."
                     (to the NARRATOR)
What does this say?

                           NARRATOR
                          (leaning in)
Innocent.

                     The NARRATOR exits.

                          KAVANAUGH
                          (reading)
"Don't forget to tell them that you're innocent."
                     (looking up, angry)
Innocent. I'm innocent, I tell you.

                           GRASSLEY
Well, it has me convinced.

                            CRUZ
Chair, if I could suggest? I don't think we need to hear
anything else here today.

                           GRASSLEY

I quite --

                          FEINSTEIN
No. I've got questions.

                          KAVANAUGH
WHAT? How can you have questions? The word of my people has
been good for centuries. How can you not believe me? For
centuries, I'm telling you.

                           GRASSLEY
Judge Kavanaugh does have a point.

                          FEINSTEIN
I've got questions.

                                              (CONTINUED)

                         GRASSLEY
Okay then. Ranking Member Feinstein, what are your
questions.

                         FEINSTEIN
Thank you.
                    (to KAVANAUGH)
Mister Kavanaugh, today we have heard first-hand testimony,
and over the past few weeks, we have heard of many accounts
by other strong women, all of which corroborate. If you
really are as innocent as you claim, why aren't you
agreeing to a formal investigation?

                         KAVANAUGH
I want an investigation. I called for an investigation.

                         FEINSTEIN
So you are asking for a formal F-B-I investigation?

                         KAVANAUGH
We don't need an investigation. Why would we need an
investigation?

                         FEINSTEIN
You don't want to prove that you're innocent?

                         KAVANAUGH
I have already proven that I'm innocent. Have you not seen
my calendars?

                         FEINSTEIN
I was just about to get to those.

                              FEINSTEIN holds up a collection
                              of calendars featuring beach
                              models.

                         FEINSTEIN
Mister Kavanaugh, are these your calendars?

                         KAVANAUGH
If they have extreme ironing every Tuesday at eight with
Squee, then yes.

                                             (CONTINUED)

                          FEINSTEIN
Okay, so my first question is why have you stuck our face
over the faces of all of these male models?

                          KAVANAUGH
Duh. It's what we all used to do.

                          FEINSTEIN
My second question is whose face have you stuck over the
female models?

                          KAVANAUGH
That's Squee. Yeah, me and P-J thought he looks funny with
boobs.

                          FEINSTEIN
Mister Kavanaugh, what sort of person keeps all of their
calendars from their youth just in case hey may need them
to try to prove they never sexually assaulted anyone --

                          KAVANAUGH
I --

                          FEINSTEIN
Hold on. I have a follow-up. What sort of person does that?
And why would you want to admit to being that person?

                          Beat.

                          KAVANAUGH
Are you drunk?

                          FEINSTEIN
If I wasn't at the start I will need to be by the end. Can
we return to my question?

                                   GRAHAM begins to bang his fist
                                   on the desk in protest.

                          GRAHAM
Chair, I must object to this line of questioning. It is
inappropriate at best and discrimination at its worst.

                                                  (CONTINUED)

                         FEINSTEIN
I'd still like an answer.

                    GRASSLEY bangs a gavel.

                         GRASSLEY
Lindsey Graham has the floor.

                         GRAHAM
Thank you, Mister Chairman. You know, this whole situation
here reminds me of a documentary I once watched on the
great Fox network.

It was a piece that told the story of a hardworking and
self-made white man who had made many sacrifices to get
where he was. And you know, people hated him for it. They
hated that a white man could still be successful in
America.

But let me tell you, this is America and he was still
successful. And when opportunity came, he took it and he
drilled for that oil to keep it in the hands of the
hardworking and deserving white American patriot.

But the people, they got real angry about it. They were
mad. And what did they do? I'll tell you what they did do.
They shot him. But no one could work out who had shot him
because every last person hated this white man's guts.

He was persecuted, just like Judge Brett Kavanaugh here. In
the end, it turned out that a baby had shot him. That's
right, a baby. And that is why we need --

                         FEINSTEIN
Senator Graham, are you talking about the Simpson's episode
where someone shot Mister Burns?

                         Beat.

                         GRAHAM
I want it on the record that it was a convincing portrayal
from all involved.

                                              (CONTINUED)

PERFORMANCE LICENSE EDITION   LICENSE # _ _ _ _ _ _ _ _

                         FEINSTEIN
Nineteen ninety-five called, they want their cultural
references back.

                    GRASSLEY bangs a gavel.

                         GRAHAM
I Yield my time.

                         GRASSLEY
Senator Flake. You've been quiet so far.

                         FLAKE
I'm just sitting here watching and thinking that this has
got to be a turning point. This is not a time for us to be
putting party over country. I've looked at all the
evidence, and I've listened to comments from my
constituents who have genuine concerns about this man here.

I'm also in a unique position, stepping down in just a few
months, so I don't need to worry about how my decision
plays with the Republican base. All things considered, I
think that the only right thing to do is not to vote in
favor.

                         FEINSTEIN
I always knew that you had a heart --

                         FLAKE
And that is why I will be voting to confirm Judge Brett
Kavanaugh.

                         FEINSTEIN
You're a real asshole, Jeff.

                    GRASSLEY bangs a gavel.

                         FLAKE
I yield my opinions.

                         GRASSLEY
I think that brings us nicely to voting. Senator Cornyn?

                                              (CONTINUED)

                          CORNYN
Aye.

                          GRASSLEY
Senator Cruz?

                          CRUZ
Aye.

                          GRASSLEY
Senator Feinstein?

                          FEINSTEIN
No. Obviously.

                          GRASSLEY
Senator Flake?

                          FLAKE
Aye.

                          GRASSLEY
Senator Graham?

                          GRAHAM
Let me tell you right now, Chair. This is an honor for me
to vote for this man. Aye, it is. Aye is most definitely
is.

                          GRASSLEY
Senator Hatch?

                          HATCH
Aye.

                          GRASSLEY
And finally, Judge Kavanaugh?

                          KAVANAUGH
I vote in favor.

                          FEINSTEIN
Wait a minute, why does he get a vote?

                                                    (CONTINUED)

                    GRASSLEY bangs a gavel.

                         GRASSLEY
Judge Brett Kavanaugh, I think you're going to be our next
Justice of the Supreme Court.

ACT III, SCENE FOURTEEN | FLAKE & COLLINS

                              On stage, a single ELEVATOR
                              sands in a CAPITOL CORRIDOR.

                         NARRATOR
                        (entering)
And so to the Senate moves Kavanaugh's confirmation, not
least due to Jeff Flake's sudden spinal ablation. But from
no Republican comes the hope of any salvation, for not one
of them finds all that they are learning the least bit
concerning to be towards the nomination anything but
discerning. But the reality is that when it comes time for
all to vote, the people outside are sat taking note. And
for no one elected, is there a place left to hide, not now
their political careers have all but died.

                              As the NARRATOR exits, FLAKE
                              enters and goes to call the
                              elevator.

                              The elevator doors open, and
                              FLAKE steps inside as SUSAN
                              COLLINS enters after him.

                         COLLINS
Can you hold it for me?

                              As the doors begin to close,
                              FLAKE pushes a button, and they
                              reopen for COLLINS to join him.

                         COLLINS
Good afternoon, Jeff. We really got them all today, didn't
we? For a moment, they actually believed that we were going
to do the right thing and vote against Kavanaugh.

                                             (CONTINUED)
PERFORMANCE LICENSE EDITION   LICENSE # _ _ _ _ _ _ _

                              As the doors begin to close once
                              more, voices of protest come
                              from offstage, and FLAKE holds
                              them open.

                    FLAKE
You know, Susan. I think I'm going to take the stairs.

                    COLLINS
I think I'll join you.

                              COLLINS and FLAKE exit together
                              as the lights fade out.

                    COLLINS (OFF)
I'm going to write a letter to someone about this. I really
disapprove of voters having their own opinions.

END OF ACT III

ACT IV : "THE THIRD YEAR"

ACT IV, SCENE ONE | OBAMA IN TAHITI

>   With the audience seated for the
>   final act, the auditorium falls
>   dark and silent as the gentle
>   sound of crashing waves and
>   tropical music grows in volume.

                            NARRATOR
                          (entering)
With the half-way point of the Trump presidency now fast
approaching, soon to come are the Midterms where Democrats
hope to capitalize by undertaking Republican seat poaching.
All the while, the situation for Donald himself becomes
ever more serious, and his ability to try to stand tall
above it all ever more increasingly less imperious.

For on each every side come new allegations and
investigations that raise questions he fights hard to duck,
not so stressful though is the life of his predecessor. For
his life is calm on a South Pacific island where he lies
back to enjoy the sun not having to give a fu --

>   A loud beep interrupts.

                            NARRATOR
                        (shouting out)
Oh, come on! There are four acts to this show. Can't I just
say it once?

>   The NARRATOR exits as lights go
>   up on a BEACHFRONT RESTAURANT
>   where a table stands waiting.
>
>   ANDERSON COOPER and BARACK OBAMA
>   enter, both dressed for warm
>   weather.

                            OBAMA
                     (gesturing at the table)
You know, Anderson...
                          (MORE)
                                                    (CONTINUED)

CONTINUED:
                              OBAMA (CONT'D)
I would say take this seat here, but... they belong to the
establishment that we have chosen to feast in this
afternoon... You could always borrow it... but it is not
mine to permit you leave of for any period of time.

                                   COOPER and OBAMA take their
                                   seats and pick up menus.

                         OBAMA
If I could make a small request?... Please refrain from
communicating with those at Fox News that I am borrowing
this chair here... For eight years, they never really
forgave me for temporarily acquiring with the intention of
later returning to the owner... anything at all.

                                   COOPER looks across the stage as
                                   though to address a camera.

                         COOPER
                    (to the "camera")
Welcome to this special edition of Anderson Cooper Three
Sixty. Today, I am on the beautiful island of Tahiti in
French Polynesia to meet with former President, Barack
Obama, to bring you an exclusive interview live... at the
time of recording, which we will later edit and broadcast
to you, our viewers, not live.

                                   OBAMA attempts to look in the
                                   same direction.

                         OBAMA
Anderson... with whom is it that you are trying to solicit
a consultation with?... There is no one in that location.

                                   A WAITER enters and approaches
                                   their table.

                         WAITER
Good evening. I will be your waiter for your meal.

                         OBAMA
Waiter?

                                                      (CONTINUED)

                         WAITER
That is correct, your waiter.

                         OBAMA
                    (pointing)
But what if we want to wait... over in that nearby locality
instead?
                    (beat, then to COOPER)
It really is a great dining facility here, Anderson... You
know, I was in here just a couple of moons back, and I saw
five people walk into the bar... In just as many sixty-
second increments... of time... The sixth person was much
luckier as they remembered... to duck.

                         COOPER
We sure are missing that sense of humor, Mister President.

                         WAITER
Can I take your orders?

                         OBAMA
Will we get them back again later on?

                         COOPER
                    (to the WAITER)
I'll take the steak.

                         OBAMA
And I will also take the tenderloin... of a cow or a bull.
But make my own lean... and by that, I mean that I want the
chef to cook it... while stood on just one of their lower
limbs.

                         WAITER
                    (to COOPER)
And would you like the soup or the salad to start?

                         COOPER
I'll take the salad.

                         WAITER
                    (to OBAMA)
And for you, sir? Would you like the soup or the salad?

                                              (CONTINUED)

                          OBAMA
Super salad?... I will be okay with the regular, standard,
ordinary selection... of prepared greeneries and selected
vegetables... thank you.

                    The WAITER exits.

                          COOPER
So, Mister President, how have things been?

                          OBAMA
Well... there have been some tenacious winds causing quite
a number of disheveled asperous crests out on the aqua on
some days... but most of the time... the circumstances
surrounding the briny deep... are more than ideal for some
surfing... and if the temperament is most agreeable... even
some paragliding also.

                          COOPER
And have you been keeping up with everything that's been
going on around the world? Do you have any concerns about
the recent developments with the situation in North Korea?

                          OBAMA
North Korea?... Not my problem... That nation is no longer
a complication, nor a dilemma... that gives me a headache
anymore... Fuck them.

                    The NARRATOR returns.

                          NARRATOR
                     (shouting out)
He's allowed one.
                          (beat)
Yes. I know who he is.

                          OBAMA
Narrator... could you please acquire on my behalf the wine
list?... And by that, I don't infer a printout... of Donald
Trump's ante meridiem Twitter feed.

                    The NARRATOR exits.

                                        (CONTINUED)

COOPER
Is there anything that concerns you anymore?

OBAMA
Well, now I have glanced over the news and noted a couple
of cases... in Wisconsin, the elected chamber there were
attempting to pass a law... to make spherical hay bails
illegal... It was something about cattle not getting... a
four-sided square meal... And then was also a story of a
kidnapping... over in a school in Massachusetts.

COOPER
I don't remember reading about that.

OBAMA
You wouldn't have heard... It ended quite amicably... The
kid awoke from his slumber before the teacher... observed
that he was sleeping.

                        The WAITER returns with their
                        starters, which they place on
                        the table.

WAITER
Please accept my apologies for your wait.

OBAMA
Weight?... Hey, are you calling Obama fat?
                    (beat)
I'm just jesting with you.

                    The WAITER exits.

COOPER
It looks like they do a good salad at this place.

OBAMA
You should wait for the steaks... The steaks rank very
highly... The chef who prepares them for our consumption
does not get paid... if they are not very good.
                    (beat)
I'm not such a fan of the Sushi, though... I never have
been. There is something just too fishy about food that
comes... from Davy Jones' back garden ornamental fish pond.

                                            (CONTINUED)

                         OBAMA laughs to himself.

                              OBAMA
Discussing the subject of salads, Anderson, you really
should consider... the possibility of remaining seated for
a dessert course... The juicy fruity harvested produce
salad is the best... That reminds me of a joke that Joe
once expressed to me... What was Beethoven's favorite
fruit?... It was a ba-na-na-na.

                         OBAMA laughs again.

                              OBAMA
Hey, Anderson, here are a few that I can disclose to you
without any consequence... while my daughters are not
currently... in attendance at this place... Were you ever
informed about the coffee that was filing a police
report?... It alleged that it had just... been mugged... Or
how about this one?... How many apples grow on trees?...
The answer is, of course... all of them.

                              A beat as OBAMA stops laughing
                              and sighs to himself.

                              COOPER
So, Mister President. What are your plans for the Midterms
next week?

                              OBAMA
Well, I am going to be spending the entire seven day period
of that democratic exercise... out here in the sun... My
two feet will be up... My surf will rise to a level above
its current trajectory... And my mini-bar bill will be
significantly increased within fiscally responsible
limits... for my checking account... There is a substantial
measure of political activity back at home, and it's nice
to be absent from the proceedings and... not find them a
burden.

                              COOPER
And what about Joe? Do you still hear anything from him?

                                                    (CONTINUED)

OBAMA

Now that is a stimulating inquiry that you put forth in
your question... I can confirm that on this occasion... We
do still exchange thoughts and words with one another both
in an electronic format... and face to face in a manner
such as we ourselves are doing at this moment...

Joe wanted to join me out here for a period, but the
problem is... Amtrak only goes so far... I have packaged
and shipped to him a parcel containing an inflatable
dolphin and a costume, however... so that he can dress up
as a choo-choo driver and then swim... the rest of the
way... Now that really would be some-fin.

                    The lights begin to fade.

OBAMA

Hey, Anderson... Here are a few more...

ACT IV, SCENE TWO | TRUMP PLAYS GOLF

                         The sound of heavy rain and
                         thunder fills a stage that is
                         dark except for brief flashes of
                         lightning.

NARRATOR
(entering)
While on vacation relaxes the nation's forty-fourth soaking
up the sun in a state of release, back home in Washington,
the pressure on his successor still only does increase.

Up early each morning is Donald J. Trump to tweet to the
world on it his thoughts. A witch-hunt, fake news, and all-
around a dishonest fake media of aughts.

But while criticism of Kavanaugh is still much in vogue,
and even though the opinions of his foreign policies is
that he's gone rogue, the President feels still that in the
upcoming election his brand remains a fighting force, and
so he retires for a day to place a round of golf upon his
Florida course.

                                            (CONTINUED)

                              The NARRATOR exits as the lights
                              go up on a ROOM at MAR-A-LAGO,
                              where TRUMP stands by a set of
                              open doors looking out at the
                              heavy rain.

                              A soaked JUNIOR enters through
                              the doors carrying a paper bag.

                    JUNIOR
Okay, you know, I think that it might be raining.

                    TRUMP
Did you get them, Donald Trump Junior?

                              JUNIOR holds the bag out in
                              front of him.

                    JUNIOR
Two cheeseburgers with extra salad, two extra slices of
cheese, doubled up with a slice of bacon, two nuggets, and
a bed of lettuce on the top, a side of fries, a side of
nuggets with extra nuggets, holding the salad on all of
that, and two diet colas?

                              TRUMP takes the bag.

                    TRUMP
Very good. All of this golf is making me very hungry.

                    JUNIOR
But you're not playing golf right now.

                    TRUMP
Fake news.

                              ERIC, as wet as JUNIOR, enters
                              through the same doors carrying
                              a golf club.

                    ERIC
I think I wet myself.

                                                    (CONTINUED)

CONTINUED:

                    TRUMP
Did you get the ball in the hole, Eric Trump?

                    ERIC
                (counting on his fingers)
One. Two. Three. Eight. Five. Seventeen shots.

                    TRUMP
Very good.

                        TRUMP pulls a scorecard from his
                        pocket.

                    TRUMP
                (to himself, writing)
Hole number one. Donald J. Trump. Seventeen.
                (to ERIC)
Now go and take your own shot.

                    ERIC
Okay. I'll be back soon.

                        ERIC exits through the doors.

                    JUNIOR
Is Eric playing himself?

                    TRUMP
He is playing me. But he is also playing for me.

                    JUNIOR
Why?

                    TRUMP
It's raining outside.

                        TRUMP takes a damp burger from
                        the bag.

                    TRUMP
Why is my burger wet?

                                        (CONTINUED)

                         JUNIOR
It's raining outside. And I mean, why Eric? Why not someone
who knows how to play?

                         TRUMP
Because some people are saying that there is also thunder
and lightning.

                         JUNIOR
I don't get what you mean?

                         TRUMP
Would he not be your first choice to stand outside in the
middle of a huge open space with a metal golf racket during
a thunderstorm?

                         JUNIOR
Okay, so you know, that is a very good point. But don't you
mean golf club?

                         TRUMP
No. A golf club is something that is attached to a bankrupt
hotel.

                              A silent pause followed by a
                              bright flash of lightning.

                         ERIC (OFF)
                      (shouting out)
The flashy thing hurt me.

                              There is a knock on an interior
                              door, and CONWAY enters.

                         CONWAY
Mister President, sir. Donald Trump Junior.

                         TRUMP
What do you need, Kellyanne Conway?

                         CONWAY
Another chance.

                                             (CONTINUED)
PERFORMANCE LICENSE EDITION   LICENSE # _ _ _ _ _ _ _ _

                         TRUMP
What was that?

                         CONWAY
Senator Mitch McConnell is here to see you, sir.

                         TRUMP
Okay. Send him in.

                              CONWAY exits before a moment
                              later, MITCH MCCONNELL enters.

                         MCCONNELL
Good to see you, Comrade.

                         TRUMP
Mitch McConnell, what can I do for you?

                         MCCONNELL
I hope I'm not interrupting?

                         TRUMP
I am only playing golf.

                         MCCONNELL
Why are you inside?

                         TRUMP
Eric Trump is taking my shots for me because it is raining
outside and rain is wet. If I get wet, then my hair
multiplies, and my tan runs. It makes me look like a sad
Halloween pumpkin.

                         Beat.

                         MCCONNELL
Mister President, I am sorry to report that we may be about
to lose Texas.

                         TRUMP
What do you mean lose Texas? How can we lose something so
big?

                                             (CONTINUED)

                    MCCONNELL
Ted Cruz is starting to look as though he's under pressure.

                    TRUMP
Is Ted Cruz the one that looks like an elderly and
incontinent man who is angry because a child laughed?

                    MCCONNELL
No. That's Lindsey Graham.

                    TRUMP
Is he the one who looks like someone attempted to turn a
walnut into a raisin but got bored and drew a face on it?

                    MCCONNELL
No. That's Chuck Grassley.

                    TRUMP
Is he the one who looks like a cartoon villain who has a
sub-plot where he secretly collects toy dolls in a creepy
way?

                    MCCONNELL
No. That's Bill Cassidy.

                    TRUMP
Is he the one who looks like every unpopular neighbor from
a nineteen eight-eight sitcom who would run over your cat
and then charge you for clearing their car?

                    MCCONNELL
No. That's Cindy Hyde-Smith.

                    TRUMP
Is he the one who secretly let one go in the elevator and
looks really smug about it because everyone blamed Anne
from human resources?

                    MCCONNELL
No. That's Marco Rubio.

                    TRUMP
Is he the one who looks like the after photo in every
erectile dysfunction or hair loss infomercial ever?

                                        (CONTINUED)

                          MCCONNELL
No. That's Mitt Romney.

                          TRUMP
Is he the one who looks like he could do you a really great
deal on that nineteen eighty-eight Toyota and can reassure
you that it is the original door, the paint just faded
faster there?

                          MCCONNELL
No. That's Rand Paul.

                          TRUMP
Is he the one who looks like he would run you down and then
tell the police that it was your fault for jaywalking, but
would then given you directions to the emergency room out
of the kindness of his heart.

                          MCCONNELL
No. That's Jeff Flake, and he's stepping down.

                          TRUMP
Is he the one who is hated by both sides?

                          MCCONNELL
Could you be more specific?

                          TRUMP
From Maine.

                          MCCONNELL
No. That's Susan Collins.

                          TRUMP
Is he the one who always looks as though he is surprised by
something but cannot decide if it is a good surprise or a
bad surprise?

                          MCCONNELL
No. That's me.

                          TRUMP
Who is Ted Cruz then?

                                             (CONTINUED)
PERFORMANCE LICENSE EDITION   LICENSE # _ _ _ _ _ _ _ _

                         MCCONNELL
He's the one who thinks that holding hands should be saved
for marriage and has recently lost a bet that says he has
to grow a beard now.

                         TRUMP
Oh, Ted Cruz. I know him. Great guy. He loves me a lot.

                         MCCONNELL
I really think that he's going to need more help down
there. He's facing a real tough battle from a guy who has a
foreign-sounding name.

                         TRUMP
Are they part Cuban and born in Canada, and yet for some
reason, hate all immigrants?

                         MCCONNELL
No. That is Ted Cruz himself.

                         TRUMP
Who is it then?

                         MCCONNELL
Some guy called Beto O'Rourke.

                         TRUMP
I have never heard of him.

                         MCCONNELL
Well, neither have I. But I asked the intern who works in
my office about him, and she went bright red and said he
was a real hot dude.

                         TRUMP
So what do you --

                         MCCONNELL
She said he's a guy who has really got it going on.

                         TRUMP
What do you --

                                                    (CONTINUED)

                          MCCONNELL
And that he has a sweet piece of ass on him.

                          TRUMP
What do you suggest we do?

                          MCCONNELL
I think we need to send reinforcements and fight ass to
ass. As we both know, Ted Cruz himself looks like --

                          TRUMP
A rejected cartoon villain going through a mid-life crisis.

                          MCCONNELL
Exactly.

                          TRUMP
So are you saying that we should send our own ass down
there?

                          MCCONNELL
That's right.

                          TRUMP
                      (to JUNIOR)
Donald Trump Junior, what are you doing this weekend?

                          JUNIOR
I was going to go on a hunting trip to shoot cute animals
to prove how much of a real man I am.

                          TRUMP
Cancel it. You are going to Texas.

                          JUNIOR
Am I going alone?

                          TRUMP
You can take your brother.

                              Another flash of lightning
                              followed by a pause.

                                              (CONTINUED)

                          ERIC (OFF)
Ouch.

ACT IV, SCENE THREE | THE DEMOCRATIC PRESS CONFERENCE

                              In front of a United States
                              flag, a podium stands in a PRESS
                              CONFERENCE ROOM somewhere in the
                              CAPITOL.

                              At the front of the scene, the
                              ENSEMBLE (as PRESS) wait.

                          NARRATOR
                        (entering)
Despite worries in the South, the talk from the President
and his Senate leader remains on the line that their party
is strong, and so it is for Democrats to prepare for a
fight on all fronts to show the voters that the Republicans
are all wrong. For they seem now, a party united together
down in their trench, especially since Brett Kavanaugh took
his place upon the Supreme Court bench. While Trump's past
and his views remain most naught but obscene, a point that
Nancy Pelosi and Chuck Schumer wish to make clear when the
media convene.

                              The NARRATOR exits as NANCY
                              PELOSI and CHUCK SCHUMER enter.

                              Together, they take their place
                              behind the podium and begin to
                              stare straight ahead without
                              blinking.

                          PELOSI
Hello to the members of the press here today and all of the
American people watching at home. I am very pleased to get
the chance to speak to you all today with my good friend...

                              Without her focus moving, PELOSI
                              points at SCHUMER.

                                              (CONTINUED)
PERFORMANCE LICENSE EDITION   LICENSE # _ _ _ _ _ _ _ _

                          PELOSI
The Senate Minority Leader, Senator Chuck Schumer of New
York.

                          SCHUMER
We are here today to tell you why you should all vote for
us, the Democrats, in next week's Midterm elections.

                          PELOSI
And we also have some fascinating policies that we would
like to share with you all.

                     SCHUMER blinks.

                          SCHUMER
                        (to PELOSI)
Oh, damn. I owe you ten dollars, Nancy.

                          PELOSI

Why, Chuck?

                          SCHUMER
I was the first to blink.

                          PELOSI
You owe me ten dollars, and you also owe our cuss tin ten
dollars as well.

                          SCHUMER

Why, Nancy?

                          PELOSI

You said damn.

                          SCHUMER

So did you.

                          PELOSI
That's very true. You owe me ten dollars, and we both owe
the cuss tin ten dollars each.

                     Beat.

                                              (CONTINUED)

PELOSI
(to PRESS)
This here is an example of how we in the Democratic party
are always seeking to hold each other to account when we do
bad, and also how we always take responsibility for our own
actions.

SCHUMER
And holding to account is exactly what we would like to do
to Donald Trump because he is a bad person who does bad
things.

PELOSI
That's right. But he isn't the only bad person. Many of the
people that the President has surrounded himself with are
also bad people.

SCHUMER
And that is why all of America should vote for us, the
Democrats, so that we can have the power to investigate
them, the bad people, and hold them to account on behalf of
you, the people.

PELOSI
But, of course, we are not a party that is all about Donald
Trump. No, we also have plans for other things. Things like
healthcare and education. And we believe in people having
rights too.

SCHUMER
And now, we will take any questions that you may have.

PRESS #1
Hello, C-N-N here. You mentioned that you've got plans for
many things --

PELOSI
Yes. Things like healthcare.

PRESS #1
I'm just wondering if you could tell us what those plans
actually are.

(CONTINUED)

CONTINUED:

                          PELOSI
Well, I like healthcare. I think that healthcare is good.

                          SCHUMER
And I think that healthcare is good too.

                          PELOSI
We are united on this cause, and that is why we are going
to work to make healthcare good for all. Does that answer
your question?

                          PRESS #1
No. Not at all.

                          PELOSI
I think we are ready for our section question now.

                          SCHUMER
                     (to PRESS #2)
Yes, you from the New York Times. Home state represent, am
I right?

                          PRESS #2
Yeah. Sure. Whatever.

                          SCHUMER
What is your question?

                          PRESS #2
You talked about wanting to hold the President to account --

                          SCHUMER
                     (nodding)
Because he does bad things.

                          PRESS #2
Are we talking impeachment here? Because that's what some
other Democrats have been suggesting.

                          PELOSI
Impeachment? Why would we need to impeach the President?

                                              (CONTINUED)

SCHUMER
We would prefer to take a much more direct approach to hold
people like Donald Trump to account.

PELOSI
That is right. And we are prepared to do so. I have already
drafted a joint letter for us to send him so that he can
read just how much we disapprove of his actions.

SCHUMER
And I have bought a red pen so that I can sign that letter
in red ink. As we all know, red is the universal color of
telling someone that they are wrong.

PELOSI
And even more than that, I have downloaded and installed
Times Old Roman, which I used to write the letter because
it makes it look even more formal and serious than Times
New Roman.

SCHUMER
We are then going to send the letter through priority mail
so that he knows we are taking everything very seriously.

PELOSI
I think that you'll find you can't get any more direct than
that.

SCHUMER
And now we will take another question.

PRESS #3
Washington Post here.

PELOSI
Go ahead.

PRESS #3
Thank you. Together you represent the leadership of the
minority party in the world's richest and most powerful
democracy --

SCHUMER
You are very flattering.

(CONTINUED)

                          PRESS #3
Could you really not afford to have a podium each?

                          Beat.

                          PELOSI
Apparently not.

                          SCHUMER
Next question. Yes, you...

                                    Together, the voices and lights
                                    fade out of the scene.

ACT IV, SCENE FOUR | THE TEXAS CAMPAIGN TRAIL

                                    Somewhere in TEXAS, a LOCAL
                                    walks around a CONVENIENCE
                                    STORE.

                          NARRATOR
                          (entering)
Never in recent history has one election had so much at
stake, and never before has it seemed so likely that the
result will bring with it a nationwide electoral quake. For
Democrats, success is on the way, or so their supporters
indeed cry. While for Republicans, their long run in power
seems sure to dry with at least one of their majorities
soon to be nigh. Of the two, it seems the House is most
likely to flip, for the Senate class up does not favor
Chuck Schumer, not that those odds will stop one man
fighting an incumbent with his own unique brand of non-
contestable humor. It is down in the south where this
particular battle ranges strong, between one Texas state
Representative and a man living with an irrational fear of
a thong.

                                    The NARRATOR exits as CRUZ
                                    enters the store.

                          CRUZ
Good morning.

                                                        (CONTINUED)

                         LOCAL
Morning, Mister Cruz.

                         STORE OWNER
                         (entering)
Well, darn good morning to you, Senator.

                              The STORE OWNER leads CRUZ over
                              to a nearby counter.

                         STORE OWNER
And how is our fine, generous servant of the people doing
today?

                         CRUZ
Not too good today, I'm afraid. A good law-abiding
Christian man is facing some difficulties. Farmer Moore has
had issues with foxes eating his chickens for some time
now.

                         STORE OWNER
I sure am sorry to be hearing that. Do convey to him my
thoughts and prayers.

                         CRUZ
I'll be sure to.

                         STORE OWNER
It may be a stupid question, but has he done anything to
try and fix the problem at all?

                         CRUZ
I advised him last month to get his own pet fox. You know,
only a good guy with a fox can stop a bad fox.

                         STORE OWNER
And how's that working with him?

                         CRUZ
Well, his fox became friends with the first fox, and then
they started eating the chickens together.

                         STORE OWNER
So has he got rid of the fox then?

                                             (CONTINUED)
PERFORMANCE LICENSE EDITION   LICENSE # _ _ _ _ _ _ _ _

                              CRUZ
Of course not. As I told him, if more foxes weren't the
solution, then we wouldn't have the God-given right to own
as many foxes as we want. And so he's gone and bought
himself twenty more foxes.

                              STORE OWNER
And is that working?

                              CRUZ
All of his chickens are dead. But on the bright side, he is
not the owner of the largest fox farm in the state. All
part of the great plan.

                              STORE OWNER
Many thoughts and prayers for his new endeavor.

                              CRUZ
I'll add them to my own.

                              STORE OWNER
Well, anyway, Senator, what can I get you today?

                              CRUZ
I'm going to be needing some new lead.

                              STORE OWNER
Of course.

                                        CRUZ watches as the STORE OWNER
                                        takes a locked box from under
                                        the counter, unlocks it, and
                                        then removes a single pencil.

                              STORE OWNER
Some lead for you.

                              CRUZ
That's a good joke you've got there. But I meant lead
bullets, not a lead pencil.

                              STORE OWNER
My apologies, Senator.

                                                            (CONTINUED)

>   The STORE OWNER locks the pencil
>   away again.

                         STORE OWNER
Can't be too careful now.

                         CRUZ
I'm glad you're working to keep those pencils out of the
hands of the children. We don't need them getting lead
poisoning or hitting their friends with them.

                         STORE OWNER
It's always good to see you looking out for the children,
Senator. Now, how many bullets do you be wanting?

                         CRUZ
Shall we say a round two dozen?

                         STORE OWNER
Of course.

>   The STORE OWNER reaches for a
>   small cardboard box on top of
>   the counter.

                         STORE OWNER
                       (to themselves)
Two dozen.

>   The STORE OWNER counts out the
>   bullets and goes to put the box
>   back. As they do, they knock it
>   onto the floor.

                         STORE OWNER
Darn it.

                         CRUZ
Would you like some help picking them up?

                         STORE OWNER
It's fine, Senator. I'll get around to it.

                                                    (CONTINUED)

CONTINUED:

> At the other side of the stage, ERIC (holding a teddy) and JUNIOR enter.

                    CRUZ
How much do I owe you?

                    STORE OWNER
Just twenty-four bucks.

                    CRUZ
Of course.

> CRUZ takes a handful of bills from his pocket and hands it over.

                    CRUZ
Well, I'll be seeing you.

                    STORE OWNER
See you later, Senator.

> The light fades on the store as CRUZ moves to the center of the stage.

                    ERIC
Hey, Junior.

                    JUNIOR
What is it, buddy?

> ERIC holds his teddy to his ear.

                    ERIC
I don't think teddy is well.

                    JUNIOR
He's a teddy, bud. He's not real.

                    ERIC
Then why does Betsy DeVos want school children to shoot him?

                                        (CONTINUED)

                              JUNIOR
She wants them to shoot big grizzly bears, not teddy bears.

                              ERIC
What's the difference?

                              JUNIOR
Well, grizzly bears go... grizzly. And teddy bears, they
go...
                         (beat, then noticing CRUZ)
Hey, there's Ted.
                         (to CRUZ)
Hey, Ted.

                              ERIC
Teddy doesn't want to talk to you. You just said he wasn't
real.

                         CRUZ walks over to them.

                              CRUZ
Hey there, Junior. Eric. I heard that you were both coming
down to help me out.

                              JUNIOR
We're at your service, Senator. Happy to be down here,
aren't we, Eric?
                         (beat)
Eric?

                              ERIC
I'm worried about teddy.

                              CRUZ
And you're right to be. Those Democrats want to silence me,
but we're going to fight them together, right?

                              ERIC
Who are you?
                         (holding up his teddy)
I'm talking about teddy. He isn't very well.

                              CRUZ
Can I take a closer look?

                                                      (CONTINUED)

                        ERIC holds tighter to teddy.

                        JUNIOR
Come on, buddy. Let the nice man take a look. He might be
able to help teddy out.

                        CRUZ
That's what I'm here for. To help people wherever I can. So
long as they're a straight, white, God-fearing Christian
man who votes Republican and has never had sex before
marriage.

                        JUNIOR
I don't think Eric has had sex after marriage.

                        CRUZ
                     (to ERIC)
Come on, let me take a look at him.

                              Reluctantly, ERIC hands his
                              teddy over to CRUZ. CRUZ holds
                              it to his ear.

                        CRUZ
You're right. He doesn't sound too good, does he?

                        ERIC
He needs to go to the hospital.

                        CRUZ
                     (to JUNIOR)
Could you hold this?

                              JUNIOR takes the teddy from CRUZ
                              and holds it out as CRUZ pulls a
                              handgun from his pocket and
                              shoots the teddy's head off.

                              At the other side of the stage,
                              BETO O'ROURKE enters wearing a
                              casual suit, backward cap, and
                              carrying a skateboard.

                                                  (CONTINUED)

                              CRUZ
There you go. I've put him out of his misery.

                              ERIC
You shot teddy.

                              O'ROURKE
You monster!

                              CRUZ, ERIC, and JUNIOR turn as
                              O'ROURKE skates across the stage
                              toward them.

                              O'ROURKE
                          (to CRUZ)
How could you shoot this child's teddy in front of him like
that?

                              CRUZ
This child is thirty-four.

                              O'ROURKE
In the Republican Party, thirty-four makes someone a baby.

                              CRUZ
In the Democratic party, thirty-four makes someone still
young enough to be ripped from the womb.

                              JUNIOR
                          (to CRUZ)
Who is this guy?

                              CRUZ
This is the guy the Democrats have put up against me.

                              O'ROURKE
                          (to JUNIOR)
Yo! I'm Beto O'Rourke. What's up?

                              ERIC
Heaven. That's where teddy has gone.

                              CRUZ
If it's that bad, then I'll get teddy fixed.

                                                        (CONTINUED)

PERFORMANCE LICENSE EDITION   LICENSE # _ _ _ _ _ _ _ _

                         O'ROURKE
Oh yeah? And what are you going to use to fix him? Thoughts
and prayers? Because they've fixed everything else.

                         CRUZ
They have.

                         O'ROURKE
They haven't.

                         CRUZ
They have.

                         O'ROURKE
They haven't.

                         CRUZ
They have.

                         O'ROURKE
Well, have your thoughts and prayers fix this then. Vagina.

                         A beat as CRUZ goes bright red
                         and sweaty.

                         CRUZ
                       (to JUNIOR)
Come on, Junior. I'll introduce you to the rest of my team.

                         CRUZ goes to leave with JUNIOR
                         following him.

                         JUNIOR
Come on, Eric.

                         ERIC
What about teddy?

                         JUNIOR
We'll steal you another one from a small child.

                         CRUZ, ERIC, and JUNIOR exit.

                                                  (CONTINUED)

                        O'ROURKE
                  (looking after them)
Yeah, that's right. You can all get out of here.

                        O'ROURKE skates off the opposite
                        side of the stage.

ACT IV, SCENE FIVE | THE MIDTERMS

                        The stage is set as a FLORIDA
                        POLLING STATION, where the
                        ENSEMBLE (as VOTERS) cast their
                        votes. Next to them, an ELECTION
                        OFFICIAL stands by a ballot box.

                        NARRATOR
                      (entering)
November sixth, the day finally arrives. A chance for
change, not least to everyday lives. For up for contention
is the Senate's first class alongside the whole House,
giving a chance for Democrats to sweep in en masse. All
around within eyes, a sense of hope does reignite for in
the near future a vision of bright new light. Today wins
where they matter might just amount to the first real
chance to hold the President to account. And nowhere in the
nation is a race as tight as those in Florida to the south
where all sides stand close with for power a drouth.

                        The NARRATOR exits as DOOCY,
                        EARHARDT, and KILMEADE enter.

                        DOOCY
Well, hello, everyone. I'm Steve Doocy.

                        EARHARDT
That's right. You are Steve Doocy, Steve.

                        DOOCY
And you're Ainsley Earhardt, Ainsley.

                                            (CONTINUED)

                         EARHARDT
I know, Steve.
                    (to audience)
Welcome to Fox and Friends, everyone.

                          DOOCY
We're down in Florida this morning to see how all of you
are voting.

                         KILMEADE
I'm Brian, and this morning I got to meet a famous mouse in
my hotel room.

                         EARHARDT
That was a rat, Brian. And it bit you.

                              KILMEADE holds up a hand with a
                              band-aid on it.

                         KILMEADE
Look. There's a drawing of him on my band-aid.

                              COOPER enters wearing a Hawaiian
                              shirt and carrying a cocktail in
                              a coconut.

                          COOPER
I'm Anderson Cooper reporting live for C-N-N and fresh from
my vacation in Tahiti.

                              COOPER takes a drink from the
                              cocktail and begins to cough.

                          COOPER
Jesus. What do they put in this thing?

                              LESTER HOLT enters.

                           HOLT
Lester Holt for N-B-C.
                    (to COOPER)
And that, Anderson, would be tequila.

                                              (CONTINUED)

                        COOPER
Do they do a non-alcoholic version?

                        MARTHA RADDATZ enters.

                        RADDATZ
Good morning, America. Martha Raddatz here reporting for A-
B-C. It's the Midterms. Have you planned to go out and vote
yet?

                        KILMEADE
I don't need to vote today because I voted two years ago.

                        EARHARDT
This is a different election, Brian.

                                    At the back of the stage, MARCO
                                    RUBIO enters and takes a ballot
                                    paper from an ELECTION OFFICIAL.

                        COOPER
There is a total of thirty-five seats in the Senate being
contested right across the country today. And, of course,
one of those is right here in Florida where the incumbent
Democrat, Bill Nelson, is facing a close contest from his
Republican contender Rick Scott.

                                    RUBIO marks his ballot, places
                                    it in the ballot box, and then
                                    goes to join DOOCY, EARHARDT,
                                    and KILMEADE.

                        DOOCY
Joining us now, we have the state's incumbent Republican
Senator, Marco Rubio.

                        RUBIO
It's nice to be here. Would you all like to take a photo
together?

                        DOOCY
I'm okay.

                                                      (CONTINUED)

                              EARHARDT
I'm okay too, Steve.

                              KILMEADE
I'm Brian.

                                HOLT
Of course, also up for election today are all four hundred
and thirty-five seats in the House of Representatives. This
is where the Democrats are widely expected to achieve
substantial gains and a majority.

                                        DMITRY and PETROV enter. While
                                        DMITRY distracts the ELECTION
                                        OFFICIAL, PETROV switches the
                                        ballot box with another.

                              RADDATZ
A particularly close race is also expected in Wisconsin for
the Governorship today in one of the many gubernatorial
elections taking place across America.

                                        DMITRY and PETROV take the
                                        ballot box to one side and empty
                                        it onto the floor.

                               DOOCY
What is your take on today's election, Senator Rubio?

                               RUBIO
Well, Steve, I think that we should all just be putting our
trust and faith in God and believe that he knows what he's
doing. He will see us safely through these elections with
the result that the American people deserve if we just
accept him into our lives. Most importantly, our Lord will
do as he sees fit to ensure that his words and his message
are blessed upon those who are most believing of him, and
he will provide the protection of his elected messengers
who embrace his love and use it to guide their actions.

                               DOOCY
I have no idea what you just said.

                                                         (CONTINUED)

                         RUBIO
I think the Republicans will win. Also, something about
China and shoutout to my sponsor, the N-R-A.

                         KILMEADE
I think that President Trump is going to win today.

                         EARHARDT
He isn't standing, Brian.

                         KILMEADE
That's right, folks. Donald Trump has a chair in the Oval
Office.

                         DOOCY
Senator, I'm sure we can all guess, but if I can ask, how
did you vote today?

                              PETROV picks up a ballot paper
                              and looks at it.

                         RUBIO
I voted Republican.

                         PETROV
                        (to DMITRY)
Have you see this, Dmitry. This guy wrote in Marco Rubio.

                         RUBIO
If you'd excuse me. I have to go make a table reservation
at McDonald's for tonight.

                         RUBIO exits.

                         DOOCY
He left in quite a hurry.

                         EARHARDT
He did, Steve. Which is unusual because he usually stays
around for much longer than anyone wants him to.

                         The NARRATOR enters.

                                              (CONTINUED)
PERFORMANCE LICENSE EDITION   LICENSE # _ _ _ _ _ _ _

                              NARRATOR
Six hours until the polls close.

                                   As the NARRATOR exits once more,
                                   the action moves to a TEXAS
                                   POLLING STATION.

                              RADDATZ
One of the other big contests to watch closely today is
over in Texas, where Ted Cruz is facing a tough fight to be
re-elected from the Democratic challenger, Beto O'Rourke.

                                   CRUZ enters and joins RADDATZ.

                              RADDATZ
Joining me now is Senator Cruz.
                    (to CRUZ)
Senator, thank you for speaking to me.

                                   At the back of the stage, a
                                   MOTHER pushing a stroller enters
                                   and goes to vote.

                              CRUZ
Very nice to be here on A-B-C today.

                                   ERIC (with the stolen teddy) and
                                   JUNIOR enter to join DOOCY,
                                   EARHARDT, and KILMEADE.

                              KILMEADE
I just wet myself with excitement.

                              Beat.

                              HOLT
Congressman O'Rourke, the polls are showing that while you
are running a close contest, you will still be short of
securing enough votes to take the seat. How confident do
you feel that despite these numbers, you will make it over
the line?

                              O'ROURKE
Wussten Sie, dass ich Spanisch spreche?

                                                  (CONTINUED)

                              HOLT
I'm sorry.

                            O'ROURKE
I said, did you know that I can speak Spanish?

                              HOLT
Yes, I did know that, Mister O'Rourke.

                             DOOCY
Thank you for coming on the show today, Donald Junior and
Eric.

                            EARHARDT
I thank them too, Steve.

                             JUNIOR
You know, it's great to be down here in Texas.

                            KILMEADE
I've never been to text-ass before. I have butt-dialed a
few times, though.

                         Beat.

                             ERIC
I got a new teddy.

                            O'ROURKE
Could you excuse me for a moment?

                              HOLT
Of course.

                         O'ROURKE moves close behind
                         CRUZ.

                             DOOCY
So how do you think people are voting today, Donald?

                             JUNIOR
I hope that they are voting for my father. He only wants
what is best for our country, but he needs the support of a
strong Congress that will allow him to be the…

                                        (CONTINUED)

          JUNIOR   O'ROURKE
...leader...   (shouting behind CRUZ)
                        DILDO!

                    JUNIOR
... America deserves.

                    CRUZ goes red and dabs sweat
                    from his face.

                    CRUZ
                (turning to O'ROURKE)
For God's sake. Can't you stop doing that?

                    O'ROURKE
Thoughts and prayers, Ted.

                    COOPER returns to the front of
                    the stage with the MOTHER.

                    COOPER
And now, I can bring you an exclusive interview with a
voter who has actually met Beto O'Rourke in person.
                (to the MOTHER)
Ma'am, can you tell us where and when you first met the
Congressman?

                    MOTHER
Outside five minutes ago.

                    COOPER
And who did you vote for today?

                    MOTHER
Ted Cruz.

                    Beat, and then the NARRATOR
                    enters.

                    NARRATOR
Polls are closed.

CONTINUED:

>   The NARRATOR exits as the stage
>   clears except for COOPER, DOOCY,
>   EARHARDT, HOLT, KILMEADE, and
>   RADDATZ.

                              HOLT
And now we come to the part of the day that all of you at
home have been waiting for.

                              RADDATZ
Stay tuned to A-B-C for the result as they come in live.

                              COOPER
And I can now confirm that America has won in Wisconsin.

                              HOLT
You can't know that yet, Anderson.

                              COOPER
Paul Ryan is stepping down.

                              RADDATZ
There is some confirmed news coming out of Wisconsin.
Democrats have taken the Governorship in the gubernatorial
race with Tony Evers winning a slim majority over
Republican incumbent Scott Walker.

                              DOOCY
And now we can go live to Sean Hannity, who is in Florida
for an update on the counting there.

                              EARHARDT
That's right, Steve. We can.

>   HANNITY steps onto the stage.

                              DOOCY
How are things looking, Sean?

                              HANNITY
Get this, there isn't a result yet.

                              DOOCY
Great. We'll come back to you later.

                                                    (CONTINUED)

CONTINUED:

                    HANNITY steps off the stage.

                         HOLT
More good news for the Democrats now as they are picking up
House seat after House seat this evening.

                         COOPER
With just a few more results to be announced, it's looking
as though the polls were right with the Democrats set to
reclaim control of the House of Representatives.

                         RADDATZ
Things are not going as well in the contest for the Senate,
however. It looks as though Republicans will be keeping
their control in the chamber after taking seats from the
Democrats in Indiana, Missouri, and North Dakota.

                         CRUZ and O'ROURKE reenter the
                         stage.

                         HOLT
And now, we are ready to receive the result here in Texas.
And it looks as though it is going to be a narrow win for
the incumbent Ted Cruz.

                         CRUZ
Just as God intended.
                    (to O'ROURKE)
Thoughts and prayers, Beto.

                         KILMEADE
I sometimes have thoughts.

                         O'ROURKE
                    (to CRUZ)
Orgasm.

                         CRUZ goes red and wipes sweat
                         from his face.

                         CRUZ
Will you quit doing that?

                                        (CONTINUED)

                         O'ROURKE
Period. Thong. Women's rights.

                         CRUZ
Stop it.

                    Wiping his face, CRUZ exits.

                         HOLT
And now I can get a live reaction from the runner-up here
in Texas, Beto O'Rourke.
                         (to O'ROURKE)
Congressman, how are you feeling right now?

                         O'ROURKE
It's a tight result and disappointing for myself and my
team, but now I'm going to go home, get some rest, and then
take the logical next step after losing a Senate race by
running for President.

                    O'ROURKE goes to leave.

                         O'ROURKE
Beto out y'all.

                    O'ROURKE exits.

                         DOOCY
I think that we should try to find out what's going on in
Florida again.

                         EARHARDT
I agree, Steve.

                    HANNITY steps back onto the
                    stage.

                         HANNITY
Steve. Ainsley.

                         KILMEADE
What about Brian?

                                              (CONTINUED)

                         HANNITY
What about you, Brian?

                         DOOCY
Sean, do you have any new information for us?
                    (beat)
Sean?

                    Beat.

                         EARHARDT
I think there is a delay in the satellite link, Steve.

                         HANNITY
There's no delay. We just still don't have a result yet.

                         COOPER
Florida must be a Republican victory. That's the only way
they could be so far behind the rest of the country.

                         HOLT claps as HANNITY steps back
                         offstage.

                         HOLT
You know, Anderson, that was a good one. I like that one.

                         COOPER
Really?

                         HOLT
Let's call a truce and hug it out.

                         HOLT goes to hug COOPER.

                         COOPER
Okay.

                         They hug with COOPER's back to
                         the audience as HOLT pulls out a
                         large "NBC Nightly News" sticker
                         and sticks on COOPER's back.

                                                      (CONTINUED)

                              RADDATZ
And so with the final results in it looks as though the
Democrats have done what they were widely expected to do,
with substantial gains in the House to reclaim the majority
with two hundred and thirty-five seats.

                              COOPER
Big gains for the Democrats also in the gubernatorial
contests with a net gain of seven Governorships. And --

                              DOOCY
Breaking news. The Republicans have won the Midterms by
retaining control of the Senate in a nationwide endorsement
of President Trump.

                              HOLT
I've been Lester Holt.

                              COOPER
Florida has been Florida.

                              HOLT
And that's all from me.

                              RADDATZ
And from me.

                              COOPER
And me. Good night.

                              The NARRATOR enters as the stage
                              fills with light.

                              NARRATOR
Okay, can we wrap this up here? Midterms are over, and it's
time to get back to how truly terrible everything is.

                              The stage begins to clear with
                              the ENSEMBLE helping to move
                              pieces of the set off until ERIC
                              and KILMEADE are left on stage
                              alone.

                                                        (CONTINUED)

CONTINUED:

>   At first, ERIC and KILMEADE
>   don't notice each other.

ERIC	KILMEADE
Hey, where has everyone gone?	Hey, where has everyone gone?

>   They turn and notice each other.

ERIC	KILMEADE
Who are you? I'm Eric. We should be friends. Okay. Let's be friends.	Who are you? I'm Brian. We should be friends. Okay. Let's be friends.

>   KILMEADE approaches ERIC and
>   tags him on the arm.

                         KILMEADE
Tag. You're it.

                           ERIC
I don't want to be friends anymore. I'm going and taking
teddy with me.

>   The lights fade as ERIC begins
>   to walk offstage with his head
>   down.

ACT IV, SCENE SIX | PELOSI'S PRESS CONFERENCE

>   The lights go up on a PRESS
>   CONFERENCE ROOM, where PELOSI
>   stands behind a podium
>   addressing the ENSEMBLE (as
>   PRESS, except PRESS #4).

                         NARRATOR
                        (entering)
With the voting over the Midterms bring a shock result for
President Trump and his sheep-like cult. The polls might
have shown that they were likely to lose, but they had
Russia behind them, helping voters to choose. But what does
it all mean now for Donald and his presidency coddled?
                        (MORE)
                                              (CONTINUED)

NARRATOR (CONT'D)

For that is the question that many now begin to contemplate as they feel that Democrats will soon declare checkmate or, at the very least, his agenda frustrate. But the approach by Pelosi seems much tamer than others in her party who wish to take aim. And there's pressure too from voters who believe immediate action is all that is right, and so Pelosi is forced to address the press to prove against Trump she is ready to fight.

The NARRATOR exits.

PELOSI
(to PRESS #2)

We've all got a lot of work to be doing, so I've only got time to take a few short questions.

PRESS #2

Madame Representative, many in your party ran on a platform of moving toward impeaching President Trump if Democrats reclaimed the House. Now that you have succeeded in taking the House back, will you commit to this action?

PELOSI

I'm not going to get drawn into that. Next question.
(to PRESS #3)
Go ahead.

PRESS #3

There is evidence to suggest that the President has already committed what can only be described as crimes against humanity, not least with his refusal to offer fundamental human rights to millions, including some tens of thousands of innocent children seeking safety. Are you sure that you don't want to commit to impeachment?

PELOSI

I'm not going to get drawn into that. Next question.
(to PRESS #1)
Yes. New York Times.

PRESS #1

I'm actually from C-N-N.

(CONTINUED)

CONTINUED:

                        PELOSI
Well, I'm not here to get drawn into the specifics. What's
your question?

                        PRESS #1
Just a few weeks ago, alleged alcoholic sex offender Brett
Kavanaugh became the newest Justice of the Supreme Court
despite multiple allegations backed up by circumstance and
corroborating stories. His only defense was a calendar.
Given that the President nominated a man like that, don't
you think it might be time to commit to holding him to
account in the way that many in your party and many of your
voters would like to see?

                        PELOSI
Of course, I disagree with the appointment of Brett
Kavanaugh, but I'm not going to get drawn into the details.
                   (to PRESS #5)
Yes. I can take one from Fox News.

                        PRESS #5
Oh, I don't have a question. I just wanted to say thank
you.

                        PELOSI
Are there any more questions.

                        PRESS #6
I have a question.

                        PELOSI
Go ahead.

                        PRESS #6
My daughter is in third grade and has been given a home
assignment where she has to draw her favorite politician --

                        PELOSI
I'm not going to get drawn into that.
                   (beat)
Okay, are we done here? I'll be seeing you all then.

                        PELOSI exits as the PRESS shout
                        questions after her.

PERFORMANCE LICENSE EDITION   LICENSE # _ _ _ _ _ _ _ _

ACT IV, SCENE SEVEN | TRUMP'S PRESS CONFERENCE

> The scene remains the same, and
> the ENSEMBLE (as PRESS, except
> PRESS #4) remain on stage as the
> NARRATOR enters.

NARRATOR
Day two of a new dawn and for once the President feels a
need to set things straight somewhere other than the White
House lawn. And so the press are called to gather in the
famous East Room where Trump and his team hope to give
excuses to ensure the news agenda is just as they groom.
For shock is what settles in now they know the full result
and truth is that victory for him is seen by none except
his narrow cult. Among the media stands C-N-N's Jim Acosta
with a question on Trump's future vexed, though soon he is
to unexpectedly find his own left muscle somewhat flexed.

> JIM ACOSTA enters.

ACOSTA
Jim Acosta, reporting for C-N-N.

> ACOSTA joins the PRESS.

NARRATOR
But before the President can answer questions about how the
pressure on him he hopes to discount, he must first satisfy
his own boss who has arrived to ensure that any suspicious
they do surmount.

> The NARRATOR exits.

PRESS #2
How much longer do you think we'll have to wait?

PRESS #6
I think I can hear voices.

> From offstage, several voices
> become audible.

(CONTINUED)

CONTINUED:

                         PUTIN (OFF)
I leave for short time, and when I return, I find you lose
election.

                         TRUMP (OFF)
It was not my fault.

                              PUTIN and TRUMP enter without
                              being noticed by the PRESS.

                         PUTIN
How be it not fault of yours? How do you even lose election
that you be guaranteed to win?

                         TRUMP
It was the Democrats. They are traitors. They got help from
illegals.

                         PUTIN
I be illegals, and I help you, not them.

                              CONWAY enters.

                         CONWAY
Mister President, sir, the press are waiting for you.

                         PUTIN
Donald, you fix mess now.

                         TRUMP
Yes, Comrade Putin, sir.

                         PUTIN
Good.
                         (to CONWAY)
Kellyanne, please move ornament away from television at
home. Signal be interfering with microphone.

                         CONWAY
I'm sorry?

                         PUTIN
                    (ignoring CONWAY)
I go now.

                                                  (CONTINUED)

PERFORMANCE LICENSE EDITION   LICENSE # _ _ _ _ _ _ _ _

CONTINUED:

> PUTIN points at his own eyes and
> then at TRUMP before he turns
> and exits.

                    CONWAY
Mister President, would you like me to go out and introduce
you first?

                    TRUMP
That is a great idea, Kellyanne Conway. I am glad I thought
of it.

> As CONWAY and TRUMP go to walk
> to the podium, SARAH HUCKABEE
> SANDERS enters.

                    HUCKABEE SANDERS
Mister President. I am here and ready to deliver this press
conference. My daddy says it's a privilege for me to do so.

                    TRUMP
Sarah Huckabee Sanders, where have you been for the past
ninety-four days?

                    HUCKABEE SANDERS
I've just been sat in my office watching documentaries on
how to care for cute little puppy dogs and also writing my
tell-all book to sell to the highest bidder. Half a million
dollars and I will shred it.

                    TRUMP
You have no held a press conference in three months?

                    HUCKABEE SANDERS
No, Mister President, I have not. I was not aware that it
was a part of my job description.

                    Beat.

                    TRUMP
Two hundred and fifty thousand, and you have a deal.

                    HUCKABEE SANDERS
I'm not going to take a cent less than four hundred, sir.

                                        (CONTINUED)

                    TRUMP
We can negotiate later.

                              Together, all three walk toward
                              the podium.

                    TRUMP
                    (quietly to CONWAY)
Kellyanne Conway, I need you to go and burn that document.

                    HUCKABEE SANDERS
I've made multiple copies, Mister President.

                    TRUMP
                    (quietly to CONWAY)
Could we nuke her office?

                    CONWAY
It is right next to Mike Pence's, sir. There might be some
collateral damage.

                    TRUMP
We could leave him a memo?

                    CONWAY
I'll look into it, Mister President.

                              CONWAY exits as HUCKABEE SANDERS
                              and TRUMP reach the podium.

                    HUCKABEE SANDERS
Well, hello. Good morning to y'all, folks. My name is Sarah
Huckabee Sanders, or as my daddy calls me, Sarah Huckabee.
Y'all get it? Because he's Mike Huckabee.

                    PRESS #1
Sarah, we know who you are.

                    PRESS #3
What we want to know is why you haven't given us a briefing
in over thirteen weeks now.

                                                      (CONTINUED)

                    HUCKABEE SANDERS
I think that is a very unfair statement and I believe that
your daddy would be very disappointed in you for saying it.
This White House has been giving daily briefings to keep
the American people updated.

                        PRESS #2
Where have they been? We haven't been invited.

                    HUCKABEE SANDERS
We outsourced them to save the American people their tax
dollars. All you have to do is turn on Fox News at nine
eastern.

                        PRESS #5
U-S-A! U-S-A! U-S-A!

                        PRESS #1
Sarah, are you talking about Sean Hannity?

                         TRUMP
Sean Hannity is a great man. Just ask Sean Hannity.

                    HUCKABEE SANDERS
And my daddy does agree. Now if there are no more
questions, then I'm going to…

        HUCKABEE SANDERS   PRESS #2
... Introduce President   There's more questions!
Trump.

                    HUCKABEE SANDERS
                        (to TRUMP)
Mister President, it really is an honor for you to be with
us today.

                              HUCKABEE SANDERS stands to the
                              side as TRUMP takes the podium.

                         TRUMP
                  (pointing at PRESS #1)
Loser.
                  (pointing at PRESS #2)
Fake news.
                        (MORE)
                                              (CONTINUED)

                              TRUMP (CONT'D)
                    (pointing at PRESS #3)
Enemy of the people.
                    (pointing at PRESS #6)
Not so great.
                    (pointing at PRESS #5)
You from Fox News, thank you for coming. It is always great
to see our free press in action. Do you have a question?

                         PRESS #5
On behalf of all of us at Fox News I wanted to congratulate
you on your election win.

                          TRUMP
That is a great question. I did great in the election, a
lot of people are saying it. My Senators did a great job.
Mitch McConnell did a great job. I did a great job, and the
result was just so great. I think that the Democrats should
learn from the Republicans that embracing their President,
that's me, okay, is the way to be great.

                         PRESS #5
You're a real hero, Mister President.

                         PRESS #3 mimes being sick.

                          TRUMP
Okay, are we done here?

                         As TRUMP turns to leave, ACOSTA
                         stands up.

                         ACOSTA
I have a question.

                         TRUMP turns back.

                          TRUMP
Who are you?

                         ACOSTA
Jim Acosta. I'm from C-N-N.

                         PRESS #1
No, I'm from C-N-N.

                                        (CONTINUED)

CONTINUED:

                         TRUMP
Okay. I will take your question so that everyone watching
can see how not so great you are.
                    (to HUCKABEE SANDERS)
Come on, let us get this guy a microphone so everyone can
hear his sad question.

                              HUCKABEE SANDERS gestures to
                              someone offstage. A moment
                              later, an INTERN enters with a
                              microphone.

                    HUCKABEE SANDERS
                    (to the INTERN)
It's okay. Like my daddy always says to me, just don't get
too close, and you'll be safe.

                         TRUMP
It is only Jim Acosta.

                    HUCKABEE SANDERS
I wasn't warning her about him, Mister President.

                              The INTERN hands ACOSTA the
                              microphone and stands to one
                              side.

                         ACOSTA
I want to start with your claim that the Republicans won
the election.

                         TRUMP
It was a great result. Not so great for you at C-N-N.

                         ACOSTA
How can you claim to have won when the Democrats made
sweeping gains in gubernatorial contests right across the
country and also reclaimed the house?

                         TRUMP
Some people are saying that. You are saying that.

                         ACOSTA
I'm saying it because it's true.

                                             (CONTINUED)

PERFORMANCE LICENSE EDITION   LICENSE # _ _ _ _ _ _ _ _

                              TRUMP
Well, I do not know about that. It is what some people are
saying. I do not know who is saying it. But others are
saying we did great and they are right. Republicans won in
the Senate and did so great, okay?

                              ACOSTA
No one is saying that you didn't win the Senate --

                              TRUMP
Even you are saying it. It was a great result.

                              ACOSTA
But you didn't win the House of Representatives, and you
lost multiple Governorships.

                              TRUMP
Fake news. That is fake news, and you know it is fake news.
Do you have a real question?

                              ACOSTA
During the campaign, you consistently referred to asylum
seekers from South America as an invasion. Do you think
that you demonized them with those comments?

                              TRUMP
Fake news. All fake news. I do not even know what an asylum
seeker is. Some people do, but not me. Some people are
looking into it for me. They talk to Russia, and they talk
to North Korea. But they do that. Not me.

                              ACOSTA
Mister President, if I could just follow on --

                              TRUMP
You have had your time.

                              ACOSTA
Mister President --

                              TRUMP
Put down the microphone.
                    (to the INTERN)
Take the microphone.

                                                    (CONTINUED)
PERFORMANCE LICENSE EDITION   LICENSE # _ _ _ _ _ _ _ _

                          ACOSTA
Are you worried about any of the indictments against your
allies in the Russia investigation?

                          TRUMP
I told you to shut up.

                              The INTERN attempts to take the
                              microphone from ACOSTA.

                          TRUMP
Hand it over.

                          ACOSTA
                     (to the INTERN)
Excuse me, ma'am.

                              While ACOSTA holds onto the
                              microphone, the INTERN moves
                              over to the side, some distance
                              from anyone else.

                              The INTERN grabs one of their
                              arms with the other and slaps
                              their face before falling over.

                              Beat.

                          TRUMP
Okay, get him out of here. Go on, get him out.

                              HUCKABEE SANDERS grabs ACOSTA.

                          TRUMP
No one gets to treat my staff that badly except for me.

                              HUCKABEE SANDERS aggressively
                              drags ACOSTA offstage.

                     HUCKABEE SANDERS
Alright, you heard the President. You did bad. I'm going to
be writing to my daddy about this.

                                              (CONTINUED)

> As he's dragged off, ACOSTA
> drops the microphone before the
> INTERN stands up, picks it up,
> and hands it to TRUMP.

                    TRUMP
Do you have any idea how long it will take her to recover?
We don't give our employees healthcare coverage.

ACT IV, SCENE EIGHT | THE GOVERNMENT SHUTDOWN

> The back of the stage remains
> dark as the NARRATOR enters.

                    NARRATOR
So begins for America a new political era, one where the
return of balance and responsibility is ever nearer. For
with the Democrats in the House, many feel that in his
office, Donald Trump is but a scared small mouse. Though
Pelosi doesn't rush to do what many wish to see, she
nevertheless ensures he knows what she thinks by sending a
handwritten decree. But when one issue comes along, she
feels a need for action more strong...

> Behind the NARRATOR, CONWAY
> crosses the stage wearing a
> protective suit without a hood.

                    NARRATOR
... For the President is demanding the building of his wall
despite the nationwide opposition calling for the project
to permanently stall. And so as Democrats together refuse
to support, the signing of any bill is what Trump decides
in response to abort. Consequences follow and beings a
nationwide shutdown, a Government inoperable all due to one
clown.

> CONWAY returns, this time
> wearing a hood and carrying a
> stick of plutonium in each hand.

                                              (CONTINUED)

                         CONWAY
                 (muffled to the NARRATOR)
You should step back for the next bit.

                         NARRATOR
I'm sorry?

                                   CONWAY places both sticks into
                                   the same hand and uses her free
                                   hand to pull off the hood.

                         CONWAY
I said you should step back for the next bit.

                         NARRATOR
Is there any reason?

                         CONWAY
I have a job to do.

                                   CONWAY hands one of the sticks
                                   to the NARRATOR.

                         NARRATOR
I don't need both of these, but if you hold it for long
enough, you gain super-human strength.

                                   CONWAY exits as the NARRATOR
                                   throws the plutonium into the
                                   audience.

                         NARRATOR
                 (to audience member)
You can keep that. I don't need any more strength. I've
been carrying this administration for three and a half
acts.
                 (to audience)
And so with Federal buildings across the country all
shutting their doors, Pelosi and Schumer set off to the
White House to settle the scores.

                                                  (CONTINUED)

> The NARRATOR exits as lights go up on the OVAL OFFICE, where TRUMP sits on a couch opposite PELOSI and SCHUMER.
>
> As PELOSI argues with TRUMP, SCHUMER looks around with interest.

PELOSI

Mister President, I think the American people recognize that you are in the wrong here.

TRUMP

Some people are saying that, but not all people.

PELOSI

You can't expect us to fund the building of an unnecessary monument to racism at the expense of hardworking Americans.

TRUMP

We need to build that wall, Nancy Pelosi. There are a lot of illegal and bad people, some say criminal people, who want to do us bad.

PELOSI

That isn't true, Mister President.

TRUMP

It is true, I know many of them personally.

PELOSI

Mister President, we are not going to agree to build this wall.

TRUMP

It is not up to you, I am the President.

PELOSI

If I impeach you and Mike, then I will be the President.

TRUMP

No. Paul Ryan would be the President.

(CONTINUED)

                              PELOSI
Paul Ryan will soon be nothing but a departed stain on our
democracy.

                              TRUMP
Paul Ryan is a great --

                                        At the back of the stage, the
                                        desk swivels around to reveal
                                        PAUL RYAN on the reverse.

                              RYAN
I really wish people would stop saying my name three times
in a row. I was trying to stop some raccoons from eating my
car. Second time this week.
                         (beat)
How do I get out of this place?

                              PELOSI
You never will. This will follow you for the rest of your
life.

                              TRUMP
                         (pointing offstage)
Through that door and then go right.

                              RYAN
How far do I go right?

                              TRUMP
Never stop.

                                        RYAN exits as PENCE enters from
                                        the other side of the stage.

                              PENCE
Mister President, why is there a gas mask and some burn
cream on my desk.

                                        A loud band accompanies a flash
                                        of bright orange and green light
                                        from offstage.

                                                        (CONTINUED)

                         TRUMP
Mike Pence. You are going to need a new office.

                         PELOSI
This is just another example of how you have no sense of
moderation.

                              PENCE sits down next to TRUMP.

                         TRUMP
You are just jealous because you are a loser.

                         PELOSI
I won the House.

                         TRUMP
I won the White House.

                         PELOSI
The White House belongs to the American people.

                         TRUMP
The American people love me.

                         PELOSI
No, Russia loves you.

                         PENCE
I think that is an unfair statement. God also loves him.

                         TRUMP
And Mike Pence would know. He is good friends with God.

                         PELOSI
I think that Chuck might want to say something here.

                              A beat as PELOSI, PENCE, and
                              TRUMP all turn to SCHUMER.

                         SCHUMER
It's a nice place you have here.

                                             (CONTINUED)

>   Another beat and then the
>   arguing resumes as green smoke
>   begins to appear from the wings.

ACT IV, SCENE NINE | HAMBERDERS & FRIES

>   The stage is dark as the
>   NARRATOR enters.

                         NARRATOR
Unresolved is how in the weeks that follow, all problems
remain, and always the other side is to blame is what both
continue to claim.

                    TRUMP (IN DARKNESS)
                         (quietly)
/WHO WOULD HAVE GUESSED, THAT I'M SO BLESSED? SO MANY
NUGGETS HERE TO TEST./

                         NARRATOR
And so the problems caused by the Government closure only
intensify so that even the President is forced to suffer
some exposure.

                    TRUMP (IN DARKNESS)
                         (quietly)
/BEEF BERDER. CHEESE ON TOP. SOMETHING WITH FISH TO TOP THE
LOT. I CALL AND HAVE DELIVERED, A CULINARY COVFEFE./

                         NARRATOR
For as one sporting trophy finds a new shelf to call home,
Donald Trump invites the team to the place he alone calls
his Rome.

                    TRUMP (IN DARKNESS)
                         (quietly)
/I AM A JOKE. I AM A TRICK. I LIKE BIG WALLS MADE OF
BRICKS. AND IF YOU VOTE FOR ME, IT IS WHAT YOU WILL
REGRET./

                                              (CONTINUED)

NARRATOR
But with a meal planned and no chef on hand, the President
is forced to pick up his phone and order in berders, all to
be served upon silver-plated servers.

> The NARRATOR exits as lights go
> up on the WHITE HOUSE DINING
> ROOM.
>
> TRUMP sits alone at a long
> table.In front of him, fast food
> is spread out on silver plates.

TRUMP
/SO MUCH TREASON STILL TO DO. DO I HAVE ONE SON OR IS IT
TWO? WHERE ARE MY GUESTS? WHERE ARE MY GUESTS? WHERE ARE MY
GUESTS?/

> TRUMP looks around at the empty
> chairs.

TRUMP
(to no one)
Have you tried the hamberders? They are so great.

> TRUMP stands and goes to sit at
> another of the chairs.

TRUMP
I agree. They are so great. I am a big fan of all of the
hamberders. I love the hamberders, and they love me.

> Again, TRUMP stands and goes to
> sit at another chair.

TRUMP
Does anyone have any fries? I love fries. A big fan of the
fries.

> TRUMP stands and sits at another
> chair, this time grabbing a cup
> of fries in front of him.

(CONTINUED)

CONTINUED:

                    TRUMP
I have some fries.

                              TRUMP moves back to the previous
                              chair.

                    TRUMP
I will trade you six nuggets and a Berder King for some
fries.

                              TRUMP moves back again.

                    TRUMP
I will not take anything less than nine nuggets and a
barbecue cheeseberder.

                              TRUMP moves back to the other
                              chair.

                    TRUMP
How about a side salad?

                              TRUMP moves back once more.

                    TRUMP
               (to no one next to him)
Do you hear this guy? This guy wants to trade a side salad
for some fries.

                              TRUMP moves to the next chair
                              along to respond.

                    TRUMP
Sad. Such a bad deal. It should be nothing less than two-
quarter pounders with cheese.

                              TRUMP returns to the first
                              chair.

                    TRUMP
There is no need to fight. I am a generous man. Some say
the most generous. There is plenty of berders for all. Just
remember that you all owe me fifteen dollars. Now, who
wants a diet cola?

                                             (CONTINUED)

                        ERIC and JUNIOR.

                             ERIC
Hey, dad, can we have some food?

                             TRUMP
This is not food for you, Eric Trump. This is food for the
Clemson Tigers.

                             JUNIOR
So you know, it seems strange that they haven't arrived
yet.

                             TRUMP
They are on their way, Donald Trump Junior. They called me
to say they are stuck in traffic.

                             JUNIOR
When did they call?

                             TRUMP
Three days ago.

                             Beat.

                             JUNIOR
Are you sure that they're coming?

                             TRUMP
They will be here soon. Why would they not come? There is
so much great food. Great American food that is waiting for
them. We have some great American berders and also some
great American fries from France.

                             JUNIOR
Dad, it's eleven P-M.

                        CONWAY enters.

                             CONWAY
Mister President, the coach of the Clemson Tigers just
called, and he said he's sorry, but the team can't make it
tonight because...

                                              (CONTINUED)

                              CONWAY pulls a memo out from her
                              pocket.

                         CONWAY
                    (reading memo)
"Just make something up yourself and tell him that. Our
hamster died or something like that."

                         TRUMP
Kellyanne Conway, find out which of the players voted for
me and send them my condolences. It must be hard when so
many hamsters die at once.

                         CONWAY
I think only one hamster died, sir.

                         TRUMP
                    (to JUNIOR and ERIC)
Donald Trump Junior. Eric Trump. Help me eat this food.

                              There is a knock on a door, and
                              HUCKABEE SANDERS enters carrying
                              a box of office supplies and a
                              desk plant.

                    HUCKABEE SANDERS
Mister President, I have come to hand in my resignation. I
really feel that it is time for me to leave. You know, my
daddy always taught me that when your boss has your office
nuked, you should take it as a sign to move on.

                              TRUMP stands.

                         TRUMP
Who are you?

                    HUCKABEE SANDERS
I'm Sarah Huckabee Sanders, Mister President. My daddy is
Mike Huckabee.

                         TRUMP
                    (to CONWAY)
Kellyanne Conway, what did she do here?

                                             (CONTINUED)

                              CONWAY
She was your press secretary, Mister President.

                              TRUMP
                        (to HUCKABEE SANDERS)
I have never met you before, but some people say that you
did a great job. You had a real honor to work for me.

                         HUCKABEE SANDERS
Thank you, Mister President, I hope that...

                                   Ignoring HUCKABEE SANDERS, TRUMP
                                   sits back at the table and turns
                                   to JUNIOR.

                         HUCKABEE SANDERS
... despite recent --

                              TRUMP
                           (to JUNIOR)
Now tell me, how long have you been playing football?

ACT IV, SCENE TEN | COUNTDOWN TO 2020

                                   The NARRATOR enters a dark
                                   stage.

                              NARRATOR
And so pass further weeks and with them more issues mount
en masse with no clear way through the legislative impasse.
But then finally comes a break when Democrats pass measures
to allow the Government to rewake.

Meanwhile, the President claims he has a new plan to build
his wall, one that would keep his rivals from having any
final call. But he makes a mistake when an emergency he
declares for Congress are ready to remind him that the
issue is still very much within their own affairs.

And all the while just nearby a new fight kicks off, for
the Democrats now have a twenty-twenty nomination standoff.
                              (MORE)

                                                  (CONTINUED)
PERFORMANCE LICENSE EDITION   LICENSE # _ _ _ _ _ _ _ _

CONTINUED:

                          NARRATOR (CONT'D)
All around names are thrown, and many candidates step in,
all hoping to prove that this is a race where they have
skin.

                              The NARRATOR exits as the lights
                              go up on a ROOM IN THE WHITE
                              HOUSE, where TRUMP sits watching
                              a giant TV. In the giant TV,
                              HANNITY.

                          HANNITY
                         (mid-show)
Coming up next, we're going to be looking at Nancy Pelosi's
secret plan to let more hurricanes onto American soil. But
first, get this, it's the advertisements.

                              HANNITY exits to the replaced by
                              ELIZABETH WARREN.

                          WARREN
Alight. Let's do this. Hi, I'm Elizabeth Warren, and I'm
running to be your next President. Whatever your problem
is, you can trust that I have a plan for that. Perhaps
you're late for a party and have nothing to take? Give me a
call, and I'll bake you a flan for that. Feeling hungry in
the morning? Eat some bran for that. Lost your wedding ring
in some dirt? I'll come along and help you pan for that.

                          TRUMP
Sad. What else is on?

                              TRUMP presses a button on a
                              remote, and WARREN exits to be
                              replaced by JOE BIDEN.

                          BIDEN
Hello, I'm Joe Biden, and I'm running for President. You
may remember me from Barack Obama.

                          TRUMP
More sad.

                              TRUMP presses again, and BIDEN
                              exits as WARREN reenters.

                                              (CONTINUED)

                          WARREN
Perhaps you're a straight woman looking for a date? Hi, I'm
Elizabeth Warren, and if this sounds like you, I can find
you a man for that. Not sure what to wear on that date? I
recommend something in cyan for that.

                          TRUMP
Not great.

                          TRUMP presses again, and WARREN
                          exits to be replaced by BERNIE
                          SANDERS.

                          SANDERS
Yes. It's me, Bernie Sanders. I am still here, I am not
dead, and I am ready to shout even louder than before. Now,
listen up. I know that many of you think that I helped get
President Trump elected, but here are the facts, we are
going to have a **REVOLUTION!**

                          TRUMP
Why do anyone prefer this guy?

                          TRUMP presses again, and SANDERS
                          is replaced by WARREN.

                          WARREN
Hi, I'm a woman...

                          TRUMP
That is why.

                          WARREN
... and are you feeling tired after a long day at work? I
sleep in a divan for that. Or do you just need to let out
some stress by complaining about the boss? Get a friend
called Ann for that.

                          TRUMP
Why is everything advertisements?

                                                   (CONTINUED)

PERFORMANCE LICENSE EDITION   LICENSE # _ _ _ _ _ _ _ _

> TRUMP presses again, and WARREN
> exits to be replaced by the
> NARRATOR as 1950's comedy music
> begins to play.

                    NARRATOR (OFF)
                  (as a voiceover)
Coming soon. The world knows here to be the chief aid to
the President while the world knows him to burn her boss
while she's at work...

                    TRUMP
I like this show.

                    NARRATOR (OFF)
... But what really goes on behind closed doors? Find out
in our brand new sitcom, The Conways.

> A light finds GEORGE CONWAY sat
> at a kitchen table typing on a
> laptop.

                    GEORGE
                    (typing)
"The President is a danger to our nation, and we should all
be scared of what he might do next. L-O-L." And tweet.

> Canned laughter followed by the
> sound of a door opening.

                    CONWAY (OFF)
Hey, George. I'm home.

                    GEORGE
                  (to audience)
Oh. I better put my laptop away, or she'll want to see my
search history.

> More canned laughter as GEORGE
> puts the laptop to one side, and
> CONWAY enters.

                                              (CONTINUED)

                              CONWAY
Now, George, I hope that you weren't looking at anything
you shouldn't have been while I was at work.

                              GEORGE
Only a --

                                        As GEORGE is interrupted by a
                                        beep, he winks to the audience
                                        before more canned laughter
                                        plays.

                              CONWAY
Oh, George.

                                        The light on CONWAY and GEORGE
                                        go down as the music stops.

                         NARRATOR (OFF)
                        (as a voiceover)
Staring Kellyanne Conway and her husband George Conway as
they try to make their personal lives work despite their
professional lives.

                                        Light up on the table where
                                        CONWAY and GEORGE sit eating.

                              CONWAY
                             (cooly)
So, I heard what you said about the President today.

                              GEORGE
This sauce seems mild.

                              CONWAY
I thought that you'd had enough spice for today in your
tweets, George.

                              GEORGE
Can you pass me the pepper?

                              CONWAY
Get your own pepper, George.

                                                      (CONTINUED)

                         NARRATOR (OFF)
                       (as a voiceover)
The Conways, next Thursday, nine eastern.

                              The light on CONWAY and GEORGE
                              goes down as the NARRATOR exits.

                         TRUMP
Such a great show. It would be, I am in it.

                         WARREN returns.

                         WARREN
Hi, I'm Elizabeth Warren, and if you're looking for a
European city vacation, then I recommend you visit Milan
for that. Or, if you want a more cultural experience, then
why not visit Japan for that? Worried how you'll be able to
afford it? Well, under my plan, the rich won't keep getting
richer, and you'll earn more.

                         TRUMP
Fake news.

                              TRUMP presses a button again,
                              and WARREN exits to be replaced
                              by GENERIC WHITE MAN.

                         GENERIC WHITE MAN
Hi, I'm Mike Bloomberg, and I'm richer than Donald Trump.

                         TRUMP
Wait, what did that woman say?

                              TRUMP presses again, and GENERIC
                              WHITE MAN exits to be replaced
                              by OBAMA.

                         OBAMA
Good sundown to you all... I am erstwhile President, Barack
Obama, and I would like to take this occasion to tell you
all about my new venture... Barack Obama Greeting Cards...
At Barack Obama Greeting Cards, you can always find... a
printed material with a message... that is just right.

                                             (CONTINUED)
PERFORMANCE LICENSE EDITION   LICENSE # _ _ _ _ _ _ _ _

                     OBAMA puts his hand to his heart
                     and looks longingly into the
                     distance.

                     OBAMA

For Saint Valentines' day.
               (romantically)
My dear, my heart beats in a most irregular pattern...
whenever I think of the person whom you are... I have a
deep infatuation and appreciation of yourself... and I feel
amorousness... in your specific direction.

                     OBAMA looks forward once more.

                     OBAMA

For birthdays.
               (cheerful)
Happy birthday to you... Happy birthday to you... Happy
anniversary of the joyful day... on which you were born and
began to make... your contribution to our world... Happy
birthday to you.

                     OBAMA looks down thoughtfully.

                     OBAMA

For bereavement
              (sincere)
At this most difficult of times... I pass on thoughts most
forthright and genuine on behalf of myself... and my
wife... slash husband... slash partner... slash
girlfriend... slash boyfriend... slash housemate... slash
goldfish.

                     OBAMA looks forward.

                     OBAMA

And for Christmas... Happy Holidays.
               (beat)
Barack Obama Greeting Cards... Why say something in three
words when you could say it in thirty-three?

                     TRUMP
               (to himself)
What the hell was that?

                                (CONTINUED)

>   The lights on the scene fade.

ACT IV, SCENE ELEVEN | THE DEMOCRATIC DEBATE

>   A DEBATE STAGE where a spotlight
>   shines upon an unoccupied desk.
>   Behind the desk, two chairs.

                         NARRATOR
                        (entering)
And so as focus moves to the year ahead, for Democrats, the
time has come to decide which of them forward dares to
tread. With the next election now just twelve months away,
voters begin to pray as thoughts turn eager to know who has
it in them to deal the Trump presidency its final blow.

At the start, over twenty names went in, but not all can go
on as they hope to begin. But how to narrow down to those
au fait? The answer lies in a live debate presented
televised and who better to host than M-S-N-B-C who sent
their anchors who stand tall foremost. First, to cut
through the lies and help the field narrow, ordinarily live
each night, it's Rachel Maddow.

>   RACHEL MADDOW enters and waves
>   to the audience as she stands
>   next to the NARRATOR.

                         MADDOW
Good evening.

                         NARRATOR
And to stand alongside and help you see at which candidates
to nod, it's the network's --

>   CHUCK TOOD enters and stands at
>   the opposite side.

                         TODD
Chuck Todd.

                         NARRATOR
Yes. I was just about to get to that.

                                               (CONTINUED)

                         TODD
Carry on.

                         NARRATOR
And so with the stage all set, it's time to place that
final bet on who will come out top and whose campaign is
set to suffer a humiliating electoral flop.

                    The NARRATOR exits.

                         MADDOW
Hello. I'm Rachel --

                         TODD
And I'm Chuck Todd.

                         MADDOW
Welcome to this, the first Democratic debate for --

                         TODD
And now, let's meet the candidates who will be debating
tonight.

                         MADDOW
First up, it's Vermont Senator, Bernie Sanders.

                              A light shines on the first of
                              eight podiums. Stood behind it,
                              SANDERS.

                         SANDERS
Yes. Hello. I am here, and tonight I will be talking so
loud that you will still hear me at home even if you mute
your television.

                    The light fades.

                         TODD
The junior Senator from the state of California, Kamala
Harris.

                              A light shines on the second
                              podium where KAMALA HARRIS is
                              standing.

                                             (CONTINUED)

                         HARRIS
Yes, hello. Tonight, I'm going to make Joe Biden wish that
he didn't turn up.

                    The light fades.

                         MADDOW
Yes, hello. Tonight, I'm going to make Joe Biden wish that
he didn't turn up.

                              A light shines on the third
                              podium where BIDEN is standing.
                              Noticing the audience, he smiles
                              and shoots his fingers out.

                         BIDEN
Did you miss me?

                    The light fades.

                         TODD
Mayor of South Bend Indiana, Pete Buttigieg.

                              A light shines on the fourth
                              podium where PETE BUTTIGIEG
                              stands.

                         BUTTIGIEG
Remember, America, if you vote for me, then Mike Pence will
cry real tears.

                    The light fades.

                         MADDOW
Author and former independent candidate for the House,
Marianne Williamson.

                              A light shines on the fifth
                              podium where MARIANNE WILLIAMSON
                              stands.

                         WILLIAMSON
Nineteen seventy-three called. They want us to bring back
the love, y'all.

                                             (CONTINUED)

                        The light fades.

                    TODD
Democratic candidate in the two thousand and eighteen
Senate race in Texas, Beto O'Rourke.

                        A light shines on BETO O'ROURKE
                        stood behind the sixth podium.

                    O'ROURKE
I am ready to kill this thing.

                        The light fades.

                    MADDOW
Massachusetts Senator, Elizabeth Warren.

                    WARREN
Let's do this together. And after that, let's do it again.
And after that, I have signed photos of my dog to give to
all of you.

                        The light fades.

                    TODD
Representing Ohio's thirteenth district, Tim Ryan.

                        A light shines on the final
                        podium where GENERIC WHITE MAN
                        stands.

                    GENERIC WHITE MAN
Hello.

                        The light fades.

                    MADDOW
Former Colorado Governor, John Hickenlooper.

                        The light on GENERIC WHITE MAN
                        returns.

                    GENERIC WHITE MAN
Hi.

                                            (CONTINUED)

                        The light fades.

                    TODD
Also from the state of Colorado, Senator Michael Bennet.

                        The light on GENERIC WHITE MAN
                        returns.

                    GENERIC WHITE MAN
How you doing?

                        The light fades.

                    MADDOW
Mayor of New York City, Bill DeBlasio.

                        The light on GENERIC WHITE MAN
                        returns.

                    GENERIC WHITE MAN
Good to see you.

                        The light fades.

                    TODD
Former representative of Maryland's Sixth Congressional
District, John Delaney.

                        The light on GENERIC WHITE MAN
                        returns.

                    GENERIC WHITE MAN
Thanks for coming.

                        The light fades.

                    MADDOW
He's currently representing the sixth Congressional
District, this time in Massachusetts, Seth Moulton.

                        The light on GENERIC WHITE MAN
                        returns.

                                                (CONTINUED)

                        GENERIC WHITE MAN
Great to be here.

                                  The light fades.

                        TODD
Governor Steve Bullock of Montana.

                                  The light on GENERIC WHITE MAN
                                  returns.

                        GENERIC WHITE MAN
Good evening.

                                  The light fades.

                        MADDOW
Former mayor of New York City and billionaire, Michael
Bloomberg.

                                  The light on GENERIC WHITE MAN
                                  returns.

                        GENERIC WHITE MAN
I'm excited to be here tonight.

                                  The light fades.

                        TODD
Former Senator from the state of Alaska, Mike Gravel.

                                  The light on GENERIC WHITE MAN
                                  returns.

                        GENERIC WHITE MAN
Remember me?

                                  The light fades.

                        MADDOW
Billionaire hedge fund manager, Tom Steyer.

                                  The light on GENERIC WHITE MAN
                                  returns.

                                                       (CONTINUED)

GENERIC WHITE MAN
I am privileged to be here. No, really, I am **privileged** to be here.

The light fades.

TODD
Washington Governor, Jay Inslee.

The light on GENERIC WHITE MAN returns.

GENERIC WHITE MAN
What's happening.

The light fades.

MADDOW
And finally, former House Representative from the state of Pennsylvania, Joe Sestak.

The light on GENERIC WHITE MAN returns.

GENERIC WHITE MAN
Yeah. I've got nothing.

The light fades.

TODD
There are, of course, several candidates who were not able to join us up on the stage tonight. The first of these is Tulsi Gabbard from Hawaii, who refused her invitation after hearing that there might be some Democrats here.

MADDOW
Julián Castro and Cory Booker, who, despite being two of the most experienced and qualified candidates in this race, are neither white billionaires or Pete Buttigieg.

TODD
And Andrew Yang who is here tonight, but is currently busy handing out free money to strangers on the sidewalk.

(CONTINUED)

                           MADDOW
Well, you've met all of the candidates, and now it's their
time to debate.

                                    Lights go up on all eight
                                    podiums as MADDOW and TODD take
                                    their places behind the desk.

                           MADDOW
Tonight, we are going to be covering some of the major
issues that people right across America care about. Climate
change, international relations, and the economy will all
be up for discussion this evening.

                           TODD
And after that, we will follow up by ignoring many of the
other issues that people care about and bring the level of
discourse down to that of a high school debating society.

                           MADDOW
We're going to begin tonight with Elizabeth Warren.
                    (to WARREN)
Senator Warren --

                           WARREN
Yeah. I'm ready for this.

                           MADDOW
Senator, since you launched your campaign for President,
you have announced plans to offer free college, free child
care, healthcare for all, cancel existing student debt,
introduce new taxes on the wealthiest, new regulations to
protect everyday consumers, and also to break up major
corporations so that they can't exploit their position. So
my question is, who are you going to be choosing as a
running mate?

                           WARREN
That is an excellent question, and I think that it's great
that you're asking it. But if you don't mind, I'd like to
answer it while I get in my daily exercise.

                                                        (CONTINUED)

                              WARREN moves to the center of
                              the stage and begins a series of
                              exercises.

                         SANDERS
Is she allowed to do that?

                         WARREN
It would be great if you came over to join me, Bernie.

                         SANDERS
I'm okay. I put my back out while trying to open the window
in my hotel room so I could keep cool.

                         WARREN
In my room, I have a fan for that.

                         HARRIS
I put my back out carrying the knowledge that there are
still millions of disadvantaged Americans right across our
country who are not being given the rights that they're
entitled to.

                         BIDEN
I know Barack Obama.

                         MADDOW
If I can, I would like to get an answer from Senator Warren
on my first question before we move onto any other subject.

                         WARREN
So, I've not really given it much thought yet, but I know
that it needs to be someone who cares about this country
just as much as I do. It needs to be someone who wants to
see everyone get the opportunities they deserve and who
wants to see accountability for those in power...

                              WARREN begins doing a series of
                              push-ups.

                         WARREN
... It needs to be someone who, just like me, will always
keep pushing for what is right.

                                             (CONTINUED)

> WARREN does a final push-up
> before standing, rubbing her
> hands together, and returning to
> her podium.

TODD

Senator Harris.

HARRIS

Yes, that's me. America may remember me my many appearances
in the Senate. I'm the one who makes Republicans weep like
a small child.

TODD

Senator, do you think that the economy is working for
everyday people?

HARRIS

No, I do not. Not at all. And let me tell you why. When I
travel around America, I meet people who are struggling to
put food on the table for their children even though they
are working two or more jobs. And why does this happen? It
happens because in America, the system isn't fair and
wealth and opportunity is being disproportionately hoarded
by billionaires --

TODD

I'd just like to bring in billionaire Tom Steyer.

GENERIC WHITE MAN

Oh, I... It's nice to be here today.

HARRIS

If I could just add. When I go around and talk to families,
that person who is going around, that person is me.

MADDOW

Senator Bernie Sanders. The environment, what's your plan?

SANDERS

I have lots of plans, Rachel. I have plans for everything.
The economy, there's a plan for that. Trade, there's a plan
for that. Infrastructure, there's a plan for that.
                          (MORE)

                                              (CONTINUED)

CONTINUED:

                          SANDERS (CONT'D)
And if you vote for Bernie Sanders on Super Tuesday, you
can get all of my plans for the price of just one plan. But
hurry, this offer is only good for one election cycle and
perhaps another after that. And remember, you cannot pay
for Bernie Sanders in installments. Some people did not
seem to understand that last time. You must vote for me all
at once, not some in twenty-sixteen and some in twenty-
twenty.

                          MADDOW
Senator, I asked about the environment. What is your plan
for climate change?

                          SANDERS
We are going to have a revolution!

                          MADDOW
But specifically, how are you going to tackle the climate
crisis?

                          SANDERS
                      (shrugging)
Point at a bush and then shout at a tree.

                          TODD
Beto O'Rourke.

                          O'ROURKE
Yo. Or as we say in Spanish, yo.

                          TODD
Mister O'Rourke, you are currently polling at just three
percentage points in this race.

                          O'ROURKE
Yes. What is my question?

                          TODD
                      (to BIDEN)
Vice President Biden.

                          SANDERS
                  (pointing at O'ROURKE)
Hold on. I have a question for this guy.

                                          (CONTINUED)

PERFORMANCE LICENSE EDITION   LICENSE # _ _ _ _ _ _ _ _

                              TODD
Okay, well, go ahead, Senator Sanders.

                             SANDERS
Thank you.
                         (to O'ROURKE)
Are you actually a real person?

                            O'ROURKE
Hey, cool it, gramps. No need to get personal.

                             SANDERS
Gramps? Who are you calling gramps? Back in my day, if I
had called someone gramps, they would have said no, I'm
your grandmother. Have you thought about wearing glasses,
Bernie?

                              TODD
Vice President Biden.

                             BIDEN
Yes. I'm ready.

                              TODD
I'd like to yield my time over to the Senator from
California.

                    HARRIS clears her throat.

                             BIDEN
I'm no longer ready.

                             HARRIS
Thank you, Chuck.
                         (to BIDEN)
Now, Joe, I am about to take you to school. Which is a lot
more than you did for all those children, including myself,
when you opposed bussing.

                             BIDEN
Is it time yet?

                              TODD
Not yet, Vice President.

                                                  (CONTINUED)

                              WARREN pulls a bag of popcorn
                              from her pocket and begins to
                              eat as HARRIS turns to her.

                    WARREN
Would you like some?

                    HARRIS
Very kind of you.

                              HARRIS takes a handful of
                              popcorn and turns back to BIDEN.

                    HARRIS
Joe, I do not think that you are a racist. But I am going
to spend the next few minutes making everyone watching at
home think that you might be.

                              BIDEN turns to the audience and
                              smiles.

                    HARRIS
Do you remember that time that you openly defended and
called your friends, two racist Senators? Because I do
remember that.

                              BIDEN's smile turns into a
                              frown.

                    WARREN
This is so good to watch.

                              HARRIS turns to WARREN.

                    WARREN
You go, sister.

                    HARRIS
Can I get the recipe for that popcorn? It's good stuff.

                    WARREN
Sure, I'll send it to you later. We should put toffee in
the next batch to mark the occasion of Joe being in a
sticky situation.

                                                  (CONTINUED)
PERFORMANCE LICENSE EDITION   LICENSE # _ _ _ _ _ _ _ _

                           HARRIS and WARREN high five.

                    WARREN
I do try.

                    TODD
Vice President Biden, would you like to respond to Senator
Harris?

                    BIDEN
Yes, I would.
                    (to HARRIS)
Now you listen to me. You're acting like a child and
talking about things that you don't understand --

                    HARRIS
Joe --

                    BIDEN
No, you're going to listen to me --

                    HARRIS
Mister Vice President --

                    BIDEN
I simply cannot be a racist. Some of my best friends are
Barack Obama.

                         Beat.

                    TODD
Senator Harris, would you like to add anything?

                    HARRIS
I don't think that I need to.

                    MADDOW
Senator Warren. Healthcare, what is your plan?

                    WARREN
My plan is straightforward. I believe that healthcare is
one of our human rights and that all of us are human. Even
Donald Trump.
                         (MORE)

                                             (CONTINUED)

CONTINUED:

WARREN (CONT'D)

We need to cut out the insurance companies and the profit that they make and ensure that no one else ever goes broke because they needed care.

MADDOW

And what do you say to those who think that your plan will take choice away from patients and perhaps force them to seek care from professionals they don't know or trust?

WARREN

I believe that we need to build a system where we can all have trust in those who are caring for us. It's essential for us all to have confidence and trust in our doctors. You should always be able to open with them. You should be able to tell them if you're a Republican, for example. There is no cure for that, but at least they can laugh at you too.

MADDOW

It's nice to see that you're able to show a sense of humor. It's something we've certainly not seen much from our current President.

WARREN

Well, having a sense of humor while working tirelessly to make our world a better place? That's precisely what strong and independent women from Massachusetts do. And I'll tell you what else we do. We also run for President.

                    Beat.

BIDEN

I know Elizabeth Warren.

MADDOW

And finally, if I could just ask one more question. Can you tell us what distinguishes your plans for healthcare from those of Bernie Sanders and Joe Biden?

WARREN

That's an easy one. Unlike Bernie's plans, I actually know how to pay for mine. And unlike Joe's, mine actually exist.

MADDOW

Thank you, Senator Warren.

                                              (CONTINUED)

                              TODD
Marianne Williamson. On behalf of everyone watching, what
are you actually doing here?

                           WILLIAMSON
What am I doing here? What are you doing here? What are we
all doing here? Do any of us truly know our purpose? Do we
have a purpose, or are we destined to float through time as
a collection of linked atoms brought together by our desire
to move forward and do with our existence things that those
before us were not able to achieve with their own?

                            SANDERS
This is like listening to Marco Rubio if he joined the
Church of Scientology.

                            MADDOW
Mayor Pete Buttigieg. Many believe that your campaign is
facing a significant problem in attracting the support of
minority voters. What do you have to say to that?

                           BUTTIGIEG
I would say that they are correct.

                            MADDOW
Okay, but do you have a plan to bring this significant
number of voters onto your side?

                           BUTTIGIEG
I think that we need to be doing more to stop racism in
this country. We need to call our racists. Donald Trump,
our President, is a racist.

                            MADDOW
But what are you actually going to do?

                           BUTTIGIEG
I think that we should take white people and introduce
black people to them.

                             Beat.

                            MADDOW
Would you like another go?

                                                    (CONTINUED)

                         BUTTIGIEG
I'm probably good.

                         HARRIS
No, go on. Try again.
                         (to WARREN)
Have you got any more of that popcorn?

                         WARREN
I'd subscribe to H-B-O for content like this.

                    HARRIS and WARREN high five.

                         BUTTIGIEG
I have no problem with black or minority voters. They just
have a problem with me.

                         MADDOW
Okay, well, we'll move on. Actually, you know what, I've
got a question for any of the men here tonight. This
question is open to any of you. What makes you qualified to
make decisions on behalf of millions of women across
America?

                         Beat.

                         MADDOW
Nothing. No one has any answer to that?

                         GENERIC WHITE MAN
If I could just talk?

                         MADDOW
No one is interrupting you, Representative --

                         GENERIC WHITE MAN
I would prefer it if my name wasn't on the record here.

                         MADDOW
Okay, well, go ahead. What do you have to say?

                                                  (CONTINUED)

GENERIC WHITE MAN
I just want to say that I know women. I respect women. I
have, in fact, met women. My wife, for example, is a woman.
I have also read about women.

> BIDEN and SANDERS drink from two
> glasses of water.

WARREN
If I could just interrupt. I'd just like to say that I am
actually an expert in this area as I do, in fact, have a
vagina.

> BIDEN and SANDERS spit their
> water out.

SANDERS
Is she actually allowed to say that?

BIDEN
I'm sorry. I try to think of myself as a modern kind of
guy, but I simply cannot abide by women using the V-word.

WARREN
It's out anatomy, Joe. It's nothing for any of us to be
ashamed of. You sound sexist over there.

BIDEN
I cannot be sexist. Some of my best friends are married to
Michelle Obama.

> Beat.

TODD
And with that, I think that we are coming to the end of our
debate this evening. There's just time for our candidates'
closing statements. Senator Bernie Sanders, you can start.

SANDERS
Here is my pitch to America. Whatever Elizabeth Warren is
offering to you, you can have it. But at the same time, you
can also satisfy your need to vote for a man because you're
scared of a woman.

(CONTINUED)

                              MADDOW
Marianne Williamson.

                             WILLIAMSON
Lettuces are the magic fruit. Eat your greens, children.
You can fly darlings.

                              SANDERS
This is why you should never eat anything offered to you by
a stranger.

                               TODD
Beto O'Rourke.

                             O'ROURKE
Nevnte jeg at jeg snakker flytende Spansk?

                              MADDOW
Senator Warren.

                              WARREN
You know, America. I used to be a teacher, so let me all
teach you something now. By definition, a man is only sixty
percent of what a woman is.

                               TODD
Mayor Pete Buttigieg.

                             BUTTIGIEG
Thank you for having me.

                              MADDOW
Senator Harris.

                                        HARRIS looks across to make eye
                                        contact with BIDEN. As he looks
                                        back, she points to her eyes and
                                        then at him.

                               TODD
Vice President Biden.

                         BIDEN
America, you've heard many things here tonight. But what I
ask you to do is judge us not on what you hear but on our
actions. When it comes time to decide, judge me on what I
achieved during those eight years I spent in the Biden and
Co. administration. And by Co., I mean Barack Obama.

                         MADDOW
And finally, let's go to Mike Bloomberg.

                    GENERIC WHITE MAN
Well, I --

                    A buzzer interrupts.

                         MADDOW
I'm sorry, but that does mean that we are out of time.

                    GENERIC WHITE MAN
Don't I get to finish?

                         MADDOW
                  (ignoring GENERIC WHITE MAN)
Thank you all for joining us for tonight's debate where --

                         TODD
Where we hope that what you have heard and seen from our
candidates here this evening, will help you make your
decision when it comes time to vote.

                         MADDOW
And for viewers at home disappointed that I cut off Mike
Bloomberg early there, if you'd like to hear more of a
white man talking about issues that others are much more
highly qualified and knowledgeable about, then I invite you
to open your front door and step outside.

                         TODD
Good night.

                         MADDOW
Good night.

                    The light fades.

ACT IV, SCENE TWELVE | MUELLER TESTIFIES

> On stage, the scene is set for a
> CONGRESSIONAL COMMITTEE HEARING
> at the CAPITOL where DEVIN
> NUNES, ADAM SCHIFF, and ERIC
> SWALWELL sit ready to question
> MUELLER who sits in front of
> them.

NARRATOR
(entering)
While the Democrat's search for a new nominee is filled
with action, the President sits hoping that their contest
will provide to him a welcome distraction. For after many
of Trump's closest allies are handed indictment, Robert
Muller is ready to provide the nation with of hope an
incitement --

> The NARRATOR is interrupted by a
> sound similar to flatulence.

SWALWELL
Sorry. I was just moving my chair.

NARRATOR
But as could be predicted, an effort to cover up does soon
ensue, with the Special Counsel's full report permitted to
be read only by a select limited few. And so to uncover the
facts in full, while the White House continues to argue
they're null, in the House a committee date is soon set,
with Democrats hoping to make Republicans sweat. But for
more than one, the goal is not simply the truth to picket,
but instead to gain high-level respect, to gain that
complimentary game ticket.

> The NARRATOR exits.

SCHIFF
Special Counsel Mueller, I'd like to thank you for being
with us today, and if I may, I'd like to begin by going
over the main findings of your report?

(CONTINUED)

                              MUELLER
I would be happy to clarify any point that you need me to.

                              SCHIFF
Thank you. Special Counsel Muller, your report is both
methodical, and it is devastating, for your investigation
determined that the Trump campaign, including Donald Trump
himself, knew that a foreign power was intervening and not
only welcomed it but also used it. Is that correct?

                              MUELLER
                          (nodding)
That is correct.

                              SCHIFF
Your investigation found that the Trump campaign did not
inform the authorities when a foreign power offered dirt on
their opponent. Is that correct?

                              MUELLER
                          (nodding)
That is correct.

                              SCHIFF
You found that instead, they made full use of that offer.
Is that correct?

                              MUELLER
                          (nodding)
That is correct.

                              SCHIFF
Your investigation also found that Donald Trump and his
campaign staff repeatedly lied to investigators, lied to
you, lied to the F-B-I, and lied to this very committee. Is
that correct?

                              MUELLER
                          (nodding)
That is correct.

                                                   (CONTINUED)

                          SCHIFF
Specifically, you found that they lied about meeting and
negotiating with Russian agents, lied about the firing of
James Comey, and lied about wanting to fire you, Director
Mueller. Is that correct?

                          MUELLER
                     (nodding)
That is correct.

                          SCHIFF
Your investigation has already successfully prosecuted
multiple members of Donald Trump's top team, most notably
his former campaign manager, Paul Manafort, and his former
personal lawyer, Michael Cohen. Is that correct?

                          MUELLER
                     (nodding)
That is correct.

                          SCHIFF
Would you personally describe the actions of Donald Trump,
his campaign associates, and the campaign itself, to be a
betrayal of our country?

                          MUELLER
                     (nodding)
I would.

                          SCHIFF
Given your answer just now and taking into account the
findings of your report, do you believe that there are
grounds to indict the President?

                          MUELLER
I cannot answer that.

                          SCHIFF
Director Mueller, speaking on behalf of millions of
Americans, what the hell?

                          Proceedings are interrupted by a
                          sound similar to flatulence.

                                              (CONTINUED)

                         SWALWELL
Sorry. I was just moving my glass on the table.

                         MUELLER
Mister Chairman, if I may clarify? I cannot answer that.

                              MUELLER leans forward and makes
                              an obvious wink toward SCHIFF.

                         SCHIFF
I'm sorry, Director Mueller, do you have something stuck in
your eye? We could get you something for that?

                         MUELLER
No. I was just winking to make a point.

                         SCHIFF
That's the end of my questions. Ranking Farmer Nunes.

                         NUNES
Thank you --

                              NUNES turns to SCHIFF.

                         NUNES
You're not funny.

                         SCHIFF
Your concerns have been herd.

                              SCHIFF bangs a gavel.

                         NUNES
                       (to MUELLER)
Director Mueller, on behalf of my Republican colleagues and
myself, I'd like to thank you for your tireless service to
our great nation and for your patriotism, your belief in
and fight for both justice and our rights, and finally, for
conducting yourself always in an honest and honorable way.

                         MUELLER
Thank you for your words.

                                                    (CONTINUED)

                        NUNES
Now, Director Mueller, could you please explain to us all
why you're a despicable fraud, a liar, a cow --

                SWALWELL moos.

                        NUNES
...ard, and a dishonorable, freedom-hating, partisan
liberal hack that is engaging in this staining of our great
President's record and reputation with all of this, and I'm
going to say it, bull.

                SWALWELL moos.

                        MUELLER
I'm sorry.

                        NUNES
I asked --

                        MUELLER
No, I heard you, Mister Nunes. I just did not know that you
knew such big words.

                        NUNES
Director Mueller, I find your comment deeply offensive. But
the American people find your treasonous witch hunt even
more so. You were tasked with establishing the facts and
instead, you butchered --

                SWALWELL moos.

                        NUNES
...those facts. Not once did you take the time to sit back
and take stock --

                SWALWELL moos.

                        NUNES
...of the full situation. Instead, you steered --

                SWALWELL moos.

                                        (CONTINUED)

NUNES

...the investigation away from its true purpose of clearing
the President and chose to focus on the Democrats wishes
for you to milk --

SWALWELL moos.

NUNES

...every small detail for lies that make the President look
bad. And not once throughout this process did you ever even
graze --

SWALWELL moos.

NUNES

...over the crimes that the Democrats have committed. Well,
let me tell you, Director Mueller, just because the
Democrats have beef --

SWALWELL moos.

NUNES

...with our President, it doesn't mean that the American
people also do. The truth of it is, anyone who believes any
of the bull --

SWALWELL moos.

SCHIFF
(to SWALWELL)
You've already done that one.

SWALWELL

It's still funny.

NUNES
(to MUELLER)
...in your report must be as thick as leather --

SWALWELL and SCHIFF moo.

NUNES

Director Mueller, it's time that you were put out to
pasture --

(CONTINUED)

> SWALWELL begins to moo but cuts
> himself off.

                    SWALWELL
That one is just too easy.

> SCHIFF bangs a gavel.

                    SCHIFF
The Ranking Member's time is up. Mr. Swalwell, two minutes.

                    SWALWELL
Thank you, Mister Chairman.
                    (to MUELLER)
Director Mueller, can I just say, it's really great to see
you here today. In fact...

> SWALWELL stands, a sound similar
> to flatulence accompanying.

                    SWALWELL
That was my chair again.

> SWALWELL approaches MUELLER.

                    SWALWELL
This really is a great day for me because it's the day I
get to meet my hero.

> SWALWELL extends his arm toward
> MUELLER, and they begin shaking.

                    SWALWELL
But you know, you're not just my hero, Robert. Can I call
you Robert? You are also the hero of many millions of
Americans.

> In silence, they continue to
> shake hands.
>
> At the side of the stage,
> unnoticed and filming themselves
> on a phone, MATT GAETZ and JIM
> JORDAN enter.

                                        (CONTINUED)

                          MUELLER
I think that we've probably shake long enough now.

                          Beat.

                          SWALWELL
I'm running for President.

                                   SCHIFF bangs a gavel, and
                                   SWALWELL returns to his chair as
                                   the action shifts to GAETZ and
                                   JORDAN.

                          GAETZ
                      (to the phone)
Yo, what is up today, guys? It's me. I'm Matt Gaetz here to
bring you another Gaetz Maetz with my good friend, it's Jim
Jordan, and you can check him our over at Jim Goes Gyming.
We're doing a collab today, isn't that right, Jim?

                          JORDAN
                      (to the phone)
That is right, Matt. We've got something really cool lined
up for all you guys at home.

                          GAETZ
                      (to the phone)
He speaks the truth. Cool is what we do here on Gaetz
Matez, and we do it each and every single day, that's
right, every single day, so you should smack that like
button and subscribe for more content. But onto what we're
showing you guys at home today, it is a big one.

                          JORDAN
                      (to the phone)
Should we tell them what's going on behind us?

                          GAETZ
                      (to the phone)
We should do just that, Jim. Well, guys, behind us is where
the Democrats --

                                                        (CONTINUED)

                          JORDAN
                      (to the phone)
Always the Democrats.

                          GAETZ
                      (to the phone)
It is always the Democrats. Jim speaks the truth. Behind us
is where the Democrats are hosting a secret interrogation
away from our eyes and, more importantly, away from your
eyes.

                          JORDAN
                      (to the phone)
And if you are a patriot who doesn't like what is going on,
then you should leave us a comment in the comment section
below.

                          GAETZ
                      (to the phone)
He speaks the truth. Always. But stick around right now
because we are going to crash this party.

                          JORDAN
                      (to the phone)
Shall we crash the party?

                          GAETZ
                      (to the phone)
Let's crash the party, Jim.

                              GAETZ and JORDAN continue to
                              film themselves as they approach
                              the COMMITTEE.

                          MUELLER
                      (mid-conversation)
... Congressman, I do not feel as though that would be an
appropriate thing for me to do.

                          SWALWELL
If you won't endorse me, can we at least get a photo
together?

                                                    (CONTINUED)

MUELLER

I can stretch to a ph --

GAETZ
(to the phone)

Guys, this is what betrayal looks like. This is the Democrats betraying our country, betraying you, in front of our very eyes.

SCHIFF bangs a gavel.

SCHIFF

What is going on here?

GAETZ

Mister Chairman, I put it to you, in front of the patriots, our great American patriots who are watching from home our fight for freedom, that you, Mister Chairman, are a traitor to our nation.

JORDAN

You are holding these secret meetings in private with no Republicans except for Congressman Nunes, but he doesn't really count, and you are not letting the American people watch. What do you have to hide?

GAETZ

He speaks the truth. What do you have to hide?

SCHIFF bangs a gavel.

SCHIFF

Congressman Gaetz, Congressman Jordan --

GAETZ

You're a disgrace to that chair and to the American people, Mister chairman.

SCHIFF

Congressmen --

JORDAN

There should be an investigation into your corruption. I want hearings. I want indictments --

(CONTINUED)

                         MUELLER
Haven't I provided enough of those?

                    SCHIFF bangs a gavel.

                         SCHIFF
Congressmen, this hearing is being broadcast on C-Span.
                    (pointing)
Look. You can see the camcorder over there. A new tape was
put in this morning.

                         GAETZ
You're still denying me and my friend here, both of us
elected representatives, that's right, elected
representatives of our great nation.

                         JORDAN
Are you elected? I didn't think so.

                         GAETZ
He speaks the truth. You are denying us our right to
interrogate...
                    (pointing at MUELLER)
...this traitor.

                         JORDAN
We were going to go all bad cop and bad cop on his ass.

                         MUELLER
Don't you mean good cop, bad cop?

                         JORDAN
No. I was going to be bad cop, and he was going to be worse
cop.

                         GAETZ
He speaks the truth.

                         SCHIFF
Congressmen, the committee on which you both sit heard
testimony from Director Muller just a few hours ago.

                         GAETZ
Don't go changing the subject on us.

                                             (CONTINUED)

> SCHIFF

I'm calling security.

> Proceedings are interrupted by a
> sound similar to flatulence.

> SWALWELL

Okay. I might need ten minutes this time.

> SCHIFF bangs a gavel.

> SCHIFF

Ten minutes.

ACT IV, SCENE THIRTEEN | TRUMP'S MISTAKE

> The OVAL OFFICE where TRUMP sits
> at the desk on the phone.

> NARRATOR
> (entering)

It is hard to imagine how Mueller could have made his point
clearer, and so it's easy to see how many believe that
impeachment should now be ever nearer. But disappointment
is strong as in the House action is put on hold, for Pelosi
still feels her party's hunt for evidence is coming up
cold. And so feeling in the clear the White House focus now
does shift, as Trump feels the time is right to ensure his
reelection chances do lift. But too far for dirt does the
President push, allowing at last for justice to ambush.

> The NARRATOR exits.

> TRUMP
> (on phone)

It is a lie. They are all lies. A witch hunt. They are
hunting witches, and they think that I am a witch. Fake
news. Robert Mueller is fake news. I did not do anything.
They all hate America. It is so sad.

> There is a knock on a door, and
> CONWAY enters.

> (CONTINUED)

                         CONWAY
Mister President.

                         TRUMP
                    (on phone)
You wait.
                    (to CONWAY)
Kellyanne Conway, do you want a pizza?

                         CONWAY
Sure, I'll take a Hawaiian.

                         TRUMP
                    (on phone)
And one Hawaiian. And charge the order to Sean Hannity.
Delivered in thirty minutes? Good.

                         TRUMP puts the phone down.

                         TRUMP
I did not think that you liked foreign food?

                         CONWAY
Hawaii isn't foreign, sir.

                         Beat.

                         TRUMP
What can I do for you, Kellyanne Conway?

                         CONWAY
Mister President, I have news about the Democratic Primary.

                         TRUMP
Did you watch the debate? I watched the debate. They were
all losers.

                         CONWAY
Yes, I did watch it, sir.

                         TRUMP
That Bernie Sanders, he looks like the kind of guy who
shouts things at strangers on the A train while everyone
tried to pretend that he is not there.

                                        (CONTINUED)

                          CONWAY
You've taken the A train before, sir?

                          TRUMP
No. I take the A-plus train because I am super smart.

                          CONWAY
Well, anyway, the latest poll numbers have come out.

                          TRUMP
Am I going to be facing Elizabeth Warren? I have already
been preparing some classic Trump for the debate. I am
going to bring back some old lines. First, I am going to
demand to see her birth certificate, and then I am going to
see her birth certificate, and finally, I am going to
pretend that I never wanted to see her birth certificate.

                          CONWAY
You're not going to be facing Warren, sir. It looks as
though there is a different frontrunner.

                          TRUMP
Who is it?

                          CONWAY
It's Joe Biden, sir.

                          TRUMP
Sleepy Joe Biden? But he is... sleepy.

                          CONWAY
Yes, sir. But he is leading in the polls right now.

                          TRUMP
But I thought that everyone liked Elizabeth Warren and felt
that she did the least worst?

                          CONWAY
Well, yes, that's true, sir. But you're forgetting
something.

                          TRUMP
To book Eric in for his monthly bath?

                                                    (CONTINUED)

                              CONWAY
I did that for you last night, sir. I meant that Elizabeth
Warren is a woman, and Joe Biden is a man.

                              TRUMP
That is a very good point, Kellyanne Conway.

                              CONWAY
I think this means that we're going to need to change our
approach. We don't have anything on Biden.

                              TRUMP
It is okay, Kellyanne Conway. I know where I can find some
dirt on Joe Biden.

                                        TRUMP stands and approaches an
                                        office window. As he does, a
                                        scene outside the window lights
                                        up where a SMALL BOY wearing a
                                        red shirt is cutting grass.

                              TRUMP
                          (to SMALL BOY)
Do you have any dirt on Joe Biden?

                           SMALL BOY
I don't. I'm sorry, sir.

                              TRUMP
Come here.

                                        The SMALL BOY approaches the
                                        window as TRUMP reaches into his
                                        pocket and pulls out a candy
                                        bar. TRUMP places the candy bar
                                        onto the SMALL BOY's head.

                              TRUMP
Have some candy.

                           SMALL BOY
Thank you, Mister President.

                                                        (CONTINUED)
PERFORMANCE LICENSE EDITION   LICENSE # _ _ _ _ _ _ _ _

> The lights on the SMALL BOY go
> down as TRUMP returns to his
> desk.

                         TRUMP
He did not have any dirt, Kellyanne Conway.

                         CONWAY
So, what now?

                         TRUMP
I have another idea.

> TRUMP picks up the phone and
> dials. A moment later, a pop
> song begins to play as a
> spotlight finds PUTIN at the
> other side of the stage.
>
> PUTIN pulls out his phone and
> answers, and the song stops as
> he does.

                         PUTIN
                      (on phone)
Donald. How be you?

                         TRUMP
                      (on phone)
Vladimir Putin, I have news.

                         PUTIN
                      (on phone)
Do tell Putin what it be.

                         TRUMP
                      (on phone)
Elizabeth Warren and Joe Biden are both sad losers, but Joe
Biden is slightly less sad and slightly less of a loser.

                         PUTIN
                      (on phone)
You mean United States voters not prefer highly qualified
woman with real ideas over man who sometime act creepy?

                                              (CONTINUED)

CONTINUED:

                         TRUMP
                       (on phone)
Yes.

                         PUTIN
                       (on phone)
I know that already. Putin know that for four years.

                         TRUMP
                       (on phone)
What are we going to do?

                         PUTIN
                       (on phone)
I have plan.

                         TRUMP
                       (on phone)
A good plan?

                         PUTIN
                       (on phone)
All plan be good of mine. In Russia I be known as Putin the
plan planner. I call back later.

                              TRUMP puts the phone down as
                              PUTIN exits.

                         TRUMP
                       (to CONWAY)
We have a plan.

                              The lights on the OVAL OFFICE
                              fade as lights go up on the
                              scene at a SUPERMARKET CASH
                              REGISTER, where OBAMA stands in
                              line behind a CUSTOMER being
                              served by the CASHIER.

                         CASHIER
That will be eleven dollars four cents.

                                                  (CONTINUED)

                                        BIDEN enters with his own
                                        shopping and stands in line
                                        behind OBAMA.

                                        As the CUSTOMER pays, BIDEN
                                        unsuccessfully attempts to get
                                        OBAMA's attention.

                            CASHIER
Thank you for shopping with us.
                      (to OBAMA)
Next, please.

                                        As the CUSTOMER exits, OBAMA
                                        moves forward and places his
                                        basket on the counter.

                            OBAMA
Just this small selection... of your most excellent items
of fresh, ripe produce, commodious goods... and tradable
essential daily commodities today please, good sir.

                                        BIDEN attempts to get his
                                        attention once more.

                            OBAMA
                     (turning to BIDEN)
Joe, I know that you're standing in that space... What are
you doing here?

                            BIDEN
Barack. I never saw you there. What are you doing here?

                            OBAMA
I'm here to tender authentic United States currency for a
variety of items... which my family and I require... What
are you doing here?

                            BIDEN
What a coincidence. I'm here doing my shopping too. We're
so alike, aren't we?

                                              (CONTINUED)

                              OBAMA
But, Joe, this establishment is a considerable distance
from... the locality in which you and your wife cohabit...
Like many hundreds of miles away.

                              BIDEN
Well, you know, I often think that this place has...

                                        BIDEN looks around and grabs an
                                        onion from a nearby stand.

                              BIDEN
The best gosh damn potatoes in America.

                              CASHIER
                            (to BIDEN)
Sir, that's an onion, and I told you yesterday, please
don't keep touching our produce. If you start sniffing the
fruit again, then I'll have to call my supervisor.

                              OBAMA
You transported yourself hundreds of miles to get yourself
a real good potato... that is actually an onion?

                              BIDEN
What can I say? I like fresh food.

                              OBAMA
Joe, have you been frequenting this branch... of a well-
known grocery store chain in the hope... that you might run
into me?

                              BIDEN
No, of course not. Though while I'm seeing you, how is
Michelle and the girls? Oh, and have you decided on that
endorsement yet?

                              OBAMA
I've already communicated my position on this matter... I'm
not making any decision... on who yet to endow with my
words of recommendation.

                                                      (CONTINUED)

                         BIDEN
Come on, Barack. I could really do with a hand, and I've
always had your back.

                         OBAMA
It wouldn't be correct or just of me to cause... any
splitting of factions, beliefs, or other ideals within...
the Democratic Party at this time.

                         CASHIER
                       (to OBAMA)
That comes to seventeen dollars and twenty-nine cents,
Mister President.

                    OBAMA hands over a bill.

                         OBAMA
Here is a twenty-dollar bill... Keep the change.

                         CASHIER
Thank you, Mister President.

                         BIDEN
                       (to OBAMA)
Well, how about we just get a photo together?

                         OBAMA
I don't currently have the availability in the schedule of
my day... to fulfill the request that you make of me...
Perhaps some other time.

                    OBAMA exits and leaves BIDEN
                    looking after him.

                         BIDEN
                       (to CASHIER)
What about you? Will you endorse me?

                    PUTIN enters dressed as another
                    cashier.

                         PUTIN
                       (to CASHIER)
You be needed at customer servicing desk.

                                        (CONTINUED)

                         CASHIER
What's happened?

                         PUTIN
There be woman called Karen there who claims she had only
ninety-nine sheets of toilet paper on roll she bought
instead of advertised one hundred. She wants to speak to
manager.

                         CASHIER
Oh, boy. I best go sort it out.

                         PUTIN
Good. I take over here.

                              The CASHIER exits as PUTIN takes
                              their place.

                         PUTIN
                       (to BIDEN)
Hello, and welcome to big shop. How can I help today?

                              BIDEN places his basket on the
                              counter.

                         BIDEN
What about you? You'll endorse me, right?

                         PUTIN
I endorse you? Sure. I endorse you.

                         BIDEN
Well, that's someone, at least.

                         PUTIN
You seem like there be stuff that bother you. Why not tell
me what it be? Perhaps you feel better after.

                         BIDEN
I'm not sure about that. I don't normally talk about this
stuff.

                         PUTIN
You trust me. I be your... greengrocer.

                                             (CONTINUED)
PERFORMANCE LICENSE EDITION   LICENSE # _ _ _ _ _ _ _ _

                          BIDEN
I'm not so sure.

                                   PUTIN pulls a candy bar and
                                   vegetable from the basket.

                          PUTIN
                     (holding up the candy)
Eat less of this.
                     (holding up the vegetable)
Eat more of this. Also, cat milk. It not come from real
cat.

                          BIDEN
I don't understand?

                          PUTIN
Now I also be doctor you can trust.

                          BIDEN
Well, alright. Recently it has just felt like even though
I'm still popular, people just don't seem to like me
anymore.

                          PUTIN
I see.

                                   PUTIN takes a melon from the
                                   basket.

                          BIDEN
And then there's my son, Hunter Biden. He's been having a
stressful time in his job in Ukraine.

                                   PUTIN drops the melon onto his
                                   foot.

                          BIDEN
And then there are the annoying neighbors next door.

                          PUTIN
What was that?

                                                        (CONTINUED)

PERFORMANCE LICENSE EDITION   LICENSE # _ _ _ _ _ _ _ _

                              BIDEN
The neighbors? A couple called Makayla and Josh.

                              PUTIN
No. Before that.

                              BIDEN
My son, Hunter Biden?

                              PUTIN
Tell me more.

                              BIDEN
Well, he does some work out in Ukraine. It's a nice job
he's got there too. Stressful at times, though.

                              PUTIN
                         (to himself)
I be sure I find way to use that.

                              BIDEN
I'm sorry?

                              PUTIN
I said shopping be twenty-three dollar.

                              BIDEN
Of course.

                                   BIDEN reaches into his pocket
                                   and pulls out a handful of
                                   quarters.

                              BIDEN
                         (to himself, counting)
One quarter. Two quarters. Three quarters. One Dollar.

                              PUTIN
Actually, today for you, special offer. It be free.

                              BIDEN
Are you sure?

                                                        (CONTINUED)

                        PUTIN
It not make difference to me. I not own store.

                        BIDEN
Well, thank you very much, young man.

                        PUTIN
Now go. I have phone call to make.

                        BIDEN
See you around.

                                    BIDEN exits with his shopping as
                                    PUTIN pulls out his phone and
                                    dials.

                                    At the other side of the stage,
                                    a phone rings out, and the
                                    lights go back up on TRUMP sat
                                    in the OVAL OFFICE.

                        TRUMP
                      (on phone)
You are through to Donald J. Trump. Calls to this number
cost thirteen Dollars a minute. Now tell me what are you
wearing?

                        PUTIN
                      (on phone)
About half a broken watermelon on left shoe.

                        TRUMP
                      (on phone)
Comrade Vladimir Putin, I did not realize it was you.

                        PUTIN
                      (on phone)
Donald, listen carefully. I have dirt on Joe Biden. He have
son who do business in Ukraine.

                        TRUMP
                      (on phone)
What is a Ukraine?

                                                    (CONTINUED)

                              PUTIN
                         (on phone)
It be part of Europe that Russia not own yet. Like Russia's
Canada.

                              TRUMP
                         (on phone)
So what do I need to do?

                              PUTIN
                         (on phone)
Dig deep. Get more dirt. Find more information and use it
against Joe Biden. Crush opponent.

                              The CASHIER returns to PUTIN's
                              side.

                         CASHIER
Excuse me, sir.

                              PUTIN
                         (on phone)
Donald, I must go. I be needed.

                              PUTIN and TRUMP both put their
                              phones down.

                         CASHIER
Sir, I forgot to check. Do you actually work here?

                              PUTIN picks up a broken half of
                              melon from the floor and hands
                              it to the CASHIER.

                         PUTIN
Here. Have present.

                              PUTIN and the CASHIER exits as
                              the lights on the SUPERMARKET
                              CASH REGISTER scene go down, and
                              action returns to the OVAL
                              OFFICE.

                                                  (CONTINUED)

                         TRUMP
                    (to himself)
Okay. I need to make this big. What do I do? I know. I
should be super smart and blackmail Ukraine.

                              TRUMP picks up his phone and
                              dials.

                              As a phone rings out, a light
                              finds OBAMA who pulls his phone
                              from his pocket and answers.

                         OBAMA
                    (on phone)
Now really, Joe, this situation is beginning to develop...
into an out of hand set of circumstances... I don't yet
know who I'm endorsing --

                         TRUMP hangs up.

                         OBAMA
                    (to himself)
He hung up on me.
                    (exiting)
Hey, Michelle. Joe hung up on me.

                              As the light goes down on OBAMA,
                              TRUMP dials again.

                         TRUMP
I will try this number.

                              As another phone rings out, a
                              light finds ERIC.

                         ERIC
                    (on phone)
Hello. You're through to Eric. My name is Eric. What's your
name?

                         TRUMP
                    (on phone)
Eric --

                                                  (CONTINUED)

                          ERIC
                     (on phone)
          Hey, that's cool. I'm called Eric too.

                          TRUMP
                     (on phone)
          Eric Trump, get off the phone. I am trying to call Ukraine.

                              TRUMP hangs up as the light on
                              ERIC goes down.

                          TRUMP
          How can it be so hard to call a country?

                              TRUMP dials again as a light
                              finds WILLIAMSON.

                          WILLIAMSON
                     (on phone)
          Are you calling to share the love?

                              TRUMP hangs up quickly, and the
                              light goes down.

                          TRUMP
          Okay. It has to be this one.

                              TRUMP dials once more as this
                              time, a light finds TIFFANY
                              TRUMP.

                          TRUMP
                     (on phone)
          Hello. This is Donald J. Trump.

                          TIFFANY
                     (on phone)
          Father?

                          TRUMP
                     (on phone)
          Who is this?

                                                      (CONTINUED)

                    TIFFANY
               (on phone)
I'm your daughter.

                    TRUMP
               (on phone)
Ivanka?

                    TIFFANY
               (on phone)
Tiffany.

                    TRUMP
               (on phone)
I do not have any money.

                         TRUMP hangs up as the light goes
                         down.

                    TRUMP
This is the last number that I have.

                         TRUMP dials a final time, and a
                         phone begins to ring out. A
                         pause follows before,
                         eventually, a voice answers.

                    PELOSI (IN DARKNESS)
               (on phone)
Hello.

                    TRUMP
               (on phone)
Now listen here. I want dirt on sleepy Joe Biden. I want to
know everything that you have got. What is he doing in
Ukraine? Why is he in Ukraine? Make it up if you have to.
Tell me everything or America will make it not so good to
be Ukraine.

                    PELOSI (IN DARKNESS)
               (on phone)
Who is this?

                                              (CONTINUED)

                          TRUMP
                        (on phone)
Do not play dumb with me. I am President Donald J. Trump of
the United States of America.

                    PELOSI (IN DARKNESS)
                        (on phone)
President Trump?

                              A spotlight shines on a table
                              where PELOSI and SCHUMER sit
                              drinking coffee.

                          PELOSI
                        (to SCHUMER)
It's the President.

                          TRUMP
                        (on phone)
Some people say the best ever President Trump.

                          PELOSI
                        (on phone)
This is Nancy Pelosi.
                        (beat, then to SCHUMER)
Chuck, I think that we've got him.

                          Beat.

                          SCHUMER
Oh, good. I'll go and change my facial expression to
something more appropriate.

                          SCHUMER exits.

                          PELOSI
                        (on phone)
Donald? Are you there, Donald?

                              Slowly, TRUMP puts his phone
                              down and stares straight ahead.

                                                    (CONTINUED)

>   PELOSI
>   (on phone)
> Donald?

>   TRUMP
> Oh no.

>   Lights out.

ACT IV, SCENE FOURTEEN | TRUMP'S FINAL EXIT

>   The NARRATOR enters a spotlight
>   at the side of an otherwise dark
>   and empty stage.

>   NARRATOR
> And so at least it seems perhaps that the President's time
> in office is soon set to lapse. For asking for dirt from a
> foreign nation can be considered by none to be an innocent
> vocation. The accurate account of what happened next is one
> that all sat here are sure to know. No justice, no truth,
> no hope, and not something we wish to show. And so instead,
> we present to you our interpretation of what we feel should
> have been, Donald J. Trump's final exit scene.

>   The NARRATOR exits as another
>   lights go up on PELOSI and
>   SCHUMER (smiling broadly) stood
>   at a podium to address the
>   audience.

>   PELOSI
> Good morning.

>   SCHUMER
> My colleague is right. It is a good morning, and that is
> why I am smiling at you all today.

>   PELOSI
> We are pleased to have this opportunity to tell you all
> about a bad thing that the President did last night. But it
> did not involve a checkbook.

>   (CONTINUED)

SCHUMER
That is right. Instead, the President called Nancy here --

PELOSI
(to SCHUMER)
Am I telling the story, or are you telling the story?

SCHUMER
Please accept my apology for interrupting you.

PELOSI
That is quite okay.

SCHUMER
And may I thank you for holding me to account.

PELOSI
(to audience)
Last night, at approximately seventeen minutes past eight,
the President called me while I was having drinks with
Chuck here. These drinks, of course, were of a strictly
professional nature.

SCHUMER
What Nancy means is that we did not go on to do the dancing
of the Paphian jig together.

PELOSI
Chuck is correct. At no point was congress amorous. We did
not, as the young people say, do the blanket hornpipe, ride
below the crupper, or even make butter with one's tail.

Beat.

PELOSI
The nature of the President's call was to ask Ukraine for
incriminating information on Joe Biden.

SCHUMER
Which is a bad thing to do.

PELOSI
It is a bad thing to do, and that is why earlier this
morning, I informed the authorities of this phone call.

(CONTINUED)

                    SCHUMER
Which is a good thing to do.

                    PELOSI
It is a good thing to do, and I am pleased that they have
already issued warrants for the arrests of President Donald
Trump, and his son's, Donald Trump Junior, and Eric Trump.

                    SCHUMER
Which is going to be beautiful to watch.

                    PELOSI
It is going to be beautiful to watch. We hope you enjoy it.

                              PELOSI and SCHUMER exit as
                              silence and darkness falls.

                    JUNIOR (IN DARKNESS)
So, you know, I think that this way is the way out.

                    TRUMP (IN DARKNESS)
Why can we not just run away to South America again?

                    JUNIOR (IN DARKNESS)
We can't get there. Don't you remember? Last week you
pulled out a map and banned flights to and from everywhere
that you thought was China.

                    TRUMP (IN DARKNESS)
Some people say that it was a smart move.

                    JUNIOR (IN DARKNESS)
But it means that we can't escape. And this map you've
given me doesn't help.

                    TRUMP (IN DARKNESS)
What is wrong with it?

                    JUNIOR (IN DARKNESS)
Eric cut it off the back of a cereal box.

                    ERIC (IN DARKNESS)
I got to use grown-up scissors.

                                          (CONTINUED)

                         JUNIOR (IN DARKNESS)
According to this, the talking cartoon alligator should be
on our left.

                         TRUMP (IN DARKNESS)
I cannot see anything.

                         JUNIOR (IN DARKNESS)
It's too dark.

                         TRUMP (IN DARKNESS)
I have an idea. I am going to bleach my eyes to see better.

                    Beat.

                         JUNIOR (IN DARKNESS)
Does that work?

                              From the darkness comes a slight
                              dripping sound.

                         TRUMP (IN DARKNESS)
No. Everything has gone funny.

                              A thud follows as TRUMP trips
                              and hits the floor.

                         TRUMP (IN DARKNESS)
Eric Trump, what are you doing down here?

                              The scene becomes dimly lit as
                              JUNIOR lights a torch.

                         ERIC
I found a nickel on the floor.

                         TRUMP
That nickel is mine. I dropped it earlier.

                         JUNIOR
Can we talk about this later? We need to get out of here
before --

                                                   (CONTINUED)

>   As ERIC and TRUMP both stand, a
>   large, bright searchlight
>   appears on them.

                              JUNIOR
...anyone notices us.

>   A beat, and then Russian banjo
>   music accompanies their
>   suspicious movements to one
>   side. As they stop, the music
>   stops.
>
>   Another beat, and then the same
>   music as they move the other
>   way. Again, it stops as they
>   stop.

                              JUNIOR
Okay, so, you know, I think we're going to have to run.

>   A third beat, and then the music
>   continues as ERIC, JUNIOR, and
>   TRUMP run offstage.
>
>   A moment later, two FBI AGENTS
>   enter from the other side of the
>   stage and give chase.
>
>   As the two FBI AGENTS exits,
>   ERIC, JUNIOR, and TRUMP reenter
>   and stop in the middle of the
>   stage.

                              TRUMP
                           (to JUNIOR)
We need to ditch the stupid one.

                              JUNIOR
                           (to ERIC)
Okay, buddy. We're going to play a game of hide and seek.
You count first.

                                              (CONTINUED)

ERIC
Okay. Let's have fun. One... seven... four... nine...

> As ERIC stands counting with his hands covering his face, JUNIOR and TRUMP make their exit.
>
> The FBI AGENTS return and walk up to ERIC. After a moment, they grab him and begin to drag him toward the wings.

ERIC
(exiting)
...five... eight... eleven... Hey, is this an earthquake?

> With the stage one more empty, a brick wall is brought on from the wings to meet JUNIOR and TRUMP reentering from the other side of the stage.
>
> Noticing the wall, JUNIOR doubles back to the wings to bring out a ladder.
> JUNIOR begins to scale the wall, as he reaches the top, however, TRUMP takes a run-up and hits the wall with enough force to knock it, and JUNIOR, over.
>
> TRUMP makes his exit as the two FBI AGENTS return to retrieve and unconscious JUNIOR.
>
> This time, TRUMP enters the stage walking backward as the two FBI AGENTS do the same from the other side.

(CONTINUED)

>   Stopping close to each other,
>   simultaneously, they all look
>   behind each other in such a way
>   as to not notice anyone else.
>
>   As a group, they turn clockwise
>   and then back again.
>
>   Finally, at the same time, they
>   all turn around and notice each
>   other.
>
>   A beat, and then TRUMP turns,
>   takes two sarcastic steps
>   forward and then makes a run for
>   it. As he reaches the wings,
>   however, he is tackled suddenly
>   to the ground by CLINTON.
>
>   As the FBI AGENTS close in on
>   TRUMP, CLINTON stands, brushes
>   her hands together, and turns to
>   address the audience.

                    CLINTON
You have no idea how satisfying that was.

ACT IV, SCENE FIFTEEN | CLINTON IN THE OVAL OFFICE

>   The NARRATOR enters an otherwise
>   empty OVAL OFFICE.

                    NARRATOR
And so, at last, we reach the end, though certainly truth
we will now bend. For no matter how much we hope, wish, or
to you portray, at least now, accountability will not take
place on any nearby day. Our story was one neither all
accurate or whole, and as you leave, democracy still misses
its long lost soul. But while laughter was why you all
gathered in this here place, we ask that you exit with just
one message we hope you will ensure to pass along. A
message that can only be delivered by the woman who, from
the start, remained strong.

                                        (CONTINUED)

> The NARRATOR exits as CLINTON
> enters.

                              CLINTON
                          (to audience)
Be honest, you missed me, didn't you? Now, America. I do
not want to say that I told you so, but I did tell you so.

I told you all that Donald Trump would be a bad president.
I told you that he was not qualified. I told you that he
would ruin our standing in the world. I told you that he
would try to start wars with countries that he can't spell.
I told you that he would destroy our economy. And I told
you that he would try to kill us all. I guess what I am
trying to say, America, is that I was right.

Do you all remember that time you thought that a woman is
too emotional to be president? Or when you all said that I
was not likable enough. Well, let me ask you this, America.
How do you like me now?

I am not here to gloat, however. There will be an eternity
for that when we are all in hell together. Or Tampa as they
call it in some parts. I am here to give you all one final
reminder. Not about switching off your devices, but about
all of us here in this room.

We have faced difficult times under President Trump. And
many of us will indeed continue to do so because the
reality is, some people are very stupid. But this fact does
not mean that any of us should ever give up, or that we
should shut up. And you can trust me, I know about not
shutting up.

Now if you take just one thing from this here show tonight,
other than memories of the uncomfortable seats, overpriced
soda, and the strange smell coming from the end cubicle in
the bathroom, then let it be a reminder of the knowledge
that every person in this room has the power to make a
difference. Well, almost everyone. I am not so sure about
the person sat in seat E-eleven. After all, they are
responsible for that end cubicle.

                              (MORE)
                                                    (CONTINUED)

                         CLINTON (CONT'D)
But we all, in our own way, contribute to the world and the
lives of those we know and meet. And we all have the power
to stand up for what we believe in and for a future where
everyone is both equal and safe, and where our planet is
protected for people to enjoy that future.

If we all make an effort to show a little kindness and
respect, and we work to inspire and lift others, then
maybe, we can be strong enough to make it through anything.

                         CLINTON approaches the desk.

                         CLINTON
But now, it is time for the moment that you have all been
waiting for.

                         CLINTON sniffs and gently
                         strokes the desk.

                         CLINTON
It is mine. All mine. I have waited centuries for this.

                         CLINTON goes to sit in the
                         chair.

                         CLINTON
Shall I do it? I am going to do it. I am doing it.

                         CLINTON sits in the chair and
                         holds out her hands.

                         CLINTON
Ha. Ha. Ha. Finally. I AM YOUR PRESIDENT --

                         CLINTON is cut off as the desk
                         swivels around to revel PENCE
                         sat at the other side.

                    CONWAY
                 (entering)
President Pence, sir.

                         Filled with rage, CLINTON walks
                         back into view.

                                                (CONTINUED)

                              CLINTON
NO!

                    Lights out.

                    THE END

CPSIA information can be obtained
at www.ICGtesting.com
Printed in the USA
BVHW071929091120
592843BV00012B/458